COAST GUARD CITY, U.S.A.

To those who remember

COAST GUARD CITY, U.S.A.
A History of the Port of Grand Haven

David H. Seibold, D.D.S.

edited by

Dorothe Welch Seibold

LOGO: Paul Laubert
COVER PHOTO: David Kale Seibold

ISBN: 0-9614344-7-3

FIRST EDITION

TABLE OF CONTENTS

INTRODUCTION

This book has been written not only to commemorate the Bicentennial of the United States Coast Guard but also to tell the story of the remarkable respect and regard which exists between this 200 year old Service and the Lake Michigan port city of Grand Haven, Michigan, known today throughout the Service as "Coast Guard City."

The history of the Revenue Cutter Service—predecessor of today's Coast Guard—follows lockstep with the history of the then young, emerging Republic. The stories of the Service's undaunted readiness are ever inspiring; the unbelievable acts of heroism when called to duty are legend. At first it seems incredulous that a small Michigan city on inland waters could become the chosen location for such high honor from this proud Service. But as this monograph unfolds it becomes quite evident that there does exist a unique bond between the Coast Guard and Grand Haven. It is an interesting and remarkable story.

ACKNOWLEDGMENTS

COAST GUARD CITY, U.S.A.

It has taken nearly two years to do the research and synthesize the ideas in this book, but it never would have gotten between two covers without the understanding help of friends. From the start it has been a concern that when the time came to compile this page I would inadvertently omit someone— someone very important. And since everyone I talked to, interviewed, or borrowed from was important to the fiber of this story, the omission of anyone was unthinkable. To avoid this I kept a running list—or tried to. My deepest apology to any person whose name should be included here but is not. The oversight is completely unintentional.

It has become convincingly clear a history book of this sort is never done. There is always more information available to clarify a date, to support an historical fact, more people to interview, more interesting old tales to uncover—another chapter to write. The decision one has to make is not so much when is the book finished, but rather when is it time to stop. Omissions which have resulted for these reasons are also regrettable.

If a person knew up front the long hours, the countless sun rises, the complete loss of the routine of daily life or the untold sacrifices imposed upon family, it is questionable if they would set out on a enterprise such as this. But in the last analysis the whole experience has been a grand adventure. And all of you are the heros.

Most importantly, this book is dedicated to my beautiful wife and best friend Dottie, without whom it never would have been written. She has been my collaborator, editor, thesaurus, dictionary and thought processor in every phase of its development from conception through its numerous drafts. I could always count on her tolerance and loving forbearance.

I must also recognize the support of our children Dave, Marta and Mele. Their encouragement has helped keep me going.

I owe a large debt to Molly Perry for her contributions and understanding. She and Ken Scholtz patiently allowed for my forays into museum files and disruptions of their routines.

Thomas L. Jones, Executive Director of the Historical Society of Michigan, has been a hero in the truest sense of the word. He saved the whole venture during the publishing phase by offering his professional know-how. His contacts—especially his friends at Bauer Dunham & Barr who did the typesetting with great skill and record speed—were invaluable. Tom is fully deserving of a special thank you.

It is a pleasure to ackowledge those persons who lived this history and willingly recounted it. They are truly treasures of the realm: Elizabeth Fisher, Claude VerDuin, Charlie Bugielski, Glenn Eaton, Bill Herbst, Steve Vozar, Ed Lautenschlaeger, Glenn McGeorge and Helen DeYoung. Their patience with me is greatly appreciated.

Also acknowledged for their contributions in making the necessary connections among the ideas are Bill Creason, Paul Johnson, Al Jacobson, Bob Burgess, Eda Frickman, Ethel Pankowski, Helen Bruno, Jim Binns, Henry White, Sandy McBeath and the Grand Haven Area Historical Society, Earl Wolf, Mike VanHoey, Marge Boon, Larry Deetjen, Cmdr. Larry Mizell, Clarence Poel, Fred Vandenbrand, Andy Loree, Dave Alexander, Roger Morgenstern, Tammy Fritz, Bruce Baker, Dave Johnston, Marshall Johnston, Ron Baker, Jack Smant, Dave Klaassen, Jerry Witherell, Fern VerDuin, Bob VerDuin, John Walhout, Don Wessel, Jeanette Rosema, Katherine Groenevelt, Bill Bramer, Midge Verplank, Perry DeLille, Nat Robbins VII, Gene Rothi, Bob Sluka, Jack VanHoef, Hung Liang, Don Constant, Julian Hatton, Bob Landman, Dave Haan, Milt Ghekas, Mark Ames and the entire staff of the Loutit Library.

The final responsibility for what is in the book is mine, but all shared in its creation.

PROLOGUE:

The United States Coast Guard Bicentennial has been a year long event. It had its inaugural ceremony in Newburyport, Massachusetts—sight of the launching of the first Revenue Cutter, *Massachusetts*, in 1790—on August 4, 1989. The celebration will culminate in Grand Haven, Michigan—Coast Guard City, U.S.A.—August 2-4, 1990. The Revenue Cutter Service, predecessor of today's Coast Guard, came into being August 4, 1790 and is the Nation's oldest seagoing force—there being no Navy until 1798.

In the beginning, because the Service's main duty was to enforce custom laws, it was placed under the Treasury Department. But the Service had no official name or statutory designation. In his request to Congress Alexander Hamilton had proposed a ". . . system of Revenue Cutters" but in those early years it was referred to variably as the "Revenue Service," "Revenue Marine," "Revenue Marine Service" and "the system of Cutters." In 1832 the Secretary of the Treasury referred to it as the "Revenue Cutter Service" but it was not until 1863 that mention was made of the Service in any official document. In that year an Act called it the "United States Revenue Cutter Service," however that did not become the popularly accepted designation until 1894—more than a century after the Service came into being.

The term "coast guard" was first used by Captain Alexander Frazer, the Service's first Commandant. In his 1846 Annual Report he referred to the men and vessels of his Service as ". . . a coast guard in time of war. . . ." The term was used again in an editorial published November 26, 1864 in the "Army and Navy Journal," which also contained a variant of today's Coast Guard motto: ". . . Keeping always under steam and ever ready in the event of extraordinary need to render valuable service, the cutters can be

xi

made to form a coast guard whose value it is impossible at the present time to estimate."

The Coast Guard, per se, came into being in 1915 when the Revenue Cutter Service was united with Life Saving Service. Since then several other bureaus, boards, Acts and branches of Service have been added: the Seaman's Act in 1915, the Lighthouse Service July 1, 1939, Marine Inspection and Navigation in 1942, the Motorboat Acts of 1940 and 1958 all add to the grabbag of duties and responsibilities of today's Coast Guard. As it is musingly said, it has gotten to the point anything with a damp bottom—babies and ducks excluded—is the responsibility of the "Coasties." Of the 40,000 in active service today—the smallest of all the military—94 have the duty of inspecting bridges!

Grand Haven has had an association with the Coast Guard for 151 of the Service's 200 years. The first lighthouse was placed at Grand Haven in 1839, the first Life Saving Station in 1876 and the first Cutter arrived in 1932. In the ensuing chapters the pasts of those 3 Services as well as Grand Haven will be reviewed with the ultimate objective of showing how their respective histories became mortised together to form a most unusual alliance of mutual esteem and admiration.

CHAPTER 1

PIRATES AND SCALAWAGS

After a while smuggling became a habit. Clandestinely smuggling goods in and out of the colonies in the 1700's was a means of beating the odious British tax or duty. British taxes were a constant reminder of Royal domination and therefore dealing in contraband to avoid them was considered downright patriotic. Patriots were smugglers, smugglers were patriots. It was practiced blatantly. John Hancock and Samuel Adams, both signers of the Declaration of Independence, did their share of trading in contraband. It was a deadly game, but then so was the quest for freedom by any name.

Because of smuggling, the history of the Coast Guard coincides with the beginning of the United States. For most of us July 4, 1776 is considered the date our country gained its independence. Actually that was the date we threw down the gauntlet by issuing a signed Declaration of Independence to Great Britain and, by so doing, officially set out on the road toward independence—a road which took the colonies many tortuous miles. General Cornwallis surrendered at Yorktown October 19, 1781 after 5 long years of war, and only then had we gained our freedom.

After gaining independence this country had the burdensome responsibility of organizing a government for the new Republic. That took another 8 years—the new Constitution taking effect January 1, 1789. George Washington was inaugurated April 30, 1789 and so 13 years after 1776 the new Government was finally ready for business.

Generating a livelyhood was paramount. The most pressing problem was money because the war had left the fledgling Nation over $50 million in debt and revenues could best be described as inadequate. Congress passed a protective tariff which imposed a customs duty on tonnage entering the Country. But saying it was one thing—enforcing it was another. Prior to 1776 the merchants in port towns, in support of independence, had signed

1

Alexander Hamilton, first Secretary of Treasury and founder of the U.S. Coast Guard.

non-importation agreements, so the ordinary citizen had for years relied upon the ubiquitous smuggler to keep him supplied with tax-free goods. After 1781 these same people continued to do some "importing." So now the shoe was on the other foot!

Alexander Hamilton was this Country's first Secretary of the Treasury and as steward of the purse strings he knew there could be no allowance for financial leakage. And smuggling created a sieve. What had been a patriotic activity prior to independence suddenly loomed as a crisis which could bankrupt the young Nation. But breaking the habit was not to be a simple matter. It was easy enough to show the fellow countrymen that the custom duties imposed by Congress was taxation with representation, but it was not easy to make people see smuggling as a crime and smugglers as criminals. Domestic and foreign apathy—if not outright sympathy—toward dealing in contraband was, in a way, understandable. Business as usual was more profitable when shippers and merchants did not have to share their profits of trade with government. Sailing right past the Custom House when making port was easy. There was no one to stop them!

Alexander Hamilton decided to resort to a floating police fleet to enforce the customs laws—friendly persuasion of sorts. He requested 10 vessels of the cutter class to patrol the coast from New Hampshire to Georgia. "Boats of from 36 to 40 feet keel will answer the purpose," Hamilton told Congress. "The first cost of one of these boats, completely equipped, may be computed at one thousand dollars." And as part of the equipment he wanted his police fleet, ". . .armed with swivels." He knew he could get more with a kind word and a gun than with a kind word alone. Hamilton was the kind of gentleman you would be inclined to address as "sir"—the sort of traditional attitude retained in the Service today.

Congress recognized the urgency of Hamilton's request and on July 31, 1789—just 3 months after the Government was completely organized—approved "An act to regulate the collection of duties imposed by law on the tonnage of ships or vessels, and on goods, wares, and merchandises imported into the United States," and made available for each port surveyor the "employment of the boats which may be provided for securing the collection of the revenue." However, Congress was hard pressed for cash so no appropriations were made for the boats. Finally their parsimony abated and on August 4, 1790 construction of the 10 Cutters was authorized. With that the Revenue Cutter Service was born! Hamilton was to have his floating police force. (For the record, the Lighthouse Service had been authorized just 5 months before on March 4, 1789 but Congress appropriated no funds for it until August 7, 1789. It too was placed under Hamilton's jurisdiction.)

The first Cutter was the 2 masted *Massachusetts,* built and launched at Newburyport, Massachusetts in 1791. She was 50 feet long from the Indian figurehead to her stern with a beam of 17 1/2 feet. Others were built along the Atlantic coast and when

First revenue cutter "Massachusetts" launched 1791—decommissioned 1798. Painting by Hunter Woods, courtesy USCG.

completed, in addition to the *Massachusetts,* the fleet was made up of the *Scammel, Active, Pickering, Diligence, Argus, Vigilant, Virginia, South Carolina* and *General Greene.* Crews were of "respectable character" and received rations of rum, brandy or whiskey, salt, vinegar, soap and candles. Congress authorized ship crews of 1 master, not more than 3 mates, 4 mariners and 2 boys for each Cutter. A master's pay was $30 a month, 1st mate $20, 2nd mate $16, 3rd mate $14, mariners $8 and a boy received $4 a month. Hamilton fought to keep the pay high enough to avoid the temptation to conceal rather than detect fraud.

Hamilton wanted the officers to receive commissions that would ". . . not only induce fit men the more readily to engage, but will attach them to their duty by a nicer sense of honor." On March 21, 1791, Hopely Yeaton of New Hampshire was the first man commissioned as "Master of a Cutter in the Service of the United States." He took the double oath, ". . . to support the Constitution and detect and prevent frauds against the revenue"—just as the Coast Guard officers do today. His commission was signed by President Washington and Captain Yeaton was given command of the Cutter *Scammel*.

Cutter crews were authorized to board any vessel within the coast territorial limit of 4 leagues—12 miles. The ranks of master and mates were changed in 1799 to captain, first, second and third lieutenant, equivalent of the Navy's lieutenant commander, lieutenant, lieutenant junior grade and ensign, which came into Coast Guard usage in 1915. But regardless how they were addressed, there can be no doubt about the seamanship and fighting capabilities of these early cuttermen. They were good at both and made smuggling less profitable and less popular. Soon 92 per cent of the nation's income was coming through the Custom Houses. Congress was so impressed by the infant fleet of Cutters that in 1794 it granted the master's pay of $40 a month—the pay Hamilton had originally requested—and between 1793 and 1801 the 10 original Cutters were replaced with 13 larger ones. By 1796 the Country's entire foreign debt had been paid.

Hamilton's fleet of Cutters was the young Nation's only navy until 1798. After a Navy had been formed, Congress decreed that "Revenue Cutters shall, whenever the President of the United States shall so direct, cooperate with the Navy of the United States." On August 4, 1949 Congress restated that 150 year old

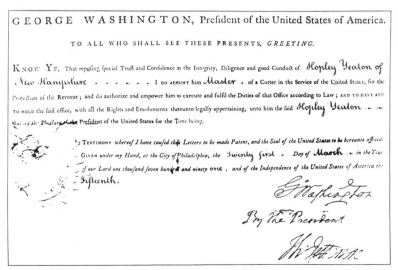

First officer commissioned in Revenue Cutter Service March 21, 1791. Courtesy USCG.

policy: "The Coast Guard established January 28, 1915, shall be a military service and a branch of the armed forces of the United States at all times. The Coast Guard shall be a service in the Treasury Department, except when operating as a service in the Navy." Other than the fact the Coast Guard was reassigned to the Department of Transportation in 1967, this policy still stands. Interestingly the Service of today and the Service of 1790 are amazingly similar in the most fundamental ways. It was and is military but with a civil and humanitarian function.

The Revenue Cutter Service aided the Navy as needed in every war, conflict or police action from 1799 until 1915: against the French privateers and pirates in 1799, the War of 1812, the war against piracy and slavery from 1815 to 1822, the Seminole Indian Uprising in 1836, the Mexican War in 1846 and the Spanish-American War in Cuba and the Philippines. After 1915 the newly formed Coast Guard served in WW I, WW II, the Korean and Viet Nam conflicts. Accounts of self-abnegation, valor and superb seamanship could fill a volume. However, two accounts from those early years are particularly noteworthy.

In 1799 the newly formed Navy put together a fleet of 20 ships to combat French pirate raiders along our coast. There were 8 Cutters among them. Of 20 French ships captured by the combined fleet, 16 were taken by Cutters. The Cutter *Eagle* set something of a record by capturing 5 French ships, assisting in capturing 10 others and recapturing 7 American ships.

In the War of 1812 the Revenue Cutter Service's greatest fame of the conflict was brought about by another *Eagle*. (The Coast Guard has a tradition of naming ships after predecessor vessels which can be confusing.) In 1814 the *Eagle* found herself up against 2 much larger British ships. A disadvantaged position as well as a huge mismatch of fire-power—the *Eagle's* six two and four pounders versus the British eighteen thirty-two pounders—left the crew no choice but to go ashore. However they carried the guns and ammunition with them and mounted the artillery in the hills, thus gaining an advantage of position. For hours the little guns yapped at the roar of the big guns. The *Eagle* was finally taken but that great display of courage raised American spirits. Today the Academy training bark *Eagle*—named for its predecessors—carries on this great tradition.

It is also of historic interest that during the 1836 Seminole Indian Uprising in Florida, the Cutter *Washington,* in coopera-

Left to right: Sandy McBeath, President of Grand Haven Area Historical Society and Commander Lawson Brigham, Commander of "Escanaba III".

tion with the Army and Navy, landed men and guns to save Fort Brook after the Seminoles had ambushed and killed all but one of the garrison. This is credited as the first amphibious landing by combined forces in the United States history and would not be duplicated again for more than 100 years—again by the Coast Guard during WW II.

The ensign of the Service had its origin in those early formative years. It was described in 1799 as "consisting of sixteen perpendicular stripes, alternate red and white, the Union of the Ensign to be the Arms of the U.S. in dark blue on a white field." At that time the Nation was comprised of 16 states—Vermont, Kentucky and Tennessee having joined the original 13—thus one stripe for each state. The Revenue Cutter Service ensign became the Coast Guard ensign after 1915.

The familiar Coast Guard Seal of crossed anchors was authorized for the Revenue Cutter Service in 1910 and then adopted by the Coast Guard after 1915. However, it was not until 1927 that the design of the emblem was officially designated as a shield within 2 concentric circles superimposed upon 2 crossed anchors. The seal has gone through some evolutionary changes to update the artwork from time to time.

Authorized in 1910

Adopted in 1927
Revised in 1957

Revised in 1967—Today's version

Evolution of the U.S. Coast Guard Seal

The U.S. Arms in the union of the ensign has also changed to stay with the logo of the times but the only major ensign design change made since 1799 took place in 1910 when the Revenue Cutter Service emblem was placed in the middle of the 7th red stripe. The Coast Guard Seal took the same position in 1927 and is the ensign we see flown today.

Adding to the great Coast Guard tradition is perhaps the finest of all Service marches—Semper Paratus—written in 1928 by Francis S. VanBoskerck, Jr., a graduate of the Coast Guard Academy at the turn of the century.

Most officers of the Coast Guard are trained at the Academy in New London, Connecticut. Built in 1932 the Georgian-style brick buildings and meticulously kept lawns which rise high from the shores of the Thames River make the campus one of the most beautiful in the country. Each candidate gains admittance by a nationwide competitive examination given in December. Unlike the other services there are no Congressional appointments. Today's Academy is a far cry from the spartan training arena for the original 1876 cadets which was located aboard the revenue cutter *Chase* sailing out of the historic old whaling town of New Bedford, Massachusetts. The *Chase* replaced the *Dobbin* in 1878 and remained at New Bedford until 1900 at which time it was quartered at Ann Arundel Cove, Curtis Bay, Maryland. There a 2 story wooden school was built to expand the curriculum to accommodate the ever increasing duties required of the Service. In 1910 the school moved to Fort Trumball, New London, Connecticut and finally in 1932 settled permanently a little farther up the Thames River—today's United States Coast Guard Academy. The Academy motto is "Scientiae cedit mare"—the sea yields to knowledge.

Traditional seamanship continues to be a part of Cadet training today aboard the three-masted sailing bark *Eagle*. Built in Hamburg, in 1936 she sailed under the name *Horst Wessel* as a training ship for the German Navy. It was awarded to the U.S. in 1946 as a part of war reparations and renamed the *Eagle* to honor the other *Eagles* which preceded her.

Many ships have served the Coast Guard and there are many serving today. But none was as influential to our story as the Cutter *Escanaba,* as we shall see as our monograph continues.

CHAPTER 2

EARLY GRAND HAVEN HARBOR

"Ironsides", wooden hull steamer, 1864-1873. Courtesy Grand Haven Area Historical Society.

She left Milwaukee bound for Grand Haven on Sunday night September 14, 1873 with winds out of the southwest. Aboard were 19 passengers, 33 crewmen and a varied cargo. As she made her way through the night the winds increased to gale force and switched to the west. Approaching the Michigan shore the waves had a longer fetch in which to build and these mounting, following seas made steering increasingly difficult.

Ironsides was a wooden hulled steamer built in 1864 for iron industry pioneer Ever Ward with the purpose of hauling ore on the Great Lakes during the Civil War. She was 231 feet long with a 38 foot beam and had two boilers which fed steam to two pistons that in turn drove two 4-bladed propellers. Nathanial Engleman of Milwaukee purchased the *Ironsides* in 1869 along with her sister ship *Labell* and placed them on duty in his newly formed Engleman Transportation Company as cross-Lake ferries for the Detroit and Milwaukee Railroad, a service which the railroad had contracted to Engleman in 1869. *Ironsides* had been overhauled for passenger service during the winter months of 1872-73.

Waiting for the arrival of *Ironsides* at the Grand Haven terminal on that September 15th morning was Engleman Line agent George Stickney. But his wait would be in vain. This would be the 9 year old *Ironsides'* final run.

When the ship approached Grand Haven at 7:00 AM winds were at full gale force. Captain Harry Sweetman made two attempts at entering port and narrowly missed wrecking on the beach. The violent winds had already driven five other vessels ashore at Grand Haven. Sweetman aborted his third try and backed off 2 miles to wait for the storm to subside. However, water was pouring in the cargo gangways which had been pounded as *Ironsides* rolled in the troughs during her wrenching turns. And what was not known was that the tremendous racking she had been subjected to during the near broaches had opened her wooden seams and the water coming in was more than the pumps could handle. *Ironsides'* doom was sealed. By 9:00 AM the ship began to sink.

At 11:00 o'clock five lifeboats were put over and all passengers and crew made it to them safely. Captain Sweetman, the last to leave, entered a lifeboat about noon, just in time to watch *Ironsides* make her death plunge to the bottom of Lake Michigan. As the pathetic lifeboats pulled for shore through the thunderous maelstrom it was obvious to the anxious masses who had gathered along the beach that the real drama was about to unfold.

Among those on shore were Captain Richard Connell and his surfmen of the recently organized volunteer Grand Haven Life Savers. This crew consisted of John Deyoung, John Wessel, C. Haffenback, John Fisher, C. VerMullen, James Barlow, R. Carmel, J.J. Glasson and 27 year old Adrian O'Beck (1846-1932).

As the defenseless lifeboats made their final desperate dash for safety two succeeded but the malevolent seas literally devoured the other three lifeboats casting all the occupants into the boiling combers. The surfmen, aided by townspeople, formed a human chain to go out into the breakers and by this means were able to grab several from certain death. Twenty-three, however, were lost.

Among those of the crew lost were Captain Sweetman, Chief Engineer Robert McGlue and the Steward, Dan Drescoll. The bodies of Harry Hasebarth and his bride later washed ashore in each others arms. Another victim was Gerald Smith, a Grand Haven cigar maker returning from a business trip in Milwaukee, who has the dubious distinction of being the first person buried in the City's new Lake Forest Cemetery.

In 1966 divers Gene Turner and the late David Groover found *Ironsides'* remains southwest of the Grand Haven pier in 120 feet of water. The painted scroll-work could still be seen on her two pistons, which were named Jack, for starboard, and Jill, for port. Artifacts recovered from this wreck are on display at Grand Haven's Tri-Cities Museum.

Grand Haven Harbor has recorded its share of boat and ship wrecks over the years. That is not, however, because it is a particularly hazardous harbor. On the contrary, the Grand River currents present no more challenge than any number of rivers which find their way to Lake Michigan and, because of its channel depth and width, Grand Haven has always been considered a comfortable harbor. The seemingly greater number of wrecks which have been chronicled at Grand Haven, therefore, may more likely be attributed to frequency of use.

Gaining safe entry to any harbor is made more difficult during a running, breaking sea. Before the construction of piers shifting channel sands caused by lake currents could compound the problem. Then too, harbors which were river mouths, such as Grand Haven, presented additional shoal water created by alluvial deposits which accumulated quite naturally at the mouth of the river and were likewise very susceptible to the vagaries of storm currents. At Grand Haven, prior to pier construction, heavy seas breaking over these shoal waters made gaining safe access to the Harbor a hazardous proposition regardless of the draft of the vessel.

The earliest crafts to use the Grand River and Grand Haven Harbor were of Native American design. The type history records as being the most common was the birch bark canoe which was utilized by those early Americans for general transportation, hunting, fishing, harvesting and commerce. It was a true outgrowth of the wilderness, a design modern man has not been able to improve.

European exploration of Lake Michigan and the Peninsulas

began in 1673. Louis Joliet, Father Marquette, Robert Cavelier de LaSalle and Henri de Tonty all used the extremely efficient and readily available bark canoe. LaSalle later built the *Griffin*. Launched August 7, 1679, she was the first sailing vessel to ride the waters of the Great Lakes. Joseph LaFramboise, one of the Territory's early fur traders, began making annual journeys into the Grand River Valley in 1783 and he used—as would fur traders like him for the next half century—the ubiquitous birch bark canoe.

The bateaux, a wooden sail/row boat of French Canadian origin, was used by the traders in the spring to freight the winter fur harvest north to Mackinac Island. As many as 10 to 30 of these colorfully painted crafts would arrive at a trading post, such as Rix Robinson's at Gabagouache. (Gabagouache was the Native American name for the "Big Mouth" of the Grand River as it entered Lake Michigan.) This trading post was one of 20 in West Michigan Robinson managed for the American Fur Trading Company. There were others such as Pierre Constant's near Lamont, a British Fur Company post. Arrival of these fleets of bateaux was epical.

But both the birch bark canoe and bateaux were shallow draft vessels and therefore the shifting delta sands at the mouth of the Grand River presented no particular problem for either when it came to negotiating a safe entry into the harbor, that is except during times of heavy, breaking seas. A second advantage of these small vessels was that safe anchorage was not necessary because both could be easily pulled ashore when the need arose.

The first European style wooden boat to visit Gabagouache was the British sloop *Felicity* which anchored a short distance up the River on Sunday, October 31, 1776. However, the presence of this deeper draft style vessel would not become commonplace at Grand Haven until the 1830's. And as long as the birch bark canoe and the bateaux could handle the commerce and serve the transportation needs there was no necessity to improve or alter the Harbor. After all, in its 1776 visit the *Felicity* had reported the Harbor to be 70 to 80 yards wide and 2 to 4 fathoms (12 to 24 feet) deep which was more than adequate for those early shallow draft vessels.

The first recorded wreck at the entrance to Grand Haven Harbor occurred in 1821 following the Chicago Treaty. An influential Ottawa chief, his wife and son were returning from the Treaty by canoe when a storm developed. The seas capsized the canoe and although the chief made it safely to shore his wife and son were drowned.

The second recorded wreck involved no loss of life but was responsible for a tale of lost "treasure" which has added intrigue to the incident through the years. In October, 1826 the schooner *Andrew,* bound for Gabagouache, failed to negotiate the Harbor and was driven ashore at the mouth of the Grand River. In the ship's cargo were 20 barrels of whiskey which were being shipped to Rix Robinson's trading post. Although at that time whiskey cost only about sixteen cents a gallon, as a business commodity it was indispensable. Robinson salvaged the barrels and buried them in the sand on safe ground. Some time later when he returned for his cache the dunes had shifted enough to obliterate his land marks and he failed to locate the goods. Supposedly all one need do is dig in the correct spot at "the mouth of the Grand River" to find a "treasure" of well aged spirits which would bring far more than sixteen cents a gallon on today's market.

In the early development of the Michigan Territory, as was true of the whole Nation, water—lakes, oceans, rivers and canals— was the only practical means of transportation. Roads were used out of necessity but generally only for short distances. Consequently water navigation was an essential part of life. Descriptions of Grand Haven Harbor's first two wrecks points up the fact that a storm-mad Lake Michigan makes no discrimination as to vessel size when it claims a victim. And as the use of the Harbor increased it became apparent improvements would be needed to aid the mariners.

This brief history of Gabagouache before permanent settlers arrived has set the scene for what was to come in the way of harbor development, navigational aids and, in general, the introduction of the Lighthouse, Lifesaving and Revenue Marine Services to Grand Haven. These pages have previously covered the origins of those three Services prior to leaving their salt water roots. Next let us turn to the trials and tribulations as the Service sought to tame the yet-to-be-domesticated Inland Seas. The old salts referred to the Great Lakes as "mill ponds", but they would soon gain a healthy respect for them as they confronted the Lakes and learned first hand of these treacherous, malevolent waters. The "Eighth Sea", as the Great Lakes have been labeled, is perhaps quite accurate because the five Lakes comprise an area of some 94,510 square miles, more than twice the size of Michigan's lower peninsula.

CHAPTER 3

NAVIGATIONAL AIDS COME
TO THE GREAT LAKES

The Erie Canal was completed in 1825. This was of eminent importance to the Michigan Territory because it provided a water link from the Atlantic Ocean to the Great Lakes, thereby affording a better means of transportation for settling that western wilderness. Before the close of the 1825 season, the steamers *Superior, Henry Clay* and *Pioneer* were carrying hundreds of pioneer homesteaders from Buffalo—the western terminus of the Canal—to Detroit. The use of lighthouses to mark the coast line is as old as maritime commerce itself, so as the settlers flowed west lighthouse construction on the Great Lake coasts flourished to keep pace.

In this day of high-speed travel and communications it is difficult to comprehend the enormous amount of time it took our predecessors to move relatively short distances, not to mention the privations and dangers which accompanied them. It is evident the Erie Canal captured the pioneering imagination of this young, expanding nation, not only for the speed of travel it afforded overland but also for the manner in which it spawned technology all along the transportation chain. The advent of the Canal—referred to by some wags of the day as Clinton's Ditch, because it was New York State Governor DeWitt Clinton who pushed for completion of the Erie Canal—could be compared with the difference between train and air travel today. For example, when Rix Robinson came from Massachusetts to the Michigan Territory in 1812 it took him 26 days to travel from Buffalo to Detroit. Eleven years later—1823—Reverend William and Amanda Ferry came cross-country from Massachusetts on part of the unfinished Erie Canal and then boarded the Great Lake's first steamer, the side-wheeler *Walk-in-the-Water,* bound

**Reverend William
Montague Ferry**

For Detroit. Their travel from Buffalo to Detroit took only 5 days.

And, whereas Michilimackinac (Mackinac Island) had been the mercantile "capital" of the Territory since the late 1600's, demise of the fur trade coupled with the flood of homesteaders from the East would soon make Detroit the Territory's gathering place.

When General Lewis Cass was appointed Provisional Governor in 1815 the Michigan Territory was a community of little more than 4000 people. When he left in 1831 to become Secretary of War, his successor, Stephens T. Mason, took over a Territory which was self supporting with a population of 32,538. The Territory's success had been tied directly to water transportation.

As the expansion of the country took place from east to west so too did the maritime navigational and safety aids. The first light was on the Canadian side of Lake Ontario, built in 1804 at Mississauga Point on the west bank of the Niagara River. That light was taken down in 1814. The first American light was simply a tower attached to the messhouse in 1818 at Fort Niagara, located on Lake Ontario on the east bank of the Niagara River. But a canal around Niagara Falls was not constructed until 1829 and so ships on Lake Ontario could not reach the Great Lakes per se. At that time in order to reach the other 4 Lakes any large vessel had to be launched at some point above the Falls, such as Lake Erie. Therefore, although these two lights were on a Great Lake, they did not aid the ships which were involved in the commerce for all of the other Great Lakes.

There is still controversy over whether the Buffalo, New York or Presque Isle—today Erie—Pennsylvania light was the first one on Lake Erie. A fire in the Treasury Department in 1920 destroyed many of the records so tracing the history is difficult, however 1818 has been documented for the Presque Isle Light so let us use that date as our benchmark. Michigan Territory received

Congressional appropriations for a light on the Detroit River in 1823, the structure itself completed August 8, 1825. And although Congress had authorized the placement of lightships and the construction of lighthouses for all the Great Lakes, their beacons would not shine on Lake Michigan with any assuring consistency until the 1840's and 50's.

Lighthouses had the very obvious purpose of warning mariners of hazardous waters as well as showing them the way to a safe port. The free harvest from ship disasters brought lighthouses some cold-blooded opposition and occasional sabotage. When wrecks occurred some very useful objects washed ashore along with the corpses of the victims. Although no accounts can be found that anything of the sort happened on the Great Lakes, it is of historic interest to note that along the Atlantic coast in the 1830's and 40's "wreckers" did exist. These "moon cussers" made a livelihood of drawing vessels ashore with false lights and then plundering the wreck. A Captain who knew the waters undoubtedly also took pains to know the idiosyncrasies of the lighthouses which marked his way so as not to be duped by these pirates. The "wreckers'" prey were most likely strangers to the waters or weary seamen lulled into poor judgement.

That is not to say that people along the Great Lakes did not take

1900's Lumber Freighter. A heavy sea could easily "redistribute" the cargo. Courtesy Grand Haven Area Historical Society.

advantage of what was found on the beaches. Jeanette Rosema and Katherine Groenevelt—sisters—can recall their father taking a team and wagon out to the beach from Ferrysburg in the 1920's to collect firewood and returning with not only firewood but lumber of construction quality which had been part of a schooners cargo or grain which had washed ashore and could be gathered for feed. Helen DeYoung—daughter of John DeYoung, keeper of the Grand Haven Life Saving Station from 1881 to 1885—and William Bramer—a Ferrysburg resident who helped build the North Shore Road to the Lifeboat Station in 1928—are two persons living today who can remember the beaches being totally littered with lumber and shingle blocks which had washed off the decks of stormed tossed vessels. Bramer recalls there were times when it was piled so thick that it was difficult to walk the beach.

The exact date Revenue Marine Service came to the Great Lakes is not certain. Henry Schoolcraft recorded the Revenue Cutter *Alexander J. Dallas* as being homeported in Detroit in 1819 and J.B. Mansfield's "History of the Great Lakes"—published in 2 volumes in 1899 by J.H. Beer and Company of Chicago, available at the Lake Michigan Maritime Museum in South Haven, Michigan—refers to the Revenue Cutter *Fairplay* sailing into Chicago Harbor prior to 1819. However, the first official documentation of a cutter being assigned to the Great Lakes was the 1829 appointment of Captain Daniel Dobbins to the Revenue Cutter stationed at Presque Isle on Lake Erie. He later took command of the Revenue Cutter *Erie* which made its maiden voyage April 29, 1833. Dobbins was one of the Lakes most illustrious folk heroes. This is the same Daniel Dobbins who helped provide Commodore Perry the ships with which he defeated the British fleet on Lake Erie in the War of 1812. One of the ships in Perry's fleet was the *Porcupine* which ended her sailing days in Grand Haven. That unusually interesting story is told in Chapter 12.

Thus we have established the arrival on the Great Lakes of two of the Coast Guard's predecessors. As the narrative continues it will become apparent that lighthouses proliferated much more rapidly than did the Revenue Cutters in their respective service to the Lakes. The evolution of the two services had followed that same pattern from their inception. But this is not surprising because whereas there was a need for buoys, markers, beacons,

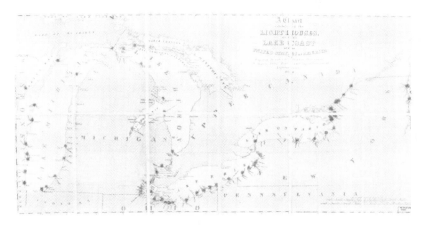

Chart exhibiting lighthouses on the Great Lakes. Courtesy USCG.

lighthouses and support personnel at every port, shoal or rocky hazard, the same could not be said for Cutters.

The Lighthouse Service traces its roots to the first light at Boston Harbor in 1716, 73 years before it became an official agency of U.S. Government in 1789. From 1818 (the date of the first light on Lake Erie) until 1865—a 36 year span—72 lighthouses sprouted up along the shores of the Lakes. As listed in "Guardians of the Eighth Sea" by T. Micheal O'Brien they are as follows:

Lake Ontario: Galloo Island, established 1820, refitted 1857
Horse Island, established 1831, refitted 1857
   (light on keeper's dwelling)
Stoney Point, established 1837, refitted 1857
   (light on keeper's dwelling)
Oswego, established 1837, refitted 1857
Big Sodus Bay, established 1825, refitted 1859
Genesee, established 1822, rebuilt 1858
Niagara Fort, established 1823, refitted 1857
   (light on messhouse - Fort Built 1813)

Lake Erie: Horse-shoe Reef, established 1856
Buffalo, established 1828, refitted 1857
   (replaced original light est. 1820)
Dunkirk, established 1837, rebuilt 1857
Presque Isle, established 1838, rebuilt 1858

(replaced original light est. 1818)

Grand River (Fairport), established 1828, rebuilt 1858

Cleveland, established 1829, refitted 1859 (lighted with gas)

Black River, established 1836, rebuilt 1857

Sandusky, established 1831, rebuilt 1858

Port Clinton, established 1832, refitted 1864

Green Island, established 1854

West Sister Island, established 1847, refitted 1857

Turtle Island, established 1831, refitted 1857

Monroe, established 1849, refitted 1855

Lake St. Clair: St. Clair Flats, established 1859

Windmill Point, established 1838, refitted 1865

Lake Huron: Fort Gratiot, established 1825, refitted 1862

Point Aux Barques, established 1847, rebuilt 1857

Ottawa (Tawas) Point, established 1853, refitted 1856

Charity Island, established 1857

Saginaw Bay, established 1841, refitted 1863

Thunder Bay Island, established 1832, refitted 1857

Presque Isle, established 1840, refitted 1857

Bois Blanc, established 1839, refitted 1857 (replaced earlier light - washed away)

Cheboygan, established 1851, rebuilt 1859 (light on keeper's dwelling)

Detour, established 1847, rebuilt 1861

Lake Michigan: Waugoshance, established 1851, (replaced lightship)

Skilligallee (Ile aux Galets), established 1850, refitted 1857 (light on keeper's dwelling)

Beaver Island Harbor, established 1856

Beaver Island, established 1851, rebuilt 1858

Grand Traverse, established 1852, rebuilt 1858 (light on keeper's dwelling)

South Manitou, established 1839, rebuilt 1858 (light on keeper's dwelling)

Point Betsey (Point aux BecScies), established 1858

Muskegon, established 1851, refitted 1856 (light on keeper's dwelling)

Grand River, established 1839, relocated 1855

Kalamazoo River, established 1852, rebuilt 1859 (light on keeper's dwelling)

St. Joseph's, established 1831, rebuilt 1859 (light on keeper's dwelling)

Michigan City, established 1837, rebuilt 1858 (light on keeper's dwelling)

Chicago, established 1859 (replaced earlier light established in 1832)

Waukegan, established 1849, rebuilt 1860 (light on keeper's dwelling)

Kenosha, established 1848, rebuilt 1858

Racine, established, 1829, rebuilt 1858

Milwaukee, established 1855

Port Washington, established 1849, rebuilt 1860 (light on keeper's dwelling)

Sheboygan, established 1839, rebuilt 1860 (light on keeper's dwelling)

Manitowoc, established 1839, refitted 1859

Bayley's Harbor, established 1852, refitted 1858

Port deMoris, established 1849, rebuilt 1858 (replaced earlier light, washed away)

Pottawatomie, established 1858, rebuilt 1858 (replaced earlier light, washed away)

Point Peninsula, established 1865

Green Island, established 1863 (light on keeper's dwelling)

Tail Point, established 1848, rebuilt 1859 (light on keeper's dwelling)

Lake Superior: Round Island, established 1855, refitted 1864 (light on keeper's dwelling)

Point Iroquois, established 1857

White Fish Point, established 1847, rebuilt 1861

Grand Island, established 1856

Marquette, established 1853, refitted 1856

Portage River, established 1856
Manitou, established 1849, rebuilt 1861
Copper Harbor, established 1848, refitted
    1848
Eagle Harbor, established 1850, refitted 1857,
    (light on keeper's dwelling)
Eagle River, established 1858 (light on keeper's
    dwelling)
Ontonagon, established 1852, refitted 1857
    (light on keeper's dwelling)
La Pointe, established 1858, (light on keeper's
    dwelling)
Rasberry Island, established 1862 (light on
    keeper's dwelling)
Minnesota Point, established 1857

Because of their obvious similarity, a tenuous amalgamation of the Lighthouse Service and the Revenue Marine was attempted in 1845 but it was to be short-lived. An unfortunate act of Congress set them apart in 1852 when the Lighthouse Board was established and the two were not to be joined again in their natural union for nearly a century.

The Lakes boasted 72 lighthouses by 1865 but by the same date only 7 cutters had served on the Lakes with just the *Erie* having had any extended tour of duty. The *Harrison* served from 1849 to 1856. In 1861 the *Thompson, Brown, Toncey, Cobb* and *Black* were ordered off the Lakes to New York for Civil War duty leaving only the *Erie*. This decided lack of presence on the Great Lakes during that pre-Civil War period may have been due in part to the Service's practice of chartering local vessels for use as Cutters rather than building new ones. It is safe to say what ever vessels were at the Revenue Marine's command at that time, their activities were concentrated on Lake Erie with apparently only temporary sojourns out of those waters. However it must be remembered the job of the Revenue Marine as it related to navigational aids was peripheral at best. The Service's primary duty remained—and until the 1900's ostensibly would remain— the enforcement of the custom laws. That responsibility was best served on Lake Erie, the spigot of the funnel as commerce and people spread west. In contrast the need for lighthouses was critical at the scores of destinations where settlers would locate throughout the Great Lakes region. Cutters on the Great Lakes would not begin to take on the humanitarian role so familiar to us today until the 1900's.

In passing it is appropriate for historic prospective to mention the Life Saving Service. Although a government operated service was not formally introduced to the Great Lakes until the United States Centennial Year—1876—this Coast Guard predecessor originated in 1785 as the concern of a few brave volunteers who sought to help preserve life by providing aid for mariners who wrecked along the coasts. The pioneer organization was the Massachusetts Humane Society, which erected the first American Lifeboat Station in 1807 at Cohasset. The first Life Saving Station, per se, was a boathouse built in 1848 at Sandy Hook, New Jersey, now a Coast Guard museum. This structure is truly a National treasure and it is fortunate that it is has been preserved.

In those early days there was inherent danger when one took to the sea in a sailing vessel; storms, fire, human error, inadequate navigational aids, unmarked underwater hazards and structural failure all played a part in early tragedies. By the 1830's about 90 American vessels were being wrecked annually, their tattered hulls littering the shores. The 1837 Congress responded by ordering the Revenue Cutters to begin winter cruising to aid ships in trouble. Still there was no Federal assistance from the shore, where it was so conspicuously needed. Other than ships aiding one another, our country had no safety procedures for disaster prevention or coping with a wreck when it did occur.

In 1847 Michigan Representative Robert McClelland—of Monroe, Michigan and State Governor 1851-53—was responsible for Congressional legislation which was to furnish lighthouses with lifeboats to aid shipwrecked mariners. This was the first Federal effort for shore based assistance. In 1854 Lake Ontario received 9 lifeboats, Lake Erie 14, Lake Michigan 23 and 1 for Lake Superior. However these were not placed at lighthouses but rather at designated land sites. There was complete lack of organization and the isolation of some of these stations made them easy prey for vandals and thieves.

But the sea disasters continued and people continued to perish. In 1854 300 persons died when the *Powhatan* was stranded just 200 yards from the New Jersey shore. Public indignation mounted and eventually forced Congress's hand. On February 1, 1871 a Revenue Marine Bureau was established by the Secretary

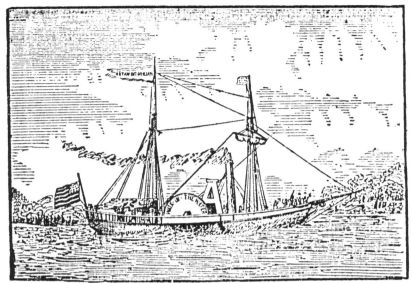

"Walk-in-the-Water", first steam vessel on the Great Lakes—1819. Courtesy Michigan Historical Commission.

of the Treasury which was to administer both the Cutters and the lifesaving stations. As we shall see in Chapter 11, 1871 was the same year a volunteer Life Saving Service would begin in Grand Haven.

Mention should also be made of the Steamboat Inspection Service. It, too, was one of the early predecessors of the Coast Guard but is the least documented therefore its date of arrival to the Great Lakes is not known. However since its authority extended to all waters plied by steam vessels it can be surmised the Service made its presence known on the Lakes shortly after it was organized in 1838. (*Walk-In-The-Water*, the Great Lakes first steamer, was making round trips between Buffalo and Mackinac Island as early as 1819) The Service was born out of calamity. Robert Fulton invented the steamboat in 1807 but it took years to perfect it. For a while it seemed that steamers were blowing up everywhere. In 1832 one out of every seven steamboats afloat exploded, with a loss of thousands of lives. Federal regulation for marine safety was needed and on July 7, 1838 the Steamboat Inspection Service came into being as another function of the Treasury Department.

CHAPTER 4

GABAGOUACHE COMES OF AGE

As early as 1821 Rix Robinson had a trading post at Gabagouache which he used as a temporary residence certain times of the year. His buildings were located on the Grand River

Rix Robinson platted Grand Haven April 14, 1835.

at the foot of Washington Street, today the approximate location of Grand Haven's Tri-Cities Museum. In 1833 the United States Government issued Robinson a patent for all of the land at the mouth of the Grand River. Even then he did not become a permanent resident but continued to live near the confluence of the Grand and Thornapple Rivers—today Ada, Michigan. Grand Haven would not have its first permanent residents until 1834.

Being a port city Grand Haven's early inhabitants either had developed—or quite naturally would develop—an intimate bond with the Grand River, Lake Michigan and all facets of water travel. Reverend William Montaque Ferry had served the Presbyterian Mission Church on Mackinac Island since 1822. In 1834, as the need for his mission came to an end, he explored Lake Michigan by canoe looking for a new home. He liked what he found at Gabagouache and returned for further exploration of the Grand River Valley. In June of 1834, starting at its headwaters near Jackson, Ferry canoed the entire length of the Grand River to Lake Michigan. He repeated this same river voyage in September and became

Grand Haven Sesquicentennial 1984. (Left to right) Dave Seibold as Rix Robinson, Dottie Seibold as Madeline LaFramboise, Marsha Witherell as Mary A. White, Jerry Witherell as Sen. Thomas Ferry, Mary Creason as Amanda Ferry, and Bill Creason as Rev. William M. Ferry.

thoroughly convinced of the Grand Valley's advantages. Reverend Ferry's 254 mile Grand River trip was relived in 1984, during Grand Haven's Sesquicentennial, in a 26 foot replica of a voyageur canoe appropriately dubbed "Gabagouache." Some of the latter-day personalities who participated in that Grand River Odyssey are pictured here.

Ferry subsequently returned to Gabagouache from Mackinac Island on November 2, 1834 with his family and 16 other homesteaders aboard the schooner *Supply*. These, then, became the area's first permanent settlers. On April 14, 1835—five months after Reverend Ferry had arrived—Rix Robinson filed the original plat of the town he named "Grand Haven." That same year-1835-Ferry built the Village's first permanent home on the south east corner of Washington and Harbor Avenue, present site of the Kirby Grill.

In 1836 the schooner *St. Joseph* arrived from Buffalo with 42 persons aboard, among them were 5 of Rix Robinson's brothers and their families. The *St. Joseph* stayed to became the first vessel

VILLAGE
of
GRAND HAVEN
Ottawa County
Michigan
Surveyed by C. Burns 1835
RIX ROBINSON
Proprietor

Territory of Michigan }
Kalamazoo County   {

Be it remembered that on this 14th day of April 1835 personally came before me, a Notary Public for said county, Rix Robinson of the County & Territory aforesaid and acknowledged the within Plat of this Village of Grand Haven to be his voluntary act for the uses and purposes therein expressed. Done and acknowledged before me this 14th day of April 1835.

THEODORE P. SHELDON,
Notary Public.

Grand Haven named. From Leo Lillie

employed regularly in lumber and passenger service between Grand Haven and Chicago. Business and shipping were picking up.

On March 7, 1838 the U.S. Government purchased from John Wright of Chicago an acre of land at the mouth of the Grand River to be used as a site for a lighthouse. The original surveyor's drawing shows "Lighthouse Acre" on the south side of the Grand River channel and fronting Lake Michigan, today the approximate location of Grand Haven's State Park.

Anyone who has witnessed the fury of a Great Lakes fall storm would question the wisdom of such a location for a free standing lighthouse. The truth of the matter is the Government's choices where not always based upon thorough knowledge of the climatic habits of a locale and therefore the positioning of

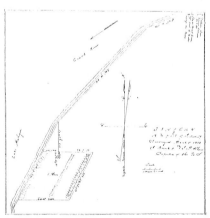

1838 Drawing of "Lighthouse Acre". From Leo Lillie

lighthouses was frequently a case of trial and error. For example the light placed on the Detroit River in 1825 was undermined and collapsed during a fall storm in November, 1828. In 1838 light-houses at Thunder Bay and Bois Blanc, both of which had been built on similar low ground, were either undermined or washed away. Higher ground was the answer for all of these. Grand Haven's turn would come. Here again the lesson would have to be learned the hard way.

It would not take long for Grand Haven to become a prominent port. As settlers moved west into the rich, open farmland of Illinois and Iowa there was need for lumber to build their homes and towns. Whereas these prairie states had only restricted reserves of timber, Michigan had a seemingly limitless supply of pine ideal for the job and no other state could furnish it either in quality or quantity with equal facility.

Reverend Ferry was, among other things, an enterprising business man and it was not by chance he had chosen Grand Haven for his new home. The Grand River is the longest river in Michigan—254 miles from its headwaters near Jackson to Lake Michigan. The Grand Valley and the River's countless tributaries had along their banks what was, presumably, an endless treasure of timber which could be cut and easily floated down to Grand Haven where it would then be processed and shipped to a waiting market.

Although Reverend Ferry had perhaps not perceived the final result to be on such a grand scale, he had, nevertheless, recognized the potential when he made his early explorations— the same potential Rix Robinson had sensed when he acquired ownership for all of Gabagouache in 1833. However, as is often the case, the pioneers of a worthy notion are not always the ones to reap its full reward. Such would be the case for both Ferry and Robinson.

The Village's first manufacturing building was a saw mill built in 1836. This was the beginning of an industry which would dominate life in the Grand Haven area for the next half century. At its zenith the mills at Grand Haven and Mill Point (renamed "Spring Lake" February 27, 1867) comprised one of the largest timber processing operations in the world at that time. Millions upon millions of board feet of lumber were to be shipped from this port annually and as the commerce grew the fleet of sailing ships to do the job grew accordingly.

By 1837 the Village of Grand Haven was a bustling "hot spot". Michigan was admitted to the Union as the 26th State on January 26, 1837. The Territorial County of Ottawa became a State County December 29, 1837, which at that time included the approximate area now occupied by Muskegon and Ottawa Counties. Grand Haven was the county seat and center of activity of a county which, according to the 1836 State census, had a population of 628.

It was a time of great speculation for eastern developers and "paper cities" seemed to abound, each with its own grandiose street and block scheme. All had some sort of river or lake frontage which made them look good on paper but in fact the majority of the development was in raw wilderness. Some were platted with over 1,000 lots which would have made the settlements larger than the original plats of Grand Haven, Holland, Zeeland or Muskegon. The lots which were sold, if indeed any were, must have been sold some distance from the actual development because if a prospective buyer were to have seen the site there is little doubt that would have been the end of the deal. It amounted to little more than wilderness homesteading and there were cheaper and better ways to do that.

And so the "paper cities" of Warren City—at the confluence of the Bass and Grand Rivers, Charlestown—opposite Lamont—and Ottawa—immediately down stream from Grand Valley State University—faded from the scene without more than a cabin or two being built on them. Both Macatawa—at the mouth of Lake Macatawa—and Superior—the present site of Waukazoo on the north side of Lake Macatawa—had a brief stint of respectability. The other exception was Port Sheldon. There, in 1836, New York and Philadelphia capitalists built a sham of a city including a hotel, boat club, a pier with a lighthouse—all with the hope of attracting settlers and reaping great land profits from this emerging frontier. It too failed.

All of this is background to explain the business climate as it related to real estate in this frontier. And Grand Haven was not immune to these "prospectors". The first platted addition to the Village of Grand Haven was the Wadsworth Addition, filed August 6, 1837. The plat was on the south bank of the Grand River at the River mouth. Its obvious intent was to make a financial gain from what was hoped would become one of the Great Lakes busiest harbors. So confident was the developer that he would strike it rich he reserved the south 100 feet of his development as the authorized terminus of the "United States Road from Detroit to the Mouth of Grand River". Interestingly this road is in direct line with Grand Haven's Pennoyer Avenue and with a little imagination—and a passel of pioneer spirit— one can envision Pennoyer extending far enough east to reach Detroit, thus achieving Wadsworth's grand scheme of joining the waters of Lake Erie to Lake Michigan. Although a little far fetched his idea did have merit.

As a matter of fact Wadsworth's machination was finally accomplished in 1858 when the Detroit and Milwaukee Railroad reached Grand Haven. Alas, the Railroad terminus was at the foot of Dewey Hill, not the Wadsworth Addition. Nonetheless the Harbor's potential was to be realized in nearly the manner Wadsworth had perceived it. And when you consider roads had been the only means available to him to accomplish his fanciful scheme—railroads being another transportation generation down the track, so to speak—at least we can credit Mr. Wadsworth with being a visionary a cut above the rest of the real estate hucksters of the day.

The Campau brothers, Louis and Toussaint, were fur traders

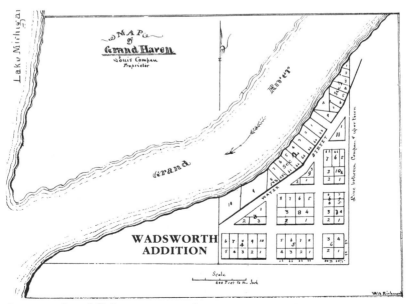

Campau's addition to Grand Haven—May 28, 1839. Future Government Pond. From Leo Lillie.

who worked the river system—the Saginaw, Bad, Maple and Grand River linkage—from Saginaw Bay to the mouth of the Grand River as early as 1826, just five years after Rix Robinson had established himself at Gabagouache. Toussaint set up a post in 1828 at a point farther down stream from Robinson in a location referred to as the "Lower Diggings"—today's Government Pond. When Reverend William Ferry made his first trip to Gabagouache in June 1834 Louis Campau sensed the meaning of the visit and purchased his brother's property at the "Lower Diggings" in July 1834 for $350. Louis built a warehouse for his trading business and then in 1839 he platted his holdings, which made it the Village's second extension—the Campau Addition. Located immediately down stream from the original town, it in effect made the contiguous link between the Wadsworth Addition and Grand Haven proper. It is shown here to provide historic background for the "Government Pond"—alias "Navy Yard", "Government Basin", "Swimming Hole", "Fish Pond" depending upon what level of sophistication a person was attempting to project or to whom one was speaking—which would one day be located at this site. Campau's trading post warehouse was located on Lot 9, Sec. 1. The River unrelentingly scoured into the Campau Addition over the years until revetments which created "Government Pond" were built in 1857-58 and put a stop to the erosion. "Water Street", shown in both the Campau and Wadsworth Additions, would not become a road to the beach until 1922.

CHAPTER 5

THE PORT OF GRAND HAVEN
IS ESTABLISHED

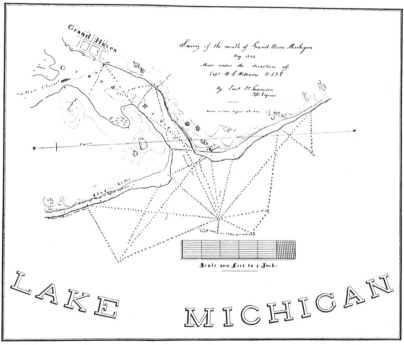

1844 Government survey of Grand Haven Harbor. From Leo Lillie.

In 1844 the Federal Government recognized the increasing importance of the Grand Haven Harbor and ordered the U.S. Engineers to survey and map the Harbor which also included charting the depth of the channel and adjacent waters. That survey, which was done under the direction of a Captain G.W.

Williams and is shown here, indicates "Warehouse Fallen" where Campau's post had been located. The River's erosive power had taken its toll in just 5 years. Still the revetment to control the erosion, thereby creating "Government Pond", would not be placed until 1857. "Shoal" is shown near the mouth of the River—a seaman's menace.

Dewey Hill is shown on the chart to be a height of 217 feet. A 1923 U.S. Government map shows this giant dune to be only 180 feet high. The sand continued to inch its way toward the Grand River so that by the 1930's it was a scant 122 feet. And then in 1941 there was an attempt to stabilize this City landmark. Construction Materials barges—formerly Michigan Materials and later to be named Construction Aggregates—were placed across the Grand River from the foot of Washington Street and on Saturday afternoon April 16, 1941 citizens, young and old, walked across the River to the top of Dewey Hill to plant 50,000 pine seedlings. Many citizens today remember their walk up Dewey Hill on that rainy spring day and can point with pride to the mature pines they helped plant which served to stabilize the erosion of this natural treasure. The sort of erosion which occurred to Dewey Hill graphically shows the "living" nature of these sand behemoths, the wind constantly recontouring our landscape legacies. Man would later see fit to the removal of these ancient dunes. And whereas the trees which had earlier been stripped clean from the State could replace themselves, the dunes, once removed, would never be replaced. Dewey Hill is mentioned here only to provide some historic reference for a landmark which will later play an important role in this story of Coast Guard City, USA.

As referrenced previously, waterways were the highways for early explorers, merchants and settlers. Understandably cities had their beginnings along these waterways and, as did Grand Haven, evolved from the water's edge inland. This is graphically revealed in the numbering system along Grand Haven's Washington Street; the addresses progress from number 1 consecutively as far as the town expanded—there being no reference to an East or West Washington address.

By 1845 Grand Haven was a village with a population of 300 while Grand Rapids had grown to 1510. In 1836 Louis Campau had started inter-city River service between Grand Haven and Grand Rapids with a pole boat he named *Young Napoleon*. A second pole boat, the *Cinderella,* owned by Rix Robinson, Thomas White and Dr. Sydney Williams was put into River service between the two cities in 1837. However these pole boats required punting as their means of propulsion and were thus slow and laborious.

The first steam boat on the Grand River was the 84 foot *Governor Mason,* which was also launched in 1837. The *Mason* had no whistle but instead had a bugler atop the pilot house to announce the boat's comings and goings. In May 1840 the *Governor Mason* was driven ashore, wrecked and burned near the entrance to Muskegon Harbor.

The steamer which had the first whistle was the 140 foot stern wheeler *Owashtanong*—Native American for "far-flowing-water" or Grand River—operated by the Grand Haven Steamship Company which had been organized by Robinson, White and Williams. Captained by Thomas White, she acquired the ridicule nickname of "Poorhouse" because of her lack of sturdy construction.

By 1845 the steam boats *Enterprise,* the 97 foot *Paragon,* 101 foot *Mishawaka* and 130 foot *Empire* were serving, or had served at one time or another, the passenger and freight needs between Grand Haven and Grand Rapids. The little steamer *Humming Bird,* built by Henry Steele at Lamont and commanded by Captain Sibley, had twin hulls and a center paddle wheel, a rather unusual design. She became part of the riverboat fleet in 1847, the same year a canal was built around the rapids at Grand Rapids. This canal made it possible for River service to reach Ionia and Lyons.

The River commerce must have been profitable because the next year—1848—the 127 foot *Algoma* began making regular runs. In 1849 the steamer *Champion* made 3 trips a week between Grand Haven and Milwaukee, connecting with these River steamers plying between Grand Haven and Grand Rapids. 1848 was the year the State capital was moved from Detroit to Lansing. Although the Grand River went through Lansing, railroads would reach the Capital City before the River boats so the romance of a stern wheeler's haunting river boat whistle and the excitement of the puffing tall stacks coming around the bend never became a common scene for the state legislators.

In those early days finding one's way into an unfamiliar harbor or along a winding river channel could be chancy business because there was no standardization of the buoy marking. This was resolved in 1850 when Congress passed an Act that provided for all buoys, which appeared on the right as you entered a harbor from seaward, to be painted red and even-numbered. Those on the left were black (green today) and odd-numbered. Those marking shoals with a channel on either side were to be painted with red and black horizontal stripes and buoys in channel ways were to be colored black and white with perpendicular stripes.

Before their demise by the railroads these Grand River steamboats could be ranked with the famed, glamorous riverboats of the Ohio and Mississippi Rivers. In their 50 year span more than 30 of these steamboats saw service on the Grand River. One of the largest was the twin-stack sternwheeler *Valley City* of Grand Rapids, owned and operated by a Captain Mitchell. Launched July 7, 1892 it was 143 feet long, 29 feet wide, had two decks with a pilot house on top of the second deck and a 5 foot cargo hold below the first deck. It cost $1.00 for a round-trip fare from Grand Haven to Grand Rapids. The *Valley City* had been built in a vain attempt to revive River traffic, however the arrival of the Detroit and Milwaukee Railroad in 1858 had already heralded the eventual end for the river boats. But history is not always a convincing teacher; in 1905 we will see this same scenario played out again. The *Valley City* was out of business by June 4, 1894—just short of 2 years after it had been placed into service. She was sold to the John Cudahy Company of Chicago, taken apart, shipped to Seattle and from there taken to Alaska's Yukon River where—still under the command of Captain Mitchell—she was used during the 1897-98 Gold Rush.

The last steamer making regular runs to Grand Rapids was the Crosby Transportation Company side-wheeler *May Graham*. The 80 foot long sidewheeler was originally owned by the Benton Harbor based Graham and Morton Line and was named for Graham's daughter, May. The *May Graham* was purchased by Crosby in 1907 and put in service on the Grand River primarily as a fruit hawler. However she also picked up clam shells from the clammers along the River for delivery to the button factory at Lamont and eventually became a very popular excursion boat. *May Graham* passed through the swing bridge at Eastmanville for the last time in 1917. Her days on the water finished, *May Graham's* upper decks and cabins were removed and served the William Bosman family as a cottage on the north

"May Graham" Courtesy Grand Haven Area Historical Society.

side of the River at the Cove. The Cove was purchased by Clare Jarecki in 1953 for development of a yacht basin, today's North Shore Marine.

Today a replica of the old steamboats—the gasoline engine powered sternwheeler *Harbor Steamer*, built in Saugatuck, Michigan in 1983—provides tourist excursions on the waters around Grand Haven, Spring Lake, Ferrysburg and the lower Grand River thus recapturing some of the nostalgia of those bygone days of the riverboats.

The River traffic is referenced here because business activity in the Grand River Valley—boat as well as the countless rafts of logs—directly reflected the business activity at Grand Haven Harbor. In the 1840's the number of saw mills in the Grand Haven area increased to six with a manufacturing capacity of 60,000 feet of lumber a day. The Village of Mill Point—which was destined to become the lumber capital of the Grand Valley—was platted by Thomas W. White—brother of Amanda White Ferry— and Silas C. Hopkins and recorded on December 10, 1849. Lumber was king and the business had nearly doubled in 10 years, keeping pace with the population of Illinois and Iowa which also had nearly doubled in that time. All varieties of lumber products left this port by schooners and funneled through the port of Chicago, which was becoming a veritable boom town. While Grand Haven's population grew from 300 in the 1840's to 600 in the 1850's, in that same time period Chicago grew from 4,479 to 38,734.

The Grand River Times, the first newspaper in Grand Haven, published its inaugural issue on July 2, 1851. The editors were James and John Barnes—twins—and William N. Angell—County Register of Deeds. It was printed in one of the upstairs rooms of the Henry Griffin Drug Store which was located on the northwest corner of First and Washington Streets. (Griffin had been the County's 2nd Sheriff, serving from 1844 to 1850. The upstairs of his drug store must have been a very busy place because in addition to the newspaper it also housed the County Offices which included the County Clerk, Register of Deeds and the Sheriff. In 1902 the building was moved to 525 Elliott where it stands today and continues its service as a residence. The structure is mentioned here as a point of historic interest because it may be the oldest building in this port city—or perhaps in the entire County.) An editorial from the first issue of the Grand River Times underscores the importance of the Harbor at that time. Reproduced here, just as it appeared in Leo Lillie's "Historic Grand Haven and Ottawa County", the vernacular of 150 years ago allows us to enjoy the full flavor of the occasion:

Grand Haven, the county seat of Ottawa County, Michigan, 213 miles west by north from Detroit, situated on the south bank of Grand River, one-half mile from its entrance into Lake Michigan, between which and the lake are sand hills 200 feet in height. Its harbor, the best on this side of this lake, could be made, by the construction of piers, superior to any on the upper lakes, and with such an improvement by the general government would open to the interior of the state by rail and plank roads to the Rapids a channel for the outlet of a vast amount of produce, the staples of a soil abounding with agricultural and mineral wealth, and the inlet of the produce of the world abroad. At the present writing there is from ten to thirteen feet depth of water in the channel which is indicated by lights and guides established at the mouth of the river. For benefit of transient vessels drawing more than eight feet, it may be well to state here that the inner and outer piers extend from the north and south past the line of ranges, presenting a straight passage out—but the buoy north of the outside pier is placed a little north of the range of the lights, in 13 feet of water; by keeping in range over the outside pier there is eight and one-half feet, and inside of it there is not less than ten feet in range.

Grand Haven contains a court house, which is used also as a church, a jail, a schoolhouse, with spacious halls above and below, with a cupola and a bell, a beautiful edifice which costs nearly two thousand dollars, and accommodates over one hundred scholars pursuing their various branches of education under an accomplished teacher, open to all classes of youth, including the penniless as well as the rich. There are three large public houses, well sustained, one of which, the Washington, is three stories high with a hall in the attic occupied by the Odd Fellows. There are five stores, three forwarding houses, two shops, several groceries, a large tannery, a tailor shop, blacksmith and carpenter shop, and several fisheries.

The principal business of the place is the manufacture and shipment of lumber. The number of steam and water mills for that purpose within the range of navigation are, and in this part of the county is, 14, five only of which are water mills, the remainder mostly double steam mills, which make an average of twenty thousand feet in twenty-four hours. The quantities of lumber shipped from this point this season will amount to nearly or quite thirty million feet besides a proportioned amount of shingles, shingle bolts, lath, wood, ceder bolts, posts, barks and so forth.

Heavy shipments of wheat, flour, and plaster have been made this season and a large amount of merchandise received for this place, and at various points in Ottawa County and Ionia. On the river two steamers ply between this place and Grand Rapids, and one connects above to Ionia, making about eighty miles inland navigation toward Lansing, the capital of the state, from which a plank road is now completed to Detroit, and is to be extended west to Ionia and Grand Rapids. Stock is now being taken in Kalamazoo for a plank road to Grand

Rapids, which improvement will facilitate travel from the east to Milwaukee.

Of interest in the forgoing editorial is the detailed description of the Harbor. Either the information was of common interest or the Editors had more than a passing fancy for boating. But the reference to piers is a bit confusing. The article first makes a plea for the construction of piers and then later refers to the extension of the inner and outer north and south piers as though they existed at that time. Later Grand River Times editorials continued the pressure for piers so it must be assumed channel improvements had not begun in 1851. Research and U.S. Army Corps of Engineer records establish 1857 as the year Harbor improvements began so that is the date which will be used for this work. However the article does mention outside buoys and range lights, which confirms evidence first seen in an 1849 Government survey of the Harbor—as an attempt at marking the channel in addition to the lighthouse.

Further insight into Harbor activity appeared in subsequent issues of the Grand River Times. A September 1851 article described the steam ship *General Harrison* passenger service from Grand Haven to Chicago, with stops at St. Joseph and Kalamazoo. The reproduction of the printed schedule shows there were 3 round trips available each week which gives further credibility to the growing importance of Grand Haven as a port.

The Marine List printed in the November 1851 edition of the paper, and reproduced here, further emphasizes the prominence of the Grand Haven Harbor. During the week November 4-10 eleven vessels arrived here while 17 schooners, loaded with

STEAMBOAT GEN. HARRISON, Capt. I. T. Pheatt, will for the balance of the season make five day trips, between Grand Haven and Chicago, touching at St. Joseph and Kalamazoo.

Leaves Grand Haven.		Leaves Chicago.	
Monday, September	29.	Friday, September 26.
Saturday, October	4.	Wednesday, October 1.
Thursday, "	9.	Tuesday, "	7.
Tuesday, "	14.	Saturday, "	11.
Monday, "	20.	Friday, "	17.
Saturday, "	25.	Thursday, "	23.
Friday, "	31.	Tuesday, "	28.
Thursday, November	6.	Monday, November	3.
Tuesday, "	11.	Saturday, "	8.
Monday, "	17.	Friday, "	14.
Saturday, "	22.	Wednesday, "	19.
Thursday, "	27.	Tuesday, "	25.
[139w.		Saturday, "	29.

SYRINGES, Metal and Glass, an assortment for sale the Mill Point Drug Store.
Sept. 20, 1851.   [13]

—Courtesy Grand Haven Tribune.

1851 Steamship Schedule.

MARINE LIST.

Steamer Empire, Fox. arrives on Mondays. Wednesdays, and Fridays of each week.

Steamer Algoma. Shoemaker, arrives on Tuesdays, Thursdays, and Saturdays of each week.

Steamer Algoma, Shoemaker. leaves on Monday, Wednesday, and Friday of each week.

Steamer Empire. Fox leaves on Tuesday, Thursday, and Saturday of each week.

ARRIVALS—Nov. 4.—10.

Nov. 4.—Schr. Roanoke. Dalton: Mariner. Irons ; S. B. Telegraph. Brown, U. S. Mail.

Nov. 5.—No arrivals.

Nov. 6.—Schr. Benton. Jones.

Nov. 7.—Schrs. Lizzie Throop. Clidesdell ; Illinois, Minskey ; New Hampshire. Warren ; Vermont, Nelson; brig Enterprise. Miller; S. B. Telegraph, Brown. U. S. Mail.

Nov. 8.—9.—No arrival.

Nov. 10—Schr. A. Harwood. Challoner.

CLEARED,

Nov. 4.—Brig Buffalo, Davidson. 4151 bushels wheat, 1856 bbls. flour, 4 sacks rags, 1 brl. cranberries, 19,000 shingles. 3,000 ft. lumber: schr. Vermont. Nelson, 100,000 ft. lumber: Wm. H. Hinsdale, Nelson, 40.000 ft. lumber; S. B. Gen. Harrison. Pheatt; S. B. Telegraph, Brown. U. S. Mail: schrs. A. Harwood, Challoner, 120,000 ft. lumber; L. P. Hilliard, Turner. 90,000 ft. lumber. 50,000 shingles; C. Walker, Hubbard, 100,000 ft. plank road stuff; Mariner. Irons, 60,000 ft. lumber: N. Hampshire, Warren 75.000 ft. lumber.

Nov. 5.—Schr. Octavia, McIntosh, 100,00 ft. lumber.

Nov. 6.—S. B. Telegraph, Brown. U. S. Mail.

Nov. 7.—No departures.

Nov. 8.—Schrs. Lizzie Throop. Clidesdell, 80.000 ft. lumber; New Hampshire.Warren. 75.000 ft. lumber; S. B. Telegraph, Brown. U. S. Mail.

Nov. 9.—Schrs. Illinois. Minskey, 50.000 ft. lumber, 50,000 shingles; Vermont, Nelson, 80,000 ft. lumber, 50,000 staves.

Nov. 10.—Schr. A. Harwood. Challoner 60 bbls. flour.

FREIGHTS.

Lumber, 14s to 16s per 1000 ft.; Lath. 2s per 1000; Shingles, 25 cts. per 1000; Staves 20s per 1000.

Shore ports 16s per 1000.

MARKETS.

GRAND HAVEN.	CHICAGO.
Lumber 4.50 a 5.00 pr. M.	Lumber 6.00 a 7.00 pr. M.
Shingles 1.13 a 1.50 pr. M.	Shingles 1.75 a 2.00 pr. M.
Lath 1,38 a 1.63 pr. M.	Lath $1.50 a 1.75 pr. M.
Staves, $5 to 6 pr. M.	Staves. $7.00 pr. M.
Shingle bolts $4,00 a 4.50 per cord.	Shingle bolts $7.00 per cord.
Saw logs 2,50 a 3,00 pr.M.	

NOTICE.

—Courtesy Grand Haven Tribune.

1851 Marine List

thousands of feet of lumber and other wood products, departed for Chicago. The schedule gave freight rates as well as the market prices on lumber and wood products at Grand Haven and Chicago.

A mail route from points along Grand River to Milwaukee had recently been established by the Postmaster General. This Marine List shows the U.S. mail steamship *Telegraph* making the Grand Haven to Milwaukee run. But let us allow the Editors of the Grand Haven Times to describe the scene in their own inimitable 1851 style:

> The Closing of Navigation. Our harbor was the scene of unusual bustle on the day of our last issue on the 19th instant. We left our sanctum at noon to witness the simultaneous departure of sixteen of the noble craft bound for Chicago for the last time this season. The merry sound of the "Heave-Ho," the cranking of the windlass, heaving the heavy anchor, and the shaking of the unfurled canvas in the wind, the stentorian voices of the officers giving their various orders, and the "aye-aye" of the active seamen were signs and sounds contrasting strangely with the unbroken stillness of nature around, which appeared barren and solitary, no more to echo these notes of preparation, or to witness men's stirring industry, till the winds of March waft back again these castles of the deep. In the van was Captain Fred with the *Telegraph* to announce the coming fleet. Next followed the *Lizzie,* making her thirty-ninth trip of 218 miles within less than thirty weeks, and averaging eighty thousand feet of lumber from this port to Chicago. Next came the *New Hampshire,* her successful rival, making as many trips in the same time; then the *Hilliard,* which is run from port to port, 109 miles in eight hours; then the three masted *Octavia* of Kalamazoo, running here on account of shallow water at her own harbor; then the *Walker,* which has walked the water successfully for numerous years, and is yet a staunch craft profitable to the owners whose name she bears. The brig *Olive Richmond,* of we say ditto; then the little *Venus,* early and late on the lake, like the morning and evening star; then the old *Tom Benton,* as great a veteran in the trade as "Old Bullion" was in the Senate. Then the light *Gazelle*

and the fleet *Reindeer*, both deserving their names, then the *Vermont,* always the favorite of passengers for her good qualities; then the *Illinois,* the *Lizzie's* sister, and ahead of her in sailing qualities—several remain to complete the list whose names we did not learn. There remains in port the brig *Enterprise* and the *Ann Winslow,* and a schooner *Amanda Harwood,* all to follow in a few hours. Besides this score of vessels there are several regular traders and two steamers on the west side of the lake, making in all a larger and better fleet than any port on this lake can boast, except Chicago. The amount of lumber exported this season cannot fall much short of thirty-five million feet, and besides this about fifteen million shingles; also large quantities of lath, wood, bark, staves, shingle bolts, and vast quantities of plaster, flour, and other produce from the upper country. Grand River is THE Grand River of Michigan and Grand Haven being THE Grand Haven, it should be the terminus of the Grand Northern Railroad to bring Milwaukee nearer to the Atlantic by way of the Canada road, than any city west of Michigan; and when the plank road connects Kalamazoo with the Rapids, we will give passengers a four hours trip to Wisconsin in a crack boat to be built this winter. It is worthy of remark here that not the slightest accident has happened at this port, during the eight months of navigation, notwithstanding such tempestuous weather in the spring and fall, the harbor being as accessible by night as by day, by the provisions of range lights. With an appropriation which we expect this winter for piers we shall become the key to unlock the stores of the wealthy resources of northern Michigan unequaled in the same extent of territory in the world. Let the upper river folks bestir themselves to put through the northern roads, and secure the counties east to the Rapids, which is soon destined to become the second city of the peninsular state.

The Editors certainly were enthusiastic about the Harbor's potential. And perhaps with good reason. The volume of products being exported from Grand Haven at that time was quite impressive. Lillie's book adds further corroboration:

Below is given a table amount of exports from the port
of Grand Haven during the season of navigation for the
year of 1851: 35,600,000 feet of lumber ($6.00 per
thousand) $312,600; 13,000,000 shingles, $16,250;
320,000 staves, $2,560; 1,200 cords of wood, $1,800;
350 cords of Hemlock Bark, $1,050; 4,500,000 pieces
of lath, $6,750; 500 dozen pails, $1,000; 105 dozen
chairs, $260.50; 150 dozen rakes, $450; 5,000 mortised
wagon hubs, $1,500; 100 bundles sash, $1,000; 650 cord
shingle bolts, $2,600; 37,800 bushels of wheat, $32,680;
17,280 barrels of flour, $60,000; 4,520 barrels of plaster,
$5,600; 300 barrels of stucco, $1,200; 900 boxes of
salertus, $5,000; 100 half barrels of saleratus, $600; 268
casks pot and pearl ashes, $3,930; 80 packs of furs,
$30,000; 11 tons of wool, $6,600; 35 tons leather,
$1,400; 34 tons of rags, $1,000; 310 barrels of cranberries,
$630; 150 barrels of whitefish and trout, $900; 1,100
bushels of potatoes, $500; 50 spars, $1,500. . . .The
above was the surplus produce of the three counties of
Ionia, Kent and Ottawa. It shows a prosperous state of
business when compared with the official statements of
the previous years.

Although it is difficult for most of us to relate to the cost of
a ton of wool or a cask of pot (my, how time can twist a language)
and pearl ashes, anyone with a fireplace today would jump at the
opportunity to pick up a cord of wood for $1.50. Mention is
made of wheat being shipped out of Grand Haven in this 1851
account. The first grain to leave this port was sent to Buffalo
aboard the brig *John Kenie* in 1836. Since there were no docks
at that time the 3,000 bushels had to be shuttled to the *Kenie* by
scows.

Some of the worst storms in years raked the Lakes in the fall
1852, the gales from November 11 to 13 being the most severe.
Most of the vessels bound for Grand Haven made port safely,
except the *N.C. Walton,* which had to be beached at the mouth.
The Editors of the Grand River Times, having full confidence in
the power of the pen, continued to lobby for Harbor
improvements as they gave this colorful account of the close of
the navigation season on December 8, 1852:

Since our last issue the fleet belonging to Grand River has arrived and laid up at winter quarters having to make more numerous and successful trips than even those of last year, which we chronicled as ranging from thirty to forty. Notwithstanding the severe gales which have wrecked many a goodly craft on Lake Michigan, our fleet have escaped harmless and our harbor, although in a state of nature, has been one of perfect safety. No thanks to Uncle Sam except so far as lighthouse expenditures have contributed to that happy result. We have no means of estimating the exact amount of exports from the valley of Grand River yet, but hope soon to be able to give the statistics. Suffice it to say that over thirty million feet of lumber has found a cash market at their prices in Chicago, the proceeds of which are distributed among our merchants, mill owners, vessel owners and lumbermen. Preparations are making for lumbering as usual, and by the opening of navigation in the spring the mills will have on hand their usual quota of stock to run their numerous saws night and day throughout the coming year. The business on the river is increasing so rapidly that steam boats are greatly in demand. It is expected that no less than six will be run in the spring between this place and Grand Rapids and probably one or more lines access the lake. It is also expected that the Northern Railroad Extension from Pontiac to this place and Grand Rapids and probably one or more lines across the lake. It is also expected that the Northern Railroad Extension from Pontiac to this place will be put in progress within the coming year. In the passage of the river and harbor bill we believe we have the assurance that the estimate of Col. Albert Abert for a harbor at this place and at Holland will be endorsed by yearly appropriations until completed, then western Michigan will become maritime, and its products will find a fast and cheap channel of export to enrich the industry of its enterprising population. We look for liberal aid by both the state and National legislatures this winter, and as in duty bound, we shall ever pray that our petitions may be granted.

The schooners *Lizzie Throop, Illinois* and *New Hampshire* came in on the 5th instant on their last trip for the season. These are probably the last arrivals from the other side of the lake this season, excepting the *Telegraph*. We hope she will be as fortunate as the rest of the fleet, and find a resting place during the winter within our harbor side by side her fellow travelers now reposing unburdened upon the elements they were designed to traverse. The *New Hampshire*, as we believe, made the greatest number of trips this season. Since the 10th of April last she has carried 40 cargoes from White's Mill. Thus 80 times has this vessel crossed Lake Michigan and the crew has handled the same number of times on an average of about seventy thousand feet of lumber.

A very colorful and poetic description of what was rapidly becoming one of Lake Michigan's most active ports. The editorial certainly makes a strong argument for Harbor improvements. One thing that can be said for the Barnes twins—as Editors they were not bashful about lobbying for a cause.

Captain George Parks—elected County Treasurer in 1854—introduced the 123 foot sidewheeler *Michigan* to the Grand Haven-Grand Rapids River fleet in 1853. Out on the Lake that same year the steamer *Detroit*—later to serve as one of the "Black Boats" for the Detroit and Milwaukee Railroad—was making three round trips a week between Grand Haven and Chicago. In 1856 the sidewheelers *Ottawa* and *Chippewa* began excursion business on the same Lake route. Captain James Dalton was in command of the *Ottawa* which departed from James R. Hugunin's dock at the foot of Franklin Street, J.A. Leggat, Clerk. These were not luxury liners as we know them today but you could not tell that from the fair they served aboard. When the *Chippewa* made her maiden voyage her menu included Haunch of Venison, Venison Ancient Style with Cypress Wine Sauce, Buffalo Tongue, Turtle Steak and Chops of Pigeon. Even today such a menu would be a gastronome's delight.

On September 2, 1854 the little steamer *Humming Bird*, which had been built in 1847, blew up in the Grand Haven Harbor. Charles Belknap, author of "The Yesterdays of Grand Rapids", gives this account of the incident:

The engineer for this boat made a practice of hanging his hat on the safety valve, and one day in a burst of speed it blew up just before it reached the city. On board was a cargo of Illinois Red Eye and Cyclone Buster from Missouri. Some of this stuff blazed when it came in contact with the river water, and the next run of mullet, the story ran, had red noses.

Also in 1854, the *Olive Branch,* one of the inter-city River boats, was wrecked at Grand Haven. Ferry and Sons built a new *Olive Branch* resembling the grandiose Ohio amd Mississippi River steamers. It was a sternwheeler 146 feet long with a 28 foot beam and a draft of only 7 1/2 inches. The 2nd *Olive Branch* and the *Empire* were on the run between Grand Haven and Grand Rapids in 1856.

Occasionally two steamboats would be going in the same direction on the River, which quite naturally called for a race. In May of 1853 the recently launched *Michigan* and the older *Algoma* were heading down river at the same time with the *Algoma* two lengths ahead as they rounded the bend at Spring Lake. Captain Parks was desperate because he had yet to lose a race with his new ship. He left the pilot house, raced to the engine room and stocked the fire with great bunches of tallow he had grabbed from a barrel. The resulting inferno pushed billows of smoke from the stacks, the pressure rose and the *Michigan* pulled ahead of the *Algoma* just as they reached Grand Haven.

Fire was an inherent danger during those logging days. A by-product of lumber manufacturing was sawdust and the ubiquitous sawdust piles along the Grand River at Spring Lake did not always mix well with river steamboats. Spring Lake had one disastrous lumber mill fire in 1871 which started within the Haire and Tolford Mill—not by a steamboat—that laid waste the greater portion of the Village. Then in 1893 sparks from the river steamer *W.H. Barrett* set fire to a sawdust pile which eventually consumed much of the east side of Spring Lake between Jackson and Meridian Streets to the water's edge—Spring Lake on the north, the Grand River on the south. People spoke of "spark arresters" but there was no one to enforce such trivial matters.

Eastmanville (formerly Scranton) flourished with the increased River traffic and on November 9, 1855 it was organized as a village by Timothy Eastman.

The propellers *Troy* and *Pocahontas* formed the Grand Haven-Buffalo passenger and freight line during the 1855 season. In that same year 45,000,000 feet of lumber left this port, most of it

"W.H. Barrett"—built in 1874. Courtesy Grand Haven Area Historical Society.

headed in the opposite direction for Chicago.

Down in New Buffalo, Michigan in 1856 a man by the name of Albert E. Goodrich purchased the wooden hull sidewheel steamer *Huron* and began a passenger service which provided daily runs between Muskegon, Grand Haven and Chicago. The Goodrich Steamship Line—more affectionately referred to in later years as the Red Stack Line—became one of the most renowned passenger-cargo systems in all the Great Lakes and at one time or another owned or leased over 50 steamships during its 75 years of operation. Some of the more famous Goodrich Line ships which became eminently involved in the history of the Port of Grand Haven were the *Orion, Alpena, Muskegon, Iowa*—ex-*Menominee, Georgia*—ex-*City of Ludington, Indiana, Atlanta, Carolina*—ex-*Charles H. Hackley, Virginia, City of Grand Rapids, Arizona*—ex-*City of Racine, Alabama* and *Wisconsin*—ex-*Naomi*. After Albert E.'s death, his son, Albert W. Goodrich, carried on the business before selling the line in 1920 for one million dollars to an H.W. Thorp. The Goodrich Line continued service until the Great Depression. On December 20, 1932 the line filed for bankruptcy and all operations were discontinued July 10, 1933.

The Village of Ferrysburg came into being on January 26, 1857, platted and recorded by William M. Ferry, Jr. and Thomas White Ferry. Grand Haven's population had jumped from 667 in 1856 to 1,100 in 1857, an increase of more than 60% in just one year. Mill Point had 4 saw mills producing more than 600,000 feet of lumber a week. All of this prosperity on the eve of one of the notable events in the history of the area—the arrival of the railroad from Detroit.

The Detroit and Milwaukee Railroad reached Mill Point on September 1, 1856. The terminus and docks for passengers and freight to Chicago and Milwaukee was situated where the bridge across the Spring Lake channel to Ferrysburg would later be located. The railroad was extended to Grand Haven November 22, 1858 and thereby, as the December 22, 1858 Grand Haven News so dramatically stated, ". . .connected Grand Haven with the outside world and put an end to its solitude." The depot was located on the west side of the River at the base of Dewey Hill directly opposite the foot of Washington Street.

The railroad had, in effect, achieved the link between the Atlantic coast and the Nation's developing mid-section much the way the Erie Canal had done it a quarter of a century earlier. The contrast between the two was speed. The Erie Canal barge transportation had achieved a quantum leap over land travel. Now the same comparison could be made for rolling stock over canal barges.

The increase in Grand Haven Harbor traffic was felt immediately. All passengers and freight had to have a means of getting across the River so a ferry service was established. Also, to complete the water crossing to Milwaukee the railroad used two "Black Boats", the sidewheeler *Detroit* and the propeller *Michigan*. A U.S. Mail contract assured regular schedules. Not affiliated with the railroad were the steamers *Cleveland* and *Huron* which, during the 1859 season, added additional service to Milwaukee and Chicago respectively.

Grand Haven would feel the effect of the arrival of the railroad in another way more indirectly; the trains and ships required 14,000 cords of wood a year to fire their boilers. At $1.75 a cord, delivered, that alone would mean quite a boost in the economy for the area.

Of interest are the fares charged by the Detroit and Milwaukee Railroad in 1859; a one way boat-rail trip from Milwaukee to New York was $12, to Boston $10, to Philadelphia $10 and Baltimore $10. The citizens of Grand Haven could now reach the "bright lights" quickly and reasonably.

With its formation in 1837 Ottawa County had extended from Lake Macatawa on the south to Ludington on the north. With the formation of Oceana and Mason counties in 1855 and Muskegon County in 1859 Ottawa County took on the configuration familiar to us today. Even with this reduced size the future of Grand Haven as a county seat and a port city looked very promising.

In this chapter we have established the credibility of Grand Haven as the second busiest Lake Michigan port in the 1850's—second only to Chicago. The point has been made and it would be redundant to verify its prominence for each ensuing year or decade. That is not the purpose of this monograph. Suffice it to say that for the next 40 years Grand Haven would share in the exuberance and wealth of the legendary lumbering era. During those years the arrival of the railroad and the beginning of a long tenure of cross-Lake ferry service (1858), a burgeoning fishing industry (1867), ship building (1867), the start of tourist trade resulting in increased Lake excursion business (1872) and the awakening of mid America's farm lands creating the start of import trade (1874) all contributed their respective share to building the illustrious reputation of Grand Haven Harbor, the decline of which did not occur until the Depression Years of the 1930's. Each will be mentioned in turn as it relates to this historic narrative but without extensive elaboration for any one of them. Rather, it is time to turn our attention to the main theme—Grand Haven's ties with the predecessors of today's Coast Guard.

CHAPTER 6

EARLY GRAND HAVEN LIGHTHOUSES

The best evidence available indicates Grand Haven's first Government lighthouse was built on "'Lighthouse Acre" in 1839. No record can be found as to the type of light it emitted, but the "magnifying and reflecting lantern" patented by Winslow Lewis in 1812 was popular at that time and in all likelihood it was this style of oil light which shone in the 1839 tower. And although accounts of its construction have not been found its demise is quite dramatically recorded. In the preceding chapter we read an account of the violent fall storms which had ushered the close of the Harbor's 1852 shipping season. The final paragraph of that Grand River Times December 8, 1852 article read as follows:

> On the night of the 6th instant the wooden wall around the lighthouse was carried away by the action of the water - the wind was blowing strong from the southwest.

As mentioned earlier the light's location on the flat beach left it exposed to the fury of a storm-mad Lake Michigan. It was just a matter of time before its fate would be sealed and on December 17, 1852 that time had come. By 4:00 A.M. the storm had become so severe the waves washed out the sand from the northwest corner of the residence of the lighthouse causing the destruction of the wall from the foundation to the roof on the north half of the building. Ice banks which formed during the day saved the tower from being undermined. Two of the auxiliary watchmen sleeping in the north room escaped and with the seas continuing to pound Keeper Torrey was finally forced to abandon the premises. By 4:00 p.m. the entire structure had collapsed. That was the end of the first Grand Haven light and the Harbor would be without another permanent lighthouse for the next three years.

Some historical accounts would lead one to believe that the lighthouse which was inundated in 1852 was actually Grand

Old Light House, Highland Park, Grand Haven, Mich.

Grand Haven Bluff Lighthouse, 1855-1905. Courtesy Grand Haven Area Historical Society.

Haven's second light. However there is no record of the 1839 light—the Port's first—being dismantled, replaced or destroyed prior to that fall storm of 1852. In J.B. Mansfield's "History of the Great Lakes" the early Grand Haven lights are referred to as follows: "Grand Haven, '39, re-built '55, fixed white light." The fact that a third is not mentioned agrees with Lillie and is also the persuasion of this author.

The second Government lighthouse was built in 1855 behind the original light but up on the bluff high above the Lake's reach. For ease of differentiation we will refer to this as the Bluff Light. The keeper's 1 1/2 story solid stone structure—which still stands today—had a tower on the south end which housed the light that shined its signal 150 feet above the Lake. A $4,000 lenticular French Fresnel lens produced the illumination which, according to the Mansfield's 1899 account, was a "fixed white light" and could be seen for 25 miles under clear conditions. On May 10, 1856 a rotating light was installed which was regulated by a clock work that produced a flash every 1 1/2 minutes. The light was moved to the 52 foot South Pier tower in 1905 when the Bluff Light was discontinued.

Fresnel (the "s" is silent and the accent is on the second "nel") lens were standard for most Great Lakes lights by 1855. They were classified into orders ranging from one to six, a first order lens being a monstrous 12 feet tall and 6 feet in diameter. A second order lens was 4 feet 7 inches in diameter, a third order 3 feet 3.38 inches, a fourth order 19.62 inches in diameter, a fifth order was 14.5 inches wide and a sixth order lens was just under 1 foot in diameter. The Fresnel style glass lens are no longer used however some of the modern reflectors are of sizable proportions. The tallest lens in use by the Coast Guard today is the 20 foot lens in the Makapuu light on the island of Oahu, Hawaii. Grand Haven's Tri-Cities Museum presently has on display in the Coast Guard exhibit the fourth order Fresnel lens which shone in the 1855 Bluff Tower and later in the South Pier tower. Replaced by a $60 American made plastic lens, the old glass lens was presented to Grand Haven during the 1979 Coast Guard Festival by Coast Guard Commandant Admiral John B. Hayes. The City then turned it over to Grand Haven's Tri-Cities Museum for display and preservation. A visit to the Museum allows a person to see first hand the remarkable artistry of the glass work used in those old lens to capture and refract every trace of luminance in those preelectric days.

Until 1862 sperm whale oil was the standard fuel for lighthouses. As sperm whale oil supplies declined Colza oil, an extract from wild cabbage seed, was tried for economy. From 1864 to 1867 lard oil was the common illuminant. But after years of experiment mineral oil was settled upon as the standard fuel for all the Service's lights.

Some of the experiments along the way ended with near disastrous but somewhat humorous results. In 1864 a Lake Michigan lighthouse keeper tried kerosene. The light it emitted was an improvement but when he tried to blow it out the kerosene exploded. He raced down the circular stairs, clothes blazing and reached the bottom just in time for a second explosion to blow the top out of the tower. Enough said for kerosene! However, properly controlled it was useful and later took its rightful place as a fuel.

A German product manufactured under the name of Pintsch gas was used sparingly as a compressed fuel for lighted buoys at the turn of the century. By 1910 compressed acetylene was the fuel of choice before the 1918 Congress ordered the electrification of all lights. Today battery and solar energy are used on some secondary pier lights and buoys.

The Great Lakes were divided into 3 lighthouse districts—the Ninth, Tenth and Eleventh; Grand Haven was in the Ninth District which encompassed all of Lake Michigan. Mansfield's 1899 "History of the Great Lakes" lists the following statistics for the Ninth District: Lighthouses and beacon lights, 96; light ships in position, 4; for signals operated by steam, 23; fog signals operated by clock work, 7; buoys in position, 93.

Keepers of lighthouses were addressed as "Captain" out of respect for the importance of their position, but that was the extent of the romance, for a keepers life was lonely and monotonous. Mundane chores such as keeping the station and equipment clean occupied most of their day. However, before the advent of electricity the keeper's overriding responsibility— the task which established his entire reputation and thus his career—was his ability to keep the light glowing properly. The wick of the lamp had to be precisely trimmed to emit the strongest light possible. Keepers were judged by how well their lamps were trimmed which led to their nickname "wickies".

Keepers were government employees under the Treasury Department and thus, as civilians, they did not receive pensions or any retirement benefits until an act of Congress was passed in 1918. Consequently prior to 1918 keepers stayed on long past the usual retirement age.

Captain Torrey was the first keeper of the Grand Haven light for which there is a record. He was keeper when the first light on the beach was destroyed by storm action in 1852. Captain Torrey was succeeded by Captain Peter Vandenberg in 1853 and therefore Vandenberg was the first keeper to serve in the Bluff Light which was built in 1855. He was followed by Captains Belger, Harm Miller, and Harry Smith. Although it is presumed they served in the order they are listed no dates have been found for the respective tours of duty of Belger and Miller. The 1882 publication "History of Muskegon and Ottawa County" lists the Grand Haven lighthouse keeper as Captain Harry Smith—born in Denmark in 1823—and that he had been keeper since 1875. From this information we know that 1875 was the year Captain Miller left the position to make way for Smith, who was, in turn, succeeded by Captain Davidson in 1883. Thus we have established Captain Smith's tenure as 1875 to 1883. However no such identifying time frames can be found for Captains Vandenberg and Belger. All of these men were former mariners and had empathy for those who carried on their old toils at sea.

The earliest verified dates for a tour of duty of a Grand Haven

Bluff Lighthouse with Capt. Frank Frega and wife. Courtesy Grand Haven Area Historical Society.

keeper was that of Captain Emanuel Davidson who served from 1883 until he retired April 1, 1900 at age 75. From Norway, he was also a Lake captain and commanded such famous ships as *Driver, Bell, Tanner* and *Constitution.* His assistant of 15 years, Frank Frega, was appointed as his successor.

Frank Frega, born in Poland, had been a whaler and so he too was a salt of the old school. His assistants were Joseph Douglas and Charles Grenell. Captain Frega died in 1911 at age 72. Although nothing is mentioned it is assumed one of the assistants succeeded him as keeper.

Further confusing the record concerning Grand Haven Light keepers is an obituary notice for Medad Spencer who died at his son's home in Crockery Township on October 31, 1919. In the article it makes reference to the fact he had been keeper of the Grand Haven Light for years before going to the light on Beaver Island. Given their penchant for lengthy tenure there doesn't seem to be room in the Grand Haven lineup for Mr. Spencer. Perhaps he had been an assistant keeper while here.

The old Bluff Light was discontinued in 1905 after flashing its reassuring beacon to seamen for half a century. The Bluff Light tower was removed from the old stone house in 1910 but the house itself—after much remodeling, as can be seen by comparing the before and after pictures—continued to serve as residence for the keeper and his family until 1939. Captain Nelson Engberg and his wife Anna were the last to reside there, Engderg having been keeper since 1926. The 13 room structure was inherited by the Coast Guard in 1939 when the Lighthouse Service was assimilated into the Coast Guard. The old stone cottage was sold at auction in 1956 and continues to serve today as a sturdy residence at 500 Harbor Avenue, a link with this Port's maritime heritage.

Grand Haven's next lighthouse would be located on the South Pier and therefore will be discussed in conjunction with the progress of the Harbor's pier construction.

Bluff Lighthouse light tower was removed in 1910. The building was extensively remodeled and served as Keeper's residence until 1939. Courtesy Grand Haven Area Historical Society.

CHAPTER 7

THE PIER CONSTRUCTION ERA

Keeping the Harbor mouth and channel open was of prime concern even in the very early days of the Port. Lake and beach sands moved freely with the waves and wind. As the ships entering the Harbor became larger and their drafts deeper some means of controlling the problem became inescapable. The 1852 session of Congress appropriated $20,000 for improvements to the Grand Haven Harbor which reflected the importance the legislators attached to this Harbor not only for commerce but, of equal importance, as a port of refuge. Revetment construction began in 1857.

Containment of River erosion and control of capricious sands were the initial concerns and because the prevailing winds were from the south west, work on the south revetments was started first. In fact serious work did not begin on the north side of the channel until 1873. Initial construction was primarily wood. The 1857 work began where today's Corps of Engineers is located, progressed down stream, thereby forming "Government Pond", continued along the River bank and ended with a short extension out into the Lake. The revetment which formed "Government Pond" narrowed and improved the channel—as well as checking the River erosion—while down stream the work helped stabilize the intrusive sands. But it was just the beginning of pier construction which would continue until 1894 at which time the South and North Piers would be completed ostensibly as we see them today.

This information has been gathered from a number of sources but it is based primarily upon current Corps of Engineer records which date back to 1857. It is inevitable historical accounts of the same subject will vary depending upon their choice of reference. For example Lillie's book gives 1881 as the date for construction of the revetment which enclosed "Government

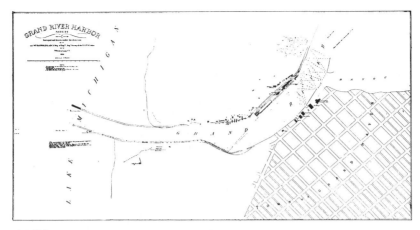

1866 government survey of Grand Haven Harbor. From Leo Lillie.

Pond." Corps documents, on the other hand, show the original substructure being built in 1857-8 with additional work in 1910-11, the superstructure erected in 1938 and the sheet piling placed in 1972. Further, the 1866 Federal survey of the Grand Haven Harbor—a copy of which is in the Loutit Library—confirms that "Government Pond" was present prior to 1881. Since we do not know what Lillie used as the basis of his research we will go with the Corps of Engineers records.

Not all the Harbor improvements were Government funded. The Detroit and Milwaukee Railroad arrived in Grand Haven in 1858—a significant chapter in the history of this Port which will be discussed in more detail later. Lillie has an interesting account of the railroad's private funds being used for pier construction in 1859:

> The Railroad company also expended $200,000 on a south pier. The length of the pier was 3000 feet. Three tiers of piles were driven, and on the inside of the piles brush was first laid down and then covered with stone.

An 1864 map by Samuel Geil of Philadelphia shows the south pier described by Lillie and also indicates that there was a "Light House" on the end of the pier. Other details of interest on the map are the Detroit and Milwaukee Railroad station, fish huts and the land based lighthouse.

Research provided by Paul Trap further corroborates the railroad's construction of the 1859 pier. In his files Trap has a copy of the Milwaukee Sentinel printed Tuesday morning August 9, 1859 which contains the following guest article from the Grand Haven Clarion:

The New Pier of the D & M Railway

The mouth of our beautiful river presents quite a busy scene, constrasting markedly with its usual quiet aspect. The Indian wigwams with their lazy denizens have disappeared, and in place thereof have been erected several large boarding houses, with kitchens, carpenters' and blacksmiths' shops, and a lodging house opposite capable of accommodating from sixty to seventy men. Immediately opposite is the nucleus of the new pier, now being erected by F.C. Ridley, Esq., for the D. & M. Railway.

The pier, when completed, will be 2,000 feet long, requiring some 3,000 piles,and 3,000 cords of stone, with an immense quantity of brush. The piles are of the best white oak and are laid six feet apart where the water becomes deeper; those are driven in some ten or twelve feet into the sand, at the rate of forty-five piles a day, three machines being now in operation. The space between the piles is filled up with alternate layers of brush, poles and stone until it reaches one foot above the level of the water; the poles are laid lengthwise.

The first eight hundred feet of the pier will be fifteen feet wide, and the remainder twenty-four feet wide, terminating in a square of fifty feet, upon which a light-house forty feet high will be placed. The stone for filling up is brought from Grand Rapids on the Railroad to the Grand Haven Depot, the trucks are then placed on scows and towed up to the works so that there is only one loading and unloading, an arrangement which saves a vast amount of labor and expense. There were three cars unloading at the time of our visit. This, owing to various contrivances, was done with the greatest dispatch.

Sixty men are employed on this pier, two hundred and fifty feet of which is finished; and should the weather continue favorable, the whole will be completed this Fall. When done, we shall have a deep channel, easy to find and accessible at all seasons of the year, thus rendering our harbor one of the best on the great Lake Coast. The generous enterprise of the Detroit and Milwaukee Railway Co., as displayed in this great undertaking, deserves the highest commendation.

It would only be an act of Justice that the United States Government should build a pier on the opposite side, so as to complete the channel.—Grand Haven Clarion.

According to Trap, newspaper articles later that year reported the pier was extended another 500 feet thus making the total length 2,500 feet, not 3,000 as stated in Lillie's book. But even the 2,500 feet meant it was 1,000 feet longer than today's South Pier, which is quite remarkable.

On May 21, 1866 the Detroit and Milwaukee Railroad's Board of Directors received word that sparks from a passing steamship had set fire to the Grand Haven pier destroying the lighthouse and burning the pier itself to the water line. Trap's research indicates that a second pier was built following the fire.

The U.S. Engineers 1866 survey map shows the South Pier and other fine details of Grand Haven Harbor at that time. The North Pier shown on the map did not exist in 1866 but was drawn in after the map was completed.

It is quite remarkable that the railroad would have financed a harbor pier in the pursuit of private enterprise. There is no doubt it was needed and when done afforded much needed protection for their cross-Lake ferry boats. But $200,000 was a huge amount of money in those days which gives us some measure of the volume of rail business that was flowing—or perhaps anticipated would be flowing—through the Grand Haven Harbor.

There is other documentation of private investments for Harbor improvements. In June 1861 (the Civil War had begun April 17, just two months earlier) E. L. Fuller & Company, dealers in lumber products, extended their docks from their place of business on the Grand River, between Franklin and Clinton Streets, down stream nearly to Government Pond—over 1000 feet of dockage.

But then docks, slips and jetties have always been considered the responsibility of those who would use them. However, it is our thinking today—and perhaps only because we have lived with the notion so long—that lighthouses and piers at major harbors are the Government's responsibility. Not only is the initial construction an expensive proposition but the ongoing maintenance can keep the pockets empty of those working on a narrow profit margin. The Detroit and Milwaukee Railroad went through foreclosure in 1860, reorganized, went through foreclosure again in 1878, emerged November 9, 1878 as the Detroit, Grand Haven and Milwaukee Railroad under the control of the Great Western Railway Company until August 12, 1882 at which time the Great Western was amalgamated with the Grand Trunk Railway Company of Canada and thereafter was known as the Grand Trunk Western System with the Detroit, Grand Haven and Milwaukee retaining its local identity. This hasty synopsis of the Detroit and Milwaukee Railroad's pedigree is to emphasize that venture capital back then was no different than it is today—risky business. There is no doubt the railroad was relieved of a heavy financial burden when the Government finally began pier construction in ernest in the 1880's.

Ship mishaps would continue to occur with or without Harbor improvements. On July 15, 1859 the little cross-river ferry operated by William Ferry and Myron Harris collided with a schooner and sank without loss of life. On September 12, 1859 the brig *Buffalo,* in command of Captain William Loutit, loaded with coal for the Detroit & Milwaukee Railroad, went aground at the end of the pier. Such was life for those who took to the Lakes in ships—it was not without its perils.

The Government had done Harbor surveys of Grand Haven Harbor in 1844, 1849 and 1856. And then ten years later—1866—there was interest in developing a major port on Michigan's west side, not only for commerce but as a port of refuge. The legislators gave Grand Haven the nod. The 1866 Congress appropriated $65,000 for harbor improvemnets, which included a complete harbor survey. From that time on, all Harbor improvements would be done by the U.S. Army Corps of Engineers. The 1866 survey shows a North Pier which had been inserted in red ink after the survey had been completed, there being no North Pier in 1866. Other than that it represents quite accurately the Harbor and the Grand Haven water front as it was in 1866. It confirms that the Government Pond had been established. It also shows the expansive Detroit and Milwaukee Railroad terminal on the west side of the River along with 25 or so fishing huts all of which created the appearance of quite a community along the River opposite Grand Haven proper. The 14 boat fishing fleet had an annual production of 765,000 pounds, primarily white fish and lake trout.

There continues to this day to be a persistent misunderstanding among some that Grand Haven "had its beginning on the other side of the River." This spurious notion must have taken root because of a misinterpretation of what the 1866 railroad station and fishing huts on the opposite side of the River actually represented. To set the record straight, few, if any, of those buildings were used as sleeping quarters or permanent addresses. Some 70 fishermen worked out of the huts during the day but went back to their homes in and around Grand Haven when they returned to port. A hotel, tavern and bakery sprang up around the rail terminal but were short lived. They, nor the depot, ever served as a permanent residence. The life saving station had not yet been built and the entire north shore area was unsettled, wide-open dune land. Perhaps the best description of the blossoming area along the Grand River would be an industrial complex. However all the buildings strung out along the River gave the whole scene an appearance of a mushrooming village so the local newspapers mounted an effort to give the area a name to provide it a degree of legitimacy. The names of "Sanford", "Cedarville" and "Muir" were offered up but each died for want of a second. The citizens of Grand Haven settled the issue on January 2, 1867 by adopting a new City Charter which extended the City boundaries from Beech Tree on the east and westerly far enough to include that development on the opposite side of the River. For anyone who cares to read history that should be the end of it but, like a bad virus, good stories die hard. Anyway, it is a romantic notion—and fun.

To further validate Grand Haven as a major port the Government established a U.S. Customs office here in 1866. The office at this port was headquarters for a Custom Collection District in Michigan which took in the west half of the Lower Peninsula and the south half of the Upper Peninsula. Duty to help support the cost of operating the ports was collected on goods which passed through the harbors. Collectors and their assistants at Grand Haven were:

H.C. Akeley with J.A. Stephenson assist.   1866-1880
David McLaughlin with J.A. Stephenson
          and C.N.A. Brower assists.   1880-1885

Dudley Watson with G.B. Parks assist.   1885-1889
George W. McBride with Andrew Thomson 1889-1893
Dudley Watson with G.B. Parks assist.   1893-1897
George A. Farr with George D. Turner   1897-1906
Walter L. Lillie with William L. Phillips   1906-1913

After 1913 all 5 Michigan Custom Collection Districts were consolidated into 1 district, with headquarters in Detroit, at which time Grand Haven became a subsidiary office. In 1913 William L. Phillips became the deputy collector for this port and remained in that position until WW II.

The original Custom House was on the River at the foot of Franklin Street. It undoubtedly also housed the 11th District Headquarters of the U.S. Life Saving Service after it was organized in 1877. The building was still being used in the 1930's by Pippel Printing and Verduin's Lunch, which, according to Claude Verduin, offered a fish sandwich lunch for 10 cents.

The $65,000 appropriation by Congress in 1866 signaled the beginning of pier construction out into the Lake. In 1867-68 work extended the South Pier out from the shore approximately 400 feet. No mention is made of the pier which had been installed by the Detroit and Milwaukee Railroad so it is assumed it had been erroded away by storms before the Corps of Engineers began its pier work.

The 1869 Congress appropriated $1,866 for Harbor improvements, in 1870 $11,885 and another $6,000 for 1871. In 1871 a red tower was placed at the end of the South Pier to display a pierhead signal which Mansfield's 1899 publication describes as a "fixed white light." However, the Bluff Light still remained the Port's primary beacon. The Government allocated $15,000 for harbor construction in 1872, $75,000 in 1873 and then an additional $50,000 for 1874.

By 1873 attention had turned to the North Pier. Revetment construction began upstream about 1,700 feet from the Harbor mouth at a point along the River bank near the terminus of today's North Shore Road. By the time that series of work was completed in 1875 the North Pier head extended approximately 400 feet from shore out into Lake Michigan. The width of the channel between the piers was 400 feet. All construction on both north and south sides of the River, was of wood, which would be the material of choice until all pier work was completed in

1894.

Work along both banks of the River, including Government Pond enclosure, was fundamentally driven wood piling. However as operations extended from shore a crib style of construction was used. The huge rectangular timber crib sections—which resembled giant open lattice work when completed—measured 50 feet long and would vary in height depending upon the depth of the water. When the first 400 feet of the South Pier was extended out into the Lake in 1867-68 the cribs were only 15 feet wide but all other construction—on the north and south sides, which included the first 400 feet of the North Pier built in 1875—would use cribs 50 feet long by 30 feet wide. The cribs were built ashore, floated out to the site and anchored into place by piling, then filed with stone for added stability. Because of its astonishing resilience to extreme forces and astounding durability when submerged, wood timbers were amazingly well adapted for the job. So amazingly well they remain today—some sections over 100 years old—as the main substructure for both the South and North Piers.

In this day of heavy, sophisticated machinery and materials it is difficult for us to conceive how these pioneers could have managed without some degree of modern technology. Such is our mentality in this age of heavy machinery. But the Grand Haven pier construction is a perfect example of what can be done with basic materials, good fundamental engineering principles, Yankee ingenuity and perseverance. There is an account of the tug *Stickney* arriving at this port on October 10, 1903 towing a barge with a full size, complete home on it which was being moved from Muskegon for owner Fred Jonker who planned to relocate it in the "Birch Tree" section of Grand Haven. Today when we read reports of such gargantuan achievements our reaction is to marvel at how they could have accomplished such feats. The Soo locks, the Erie Canal and the Niagara canal— forerunner of the Welland Canal—all in use today, are three good examples. The original construction for all of these was done without the aid of electricity, the gasoline engine, diesel power or any form of motorized vehicle. The lever, pulley, inclined plane along with wind, gravity, horse and steam power were the mechanical tools they worked with—and they used them with astonishing ingenuity.

Congress appropriated $50,000 for Harbor improvements

during their 1880 session and another $50,000 in 1881. This brought the total appropriations for Grand Haven Harbor improvements to $344,751 over a 29 year period—1852 to 1881. That same year-1881-Captain Thomas W. Kirby placed and maintained a small recognition light on the North Pier. It was a steady red light on a cross pole which could be seen 2-3 miles. This North Pier light served as a companion to the light that had been erected on the South Pier in 1871 and with the two the channel was more accurately defined.

Congress did not lose interest in this Port's development. The 1882 session appropriated another $40,000. In 1882-83 the Corps of Engineers extended the South Pier another 1000 feet making it nearly 1400 feet from shore to pier end. Congressional appropriations of $50,000 and $30,000 were made in 1884 and 1886 respectively. The North Pier received another 750 feet in 1887 which placed its pier head approximately 1150 feet from shore.

Major William Ludlow, headquartered in Detroit, was the Corps of Engineers' officer in charge of the improvements of Grand Haven Harbor at that time. On January 13, 1890 the Senate passed a resolution directing the Secretary of War, Redfield Proctor, to report to that body on the condition and estimated cost of improvements for the harbor at Grand Haven which was, according to the Senate's resolution, ". . . reported to be in a dangerous condition, whereby serious loss to the shipping interests of the lakes is imminent during the present winter: . . ." This request found its way through the Government maze and by January 17 was on Maj. Ludlow's desk in Detroit—which speaks well for the lack of bureaucratic entanglement and the speed of communications at that time. Ludlow's reply was prompt, to the point and was in itself a wonderful profile of this Port at that time. His report explained that the Grand River was the largest in the State with a drainage area of 5,300 square miles, that as the large amount of alluvium carried by the river met the Lake waves and currents the two conjoined to create a substantial harbor entrance bar, that because Grand Haven Harbor ". . . possesses the charcteristics that would fairly entitle it to be designated as a harbor of refuge, and this has continued to be its recognized status among the navigators and vessel men of the lake," it was necessary to control the harbor entrance depth and, he concluded, the way to do that was to extend the piers another 500-600 feet to reach the Lakes 20 foot depth contour. The Major

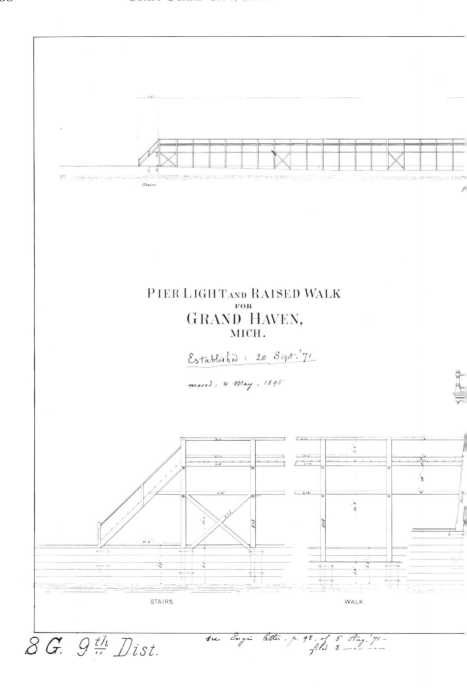

1895 South Pierhead Light. Courtesy Grand Haven Area

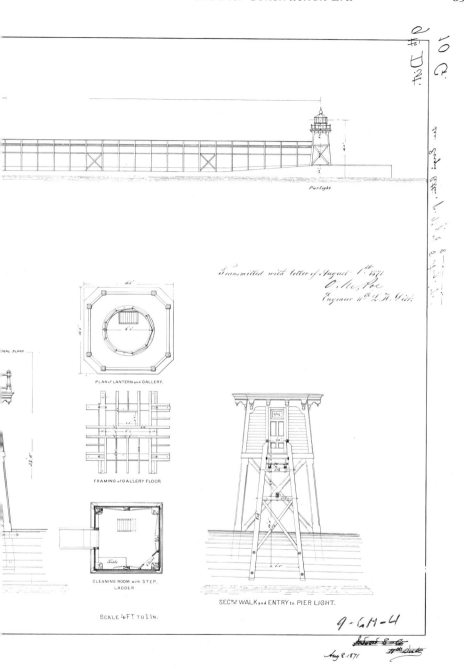

Pier Light.

Transmitted with letter of August 1st 1871

O. M. Poe
Engineer

PLAN of LANTERN and GALLERY.

FRAMING of GALLERY FLOOR

CLEANING ROOM with STEP LADDER

SEC.N of WALK and ENTRY to PIER LIGHT.

SCALE 4 FT TO 1 IN.

9-GH-4

Aug 8. 1871

Historical Society.

accompanied his report with a survey of the Harbor, shown on page 81, which has some very significant historic detail.

Major Ludlow's plan was to extend the South Pier by 11 cribs, or 550 feet, and the North Pier by 12 cribs, or 600 feet, which would have made them approximately 1950 and 1750 feet long respectively—nearly the length of the 1859 Detroit and Milwaukee Railroad pier. Ludlow estimated the project at $150,000, and here showed a bit of frustration in dealing with Washington: "It did not seem proper to reason that because $150,000 was needed and an estimate for that amount produced in 1888 only $25,000, therefore $900,000 should be asked in anticipation of the 83 per cent reduction. I preferred, on the contrary, to make half the reduction myself and so bring the estimate into somewhat closer relation to the amount which the history of the matter showed that Congress had deemed sufficient."

Major Ludlow was a remarkable detail man but his arguments on behalf of the Grand Haven Harbor must not have been persuasive enough to move Congress. His grand scheme of pier extension was reduced considerably: in 1893 and 1894 the South and North Piers received their final 100 and 50 feet respectively, far less than the 550 and 600 feet Ludlow had purposed. Thus completed the total length of the South Pier was approximately 1500 feet from shore to pier end and about 1200 feet for the North Pier. The opening between the pier heads was 450 feet which narrowed to 400 feet as ships progressed up the channel. For all practical purposes this describes the pier configuration we see today.

A fog signal house and light were installed 95 feet from the end of the south pier in 1895. Shown here is the engineer's drawing the light. The 1899 and 1904 photos shown on these pages verify the requisite catwalk was part of that construction. According to the book "Northern Lights" one of the two fog signal houses shown on Major Ludlow's 1890 chart was moved from its mid-pier position out to this new location as a better site for the fog signal. The 1899 picture shows two curved tubes extending up from the roof of the fog-house and the 1904 photograph reveals a fog "horn" on top of the house. (Photos on page 72).

Through the years several fog alert devices had been tried for American waters. Among these were cannons in the 1700's, hand rung bells, wave activated bells, in 1851 mechanically operated

**Carferry "Grand Haven" in front breaks a path through
the harbor ice for Crosby Line's "Nyack". Courtesy Grand
Haven Area Historical Society.**

bells, steam whistles by 1855 and then by 1868 sirens had been
tested. At the turn of the century the most common type alert
on the Great Lakes were steam whistles. The first steam fog signal
on Lake Michigan was installed in 1875 at the South Manitou
Island lighthouse. These were often difficult to operate because
they required firing boilers to produce the necessary steam which
could take up to 45 minutes and that much time could be critical
in a crisis situation. All of this, of course, required on-site
manpower.

Grand Haven's 1895 fog alert was a steam siren which blasted
in the key of F for 5 seconds at intervals of 35 seconds. In 1905
the power was converted to two large kerosene engines which
generated compressed air for the siren.

The 1899 and 1904 photographs show clearly the wooden
pier-head light tower which was 37 feet high and displayed a
fixed white light visible for 13 miles. Another photo from this
same period is a 1907 winter scene which shows the Crosby
Line's *Nyack* and the carferry *Grand Haven* leaving Grand Haven
Harbor past yet another South Pierhead light, which has the
"banded" appearance of today's tower and is, in fact, today's steel
tower, which, according to the book "Northern Lights", was
erected by the American Bridge Company at the end of the South
Pier in 1905. A January 12, 1905 Tribune news story adds
credibility to this line of reasoning because the article tells of the

1899 G.H. Pier and Lighthouse. Courtesy Winifred VanZantwick.

1904 South Pierhead Light and Foghorn House. Courtesy Grand Haven Area Historical Society.

Fresnal lens being transferred down from the Bluff Light to be installed in the ". . . pierhead tower." Keeper Frega and signalmen Douglas and Grinnell assured the reporter they would have the light glowing that evening—January 12, 1905. The Port's new light would flash its signal every 1 1/2 minutes and could be seen 18-25 miles. From that time on Keeper Frega and his assistants lived in shifts at the pier head to tend the light and fog horn.

Apparently the light began to send out its signal on schedule but the transfer from the Bluff to the pierhead was not without a glitch. The next day the Tribune carried a story about the confusion the skippers of the Crosby Line's *Nyack* and the

Goodrich Line's *Atlanta* had when they arrived at this Port on the night of January 12, 1905. Evidently the Captains had not been notified of the switch, as was the usual custom, and moving the light removed the range light system so familiar to them for safe entry into the harbor. One can imagine the blue air as the Captains sought an explanation for the confusion because had they not known the harbor and simply followed the charts they would have wrecked on shore. The Tribune attempted to smooth the troubled waters, ending its January 13, 1905 story with a statement that a new range system probably would be developed. Here again one can only postulate how much that salved the Captains' fury.

Later in 1907 the steel tower was moved back 600 feet from the end of the pier where today it sends out its signal 52 feet above the Lake.

At that same time the fog signal house was moved to the end of the pier. The 1908 Lake Michigan 9th Lighthouse District Light List recorded the Grand Haven South Pier front light—or pierhead light—as a 6th order Fresnel lens (the order of Fresnel lens was described in Chapter 6) sending a fixed red signal and the rear light was a 4th order Fresnel lens with a flash every 30 seconds from a 52 foot white tower with a black lantern house, tended by a red metal oil house 8 feet east of the tower. The fog signal was a compressed air sirene.

Originally the Grand Haven piers had wood decking or walkways and remained as such until 1916. In that year work was begun to build a concrete superstructure on all sections of the piers, the surface so familiar to those who walk the piers today. In 1916 the Corps of Engineers let bids to Nelson Bros. of Muskegon and John Gringel of Detroit to start part of the project but further work was halted during the World War. (It is an historic point of interest that before World War II the World War of 1914-18 did not need a modifier) Work began again in 1919 and by 1922 the concrete decking on both piers was completed. The superstructure at Government Pond was begun in 1930 and then finally completed in 1935.

Prior to convenient roads to the beach people walked to the Lake along the pier. The opening between the Government Pond piers was spanned by a pedestrian float bridge which could be easily floated out of the way to allow ships to come and go. That float bridge, with its steps up to the pier, can be seen in the 1904

1904 view of Grand Haven Harbor showing U.S. Dredge "Saginaw", footbridge across opening of Government Pond, 7 story grain elevator at South Channel and fishing shanties opposite Government Pond. Courtesy Grand Haven Area Historical Society.

picture of Government Pond. Water Street was extended from Government Pond to the beach in 1922 and following its completion the roadway became the more convenient route. Thus there was no longer the great need for the old float bridge so it fell into disrepair and was finally removed in 1934. Until 1972 the opening into Government Pond was only 65 feet wide. Les Brinkert, Captain of the dredge *Haines* from 1949 to 1961, can recall what a tight squeeze it was to maneuver the *Haines'* 40 foot beam in and out of Government Pond. This was remedied when Government Pond's West Pier was reworked in 1972 increasing the pier width itself from 20 to 30 feet and the opening between the East and West Piers from 65 to 92 feet.

Major repairs were begun on the piers and revetments in 1952. Steel sheet piling was placed on both sides of the north and south piers thus completely enclosing the wooden cribs. The work started at the pier ends and reached the shore 6 years later, in 1958. The immediate effect of the sheet piling was to widen the piers. Before placement of this new piling the pier widths were approximately 30 feet. With the concrete decking completed on the sheet piling—as we see it today—the piers were made 34 to 51 feet wide.

The sheet piling, concrete and stone work continued up the

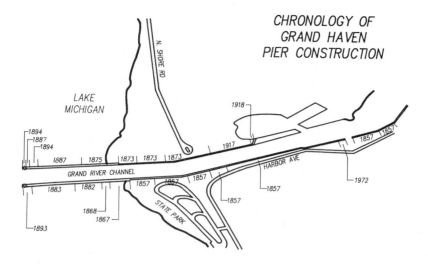

Courtesy Joe McCrea Great Lakes Design and draftsman Rod Nelson.

channel on both sides. The revetments on the south side—up to a point opposite the old Coast Guard Station—and the north side—past the old Station up to the North Shore Marina—were completed in 1963. The final phase of the sheet piling work took place in 1972. At that time the revetment-sheet piling-concrete-stone work on the south side of the channel was extended up to the Government Pond which included enclosing the Government Pond piers with the sheet piling. Before this time the Government Pond piers were a scant 22 feet wide. After the new sheet piling and its concrete decking was completed they were made—as we see them today—30 feet wide. Also the opening into Government Pond was widened to 92 feet which provided a more comfortable entrance for the larger vessels such as the *Woodbine* and the *Haines*.

Some veteran boaters agree that before the sheet piling construction the harbor entrance was more forgiving because the wave action dissipated itself within the old wooden walls and cribs. By contrast today's sheet piling is impenetrable and therefore provides a much more "stimulating" ride on choppy days.

Pier maintenance has been, of course, an ongoing expense for the Corps of Engineers. It is of interest to note that for the 42 year period from 1852 to 1894 the Federal Government appropriated $578,751, primarily for construction but undoubtedly some maintenance. By 1910 the price tag had jumped to $910,300 for a single appropriation. Thus in the first 58 years slightly more than $1.4 million had been spent on the Grand Haven piers—most of that for the original construction. The 1986 figures show the 134 year expenditures by the Corps totaled slightly over 25 million dollars; new work $1,458,000, rehabilitation work $814,000 and maintenance $22,758,000. So the $23.8 million spent in that 76 year period—1910 to 1986—was primarily for maintenance. All of these figures may seem a lot of money to a landlubber but to anyone living on Spring Lake, the Grand River, the bayous or along Lake Michigan who has had to build and maintain revetments or sea walls, the Government expenditures, proportionately, might seem like a bargain.

Lightships—lights on sailing ships anchored at hazardous shoal waters as an aid to mariners—had been stationed along the Atlantic Coast since 1820. They generally had 1 warrant officer and 10 crewmen aboard. It was dangerous, monotonous and, above all, lonely duty. The Great Lake's first lightships, *#55, #56* and *#57,* took their place at Simmon's Reef, White Shoal and Gray's Reef on October 22, 1891. They were the U.S. Lighthouse Service's first steam vessels. Through the years the number of lightships in U.S. waters grew so that by 1909—their peak year—there were 56 in service. But then as electronic warning systems became more sophisticated the lightships were retired. The last one on the Great Lakes, the *Huron,* was replaced by a navigational buoy on August 21, 1970.

The first mention that a Lighthouse Service ship had been assigned to the Port of Grand Haven was in 1900. In his work "Shipping in the Port of Grand Haven—1820-1940" author Orlie Bennett records show the steamer *Alice M. Gill* was on duty here as a lighthouse tender until June 30, 1900. Bennett also states that the Revenue Cutter on duty in Grand Haven was the *George Williams.* This is the first mention of a Cutter serving this Port. However Bennett refers to the *George Williams* variably as a "U.S. Steamer", a "government cutter" as well as a "Revenue Cutter." The Coast Guard historians in Washington have no record of a Cutter *George Williams,* and since Bennett also mentions that the *Williams* replaced the *General Gilmore* here in November of 1899, and because the *Gilmore* was probably a vessel used in hull and boiler inspection work, the *George Williams* was more likely also a Government inspection ship.

The first mention of a Revenue Cutter entering the Port of Grand Haven was in August of 1898 when the 108 foot sidewheel Cutter *William P. Fessenden* came here to return the body of Life Saving Service 11th District Superintendent Nathaniel Robbins, who had died in Bailey's Harbor, Wisconsin while inspecting stations in the district. (see Chapter 12)

In 1908 the Tribune ran a story lamenting the passing of another Grand Haven land mark. It was the "old white signal house which had stood on the south pier for 40 years" and, according to the article in the paper, had been torn down September 1, 1908. The Tribune article was most likely making reference to the white house midway out on the South Pier shown in the accompanying photograph. It was one of the two fog signal houses shown on Major Ludlow's 1890 chart. As mentioned earlier, it is quite probable that one of these two was moved nearer the pier end as a better location for the fog signal when the South Pier was completed in 1893, thereby leaving the remaining one midway out on the pier without any real function. However, if this is the "old white signal house" referred to then the "40 years" is in error. That section of the South Pier upon which the "old white house" stood was not completed until 1883 and so 25 years would be more correct for the 1908 demolition story.

Congress approved electrification of lighthouses in 1918. This was landmark legislation for the Lighthouse Service as well as the Coast Guard because it eventually led to both Services providing a higher level of protection for the mariners. It also hailed the introduction of radios and telephones to lighthouses and Lifeboat stations.

In 1921 an identification light was placed at the end of the North Pier and identified as North Pierhead Light No.1 . It was a white light which flashed every 4 seconds and was situated atop a steel lattice tower. It was powered by an acetylene tank house until 1975, at which time it was changed to a battery tankhouse. The tower was removed in 1985 and replaced with a steel cylinder which contains state of the art solar powered navigational equipment—the white column we see at the end of the North Pier today. The old lattice tower continues to send

Grand Haven Harbor c. 1906—interurban in foreground, white signal house halfway out in South Pier, Life Saving Station on north side. Courtesy Grand Haven Area Historical Society.

out its welcoming signal but in a decidedly different setting, for now it is on dry land, positioned on a pylon at the entrance to Coast Guard Park—the old Coast Guard rifle range in Ferrysburg—which was dedicated August 4, 1989.

In 1922 the end of the South Pier was rebuilt with a new concrete pierhead. The old original fog signal house—built in 1875 and still in use today—was placed on the new pierhead, provided with a covering of corregated metal to protect it from weathering, and given a fresh coat of red paint. It was then equipped with a new steam plant, coal bunker, electricity and a fog horn. The horn was a diaphone type activated by a huge air pump which was driven by an electric motor. On December 7, 1922 the fog horn emitted its first resonant, mournful "beeeeooooo" sound which became so familiar to residents within earshot of the Harbor. The horn and lighthouse required a 4 man crew to operate them. The fog signal house was also equipped with a boat, which, interestingly, harked back to the 1847 Congressional Act, initiated by Michigan Representative Robert McClelland. That 1847 law required that all lighthouses be equipped with lifeboats—the first Government appropriations for shore-based assistance to distressed mariners. There is no record of the 1922 boat ever being used for a rescue but it does indicate the thinking which still prevailed.

During the 1920's radio navigation was becoming reliable and practical. In 1927 Grand Haven was authorized to place the new equipment at the front range light on its south pier head. On August 15, 1927 it began sending a radio signal of 1 dot and 3 dashes for 60 seconds every three minutes.

The sound and feel of war were getting closer to our country's shores by 1939. Perhaps anticipating the inevitable, the Lighthouse Service became part of the Coast Guard, thus further streamlining our Nation's port security. At that time there were 2,000 aids to navigation on the Great Lakes, half of them lighted. Automation of more and more of these navigational aids spelled an end to the need for keepers as well as a very colorful chapter in the history of the Service. Today there are no manned light stations.

The 1943 Light List reported a North Pierhead light with acetylene power, a South Pier front light which was a 6th order Fresnel fixed red and a rear South Pier light which was a 4th order 30 second flash in a 52 foot tower.

The old familiar bellows type fog horn was replaced in 1969. On December 2, 1969 a new high-pitched "whistle"emanated from the fog signal house. With fog hanging in the trees and haloing every street light it had seemed right to feel the vibrations and resonance of the old bellows fog horn. When water and even land traffic were slowed by the dense stuff the romantic moan of the horn went right to the soul of this port city and let one know it was part of the tradition of the sea. The new "whine" was wimpish by comparison. Just as with the passing of the steam train whistle and its replacement by the diesel horn—it would take awhile for the local citizenry to learn to live with the new fangled fog signal.

At that time—December 2, 1969—the fog signal, as well as the lighthouse light, were automated for all atmospheric conditions. Today the navigational aids which provide the indentifying characteristics for Grand Haven Harbor's entrance are these: The South Pierhead entrance light atop the red fog signal house is 42 feet high and flashes a red light, reflected from a 190 mm lense every 10 seconds, which can be seen for 15 miles. The 52 foot red cylindrical lighthouse tower, which is 600 feet from the end of the South Pier, uses a 300 mm lense and shows a red 4 second occulting light—on 3 seconds and off 1 second—which is visible for 8 miles. The North Pierhead light is atop a 36 foot high white cylindrical tower—which contains the solar pack to power the light—and uses a 300 mm lense to flash a green signal every 4 seconds which can be seen 6 miles. (a point of explanation: by a 1983 International Agreement all white pier lights and black buoys— which were on a vessels port side as they entered a harbor—were changed to green.) The South Pier fog signal sends out 2 blasts every 30 seconds. On a frequency of 316 kilohertz a South Pier radio beacon sends out the Morse code signal of 2 dashes followed by 3 dashes, which translates as the leters "G" and "O".

All this automation eliminated the need for an onsite crew to operate the navigational aids and thus also made obsolete the catwalk which had, since 1871, allowed men to reach the pier head to tend the light and horn under all weather conditions. The catwalk was no longer needed and, therefore, was scheduled for removal. Mayor Marge Boon, the City Council and City Manager Larry Deetjen petitioned Ninth District Commander Rear Admiral Arnold Danielson to retain the catwalk but received no great encouragement that the order could be reversed. Whereas the old fog horn had been replaced before most Grand Havenites were aware what had happened, these local townspeople were not going to give up their catwalk so easily. The pier lighthouse and fog signal house were landmarks of the City and the catwalk was all part of that history and tradition. Ed Zenko spearheaded a Citizen's Committee and through organized fund raising efforts—fueled by a groundswell of public sentiment and plenty of support from City Hall—the catwalk was saved.

When the project was completed the catwalk was not only made structurally sound but, as an added touch of history, jewels were placed in the pier's crown. The *Escanaba*—the Cutter stationed in Grand Haven during the 1930's—had a mast-head light referred to as the "smoking" or "munitions loading" light. Steve Vozar was stationed on the *Escanaba* in 1940 when the ship was being prepared for war duty. In the fall of that year the *Esky* was sent to Manitowac where, among other things, its 2 wooden masts were removed and replaced with a single steel one. In the process the "smoking" lamp was never replaced and ultimately acquired by Steve Vozar. Steve gave this antique to Ed Zenko who later showed it to Catwalk Committeeperson John Harvey. John suggested that the light be replicated and the copies placed along both sides of the catwalk to give the Harbor entrance a distinctive illumination. The idea of linking *Escanaba* to the catwalk and the pier was infectious and received enthusiastic public support. Along with Zenko and Harvey many others should be mentioned who were involved in this unique civic project: Don Wessel, Hank Miller, Louie King, Warren Snyder, Wally Kasemodel, Morrie Boon and Steve Vozar. These volunteers hand produced 200 of the replicas and those latterns' soft light now connects the Boardwalk to the end of the pier. Unfortunately Ed Zenko died December 31, 1987, 11 months before completion of the venture. Ed's daughter, Terry Fenlon, took over as chairperson and guided it through to a successful conclusion. The catwalk lights were first turned on November 25, 1988. And now each night mariners are given a nostalgic *Escanaba* welcome as they enter the Port of Grand Haven. It is a beautiful, melancholy link with the Port's heritage—a fitting harbor entrance to Coast Guard City.

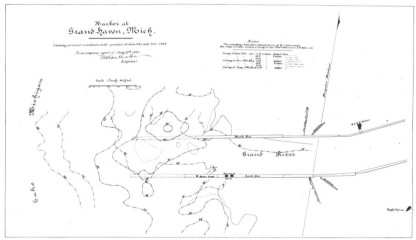

Ludlow's 1890 Survey. Courtesy Midge Verplank.

CHAPTER 8

PORT INDUSTRIAL DEVELOPMENT

The Grand Haven Area 1864 population had grown to 1,576. More lumber than ever was being shipped from Grand Haven Harbor. In the early 1860's Mill Point and Grand Haven mills were producing 4 times that which had been produced in the 1850's. From 1869 until its last log drive May 18, 1889, the Ottawa County Booming Company handled nearly two billion feet of logs, which would equate to nearly twice that much processed lumber. And as the processed lumber rolling out of the mills increased the fleet of schooners to transport it to market grew accordingly to keep pace. The following is the number of feet of unprocessed timber that came down the Grand River to the mills at Spring Lake and Grand Haven by year:

Year	Feet	
1869	47,021,355	
1870	56,017,113	
1871	73,138,886	Chicago Fire-Oct. 8
1872	61,624,512	
1873	132,764,670	
1874	68,000,764	
1875	91,218,523	
1876	40,590,843	
1877	84,628,102	
1878	47,727,042	
1879	113,245,698	
1880	149,334,891	
1881	198,009,731	
1882	171,519,152	
1883	198,092,190	
1884	159,547,465	
1885	70,559,619	
1886	91,319,192	

1887	48,360,753	
1888	56,553,911	
1889	22,288,177	last log drive May 14

River Log Drive c. 1870. Courtesy Flat River Historical Society.

The first pedestrian-vehicle bridge joining the Village of Mill Point and the Village of Grand Haven was built in 1866. It extended from the end of 7th Street—today's Beacon Boulevard—across the south channel to the present site of Grand Isle Marina—this section referred to on early maps as the old "Sawdust Road"—and then across the Grand River to the tip of Mill Point, today the location of the Holiday Inn. (This bridge served until a replacement was opened November 11, 1924. The 1924 bridge was replaced by our present U.S. 31 bridge, which was dedicated July 9, 1959) There had been a railroad bridge between Ferrysburg and Mill Point since 1858.

Mill Point's name was changed to Spring Lake February 27, 1867 and the next month Grand Haven became a city—March 16, 1867. Reverend William M. Ferry, Father of Grand Haven, died December 30 that same year and so, at least for misty eyed historians, he had lived long enough to see his progeny reach maturity.

Grand Haven was developing as a shipbuilding center. In 1855

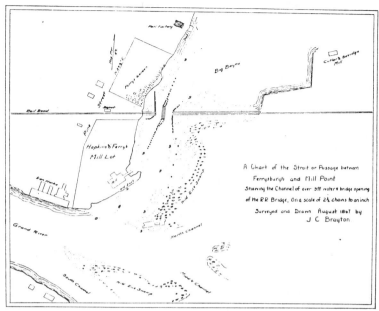

A Chart of the Strait or Passage between
Ferrysburgh and Mill Point
Showing the Channel of over 5ft water & bridge opening
of the RR Bridge, On a scale of 2½ chains to an inch
Surveyed and Drawn August 1867 by
J C Brayton

Mill Point and Ferrysburg 1867. Courtesy Carl T. Bowen, County Surveyor, and John J. Boer.

Ferry and Chandler started the Ottawa Iron Works which was located in Ferrysburg on the Grand River where the north abutment for today's US-31 bridge is situated. It manufactured, among other things, steam engines. In 1859 Thomas Turnbull organized the Thomas Turnbull Boiler Works which was located in Ferrysburg next to the Ottawa Iron Works on the Spring Lake channel near the M-104 bridge. Both of these businesses began because of the need for their products in the lumbering industry but subsequently played key roles in the shipbuilding which was to follow. Everything fit. The ships would be built locally then floated over to Ferrysburg to receive their engines, boilers and the multitude of cast metal fittings.

John Watt Johnston took over Turnbull in 1864. John's son Thomas was admitted to the business in 1875 and the name was changed from Johnston Boiler Works to John W. Johnston & Son. In 1880 another son, John B., came in, at which time the father retired and the name of the business became Johnston Brothers Boiler. Ottawa Iron Works had moved their operation to a new building on the Ferrysburg side of the Spring Lake channel but then in 1883 ceased operation. Johnston Bros. moved their boiler business into the vacated plant in 1887. A fire in 1917 destroyed the building but it was immediately rebuilt and stands today nearly as it was over a half century ago.

Johnston Bros. was capably managed by 4 generations of Johnstons; John W.—his sons Thomas and James B.—Thomas' three sons John Franklin (J.F.), Robert and James H.—and most recently James H.'s two sons David and Marshall. David's son, David, Jr.—a fifth generation—is currently an employee of today's Johnston Boiler.

In 1898 the company entered the shipbuilding business. Their first vessel was the "charcoal iron" hull *C.J. Bos,* built for William VerDuin as a fishing tug, which was launched December 21, 1898. (C.J. Bos was a celery king and also VerDuin's father-in-law) This was the beginning of a long line of ships which went down the ways at Johnston Bros. From 1898 to 1926, when Johnston Bros. discontinued the shipbuilding phase of their business, 53 ships were built—some still in service today. During WW II the Government offered the company a $6 million loan to get back into the business but Johnston decided against it.

Johnston Brothers Boiler was sold in 1970 but remains in operation today at the same location under the name of Johnston Boiler. It is of historic interest because when you consider it dates back to 1859 it is perhaps the oldest continuous manufacturing business in the Grand Haven Area. That is not to discredit those who argue that the tannery business started by Clark Albee in Grand Haven near the corner of Elliott and Second Streets in 1838 is the oldest because it was the forerunner of today's Eagle Ottawa Leather Company. The difference is in the lineage— Johnston Boiler's seems the neater of the two. Those who are inclined to jump into the debate on the side of fishing, trading or lumbering—all 3 of which were industries long before Europeons arrived on the scene—please remember that the rule of the game is "manufacturing" business.

J.F. Johnston was 82 years old when he died in 1957. He had a lifelong fascination with ships and the Lake. In 1956, during a conversation on the subject, he described how as a youth, when Grand Haven's big lumber schooners were ubiquitous, he would sit on the end of the pier and watch the Harbor traffic. He stated he could not remember a time when he could not either watch a ship leaving port or see an incoming sail on the horizon.

In 1866 H.C. Pearson of Ogdensberg, New York established a shipyard in Ferrysburg on Spring Lake just north of Johnston Boiler. In 1866-67 he built 8 boats, both schooners and steamers. In the ensuing years he built ships for owners in Wisconsin and Chicago as well as for William Ferry and other local business men. Pearson was kept so busy that at times he would have as many as 100 ships carpenters under his employment. He built his last vessel in 1872 at which time he became the region's Federal Inspector of Hulls, a position he held until 1884. Pearson had other talents as well. He improved the propeller wheel, compiled a "Manual of Navigation for the Lakes" and, for a vocation outside of boating, invented a solar attachment for the surveyor's transit. Pearson's reputation lived on through the Sping Lake Clinker Boat Manufacturing Company, organized in 1887 by C.P. Brown, Dana Brown and William Barrett—forerunner to today's Barrett Boat Works. Using patents they had acquired from Pearson the principals of the Clinker Boat Company produced a style of boat which gained world-wide fame. Mitch and Jeff Jordan, present proprietors of Barrett's, have wisely kept those old Clinker Boat Records.

Duncan Robertson, a Scotsman from Clyde, was a ship designer and naval architect. In 1867 he left his homeland and immigrated to Michigan. He established a shipyard in Grand Haven which was located on the south channel near the end of Second Street where Hardy and Bill Bedford's Wharf Marina is located today. Robertson was later joined in the venture by fellow countrymen Paul McCoil, Peter Sinclair and Captain John Budge. (Captain Budge had come from Scotland's Orkney Islands, also the birthplace of Captain William R. Loutit, a person we are soon to meet. Three other Orkney sea captains besides Captain Budge would follow Captain Loutit to Grand Haven; Captains George Robertson, Thomas Trail and Robert McKay. The latter two men are to figure prominently in ship disasters out of this port.) The first vessel Robertson built was for Thomas Heffernan of Eastmanville. In the ensuing years his shipyard launched more than 100 staunch oak sailing ships which served on the lakes far beyond the usual span of such crafts. Robertson also built the 136 foot *City of Grand Rapids,* the 160 foot *H.C. Hall,* and the *Pentland,* all wooden hull steam propellers. With the passing of wooden boats he discontinued shipbuilding and instead became the designer of most of the metal boats produced at Johnston

Mechanics Ship Yard. Courtesy Grand Haven Area Historical Society.

Bros. Boiler in Ferrysburg between 1900 and 1913. He died October 4, 1913 in Spring Lake when he was 75.

The Mechanics Dry Dock and Shipyard was organized in 1867 by Thomas W. Kirby, John W. Callister and John Neil. It was located on the island on fill land across from the sag, just upstream from the present location of the Grand Haven Board of Light and Power generating plant. Over 20 vessels were built and many more repaired here over the years. It could accommodate the largest ships on the lakes. The *H.C. Akeley* was built here in 1881 at a cost of $110,000. Its keel was 230 feet which made her the largest on the lakes at that time. But her queenly reign was to be short-lived. We will learn of her demise in chapter 11.

Another boat builder who deserves mention is Jay McCleur. The McCleur's claim to fame was not only in their wood working skills but also due to the fact that Jay's son Marshal McCleur, grandfather of Betty Moore, built and drove his own automobile around Spring Lake in 1891, one year before Henry Ford would build his first horseless carriage.

In 1884 sixty-two ships used Grand Haven as their port of registration. This was at a time when Grand Haven was one of the busiest shipping ports in the world. By 1926 the number of ships registered here dropped to 5. During 60 years of shipbuilding—1866 to 1926—Grand Haven craftsmen produced 117 wooden and 53 metal vessels.

The Dake Engine Company was organized in 1887. It manufactured a special engine referred to as the Dake double reciprocating square piston engine, which, by title, fairly well described this different but unusually dependable new product—so dependable that some are still in service today. Dake is mentioned here along with shipbuilding because its product had several uses aboard ships. The factory was located on the north west corner of Seventh and Monroe Streets which placed it conveniently near the heart of the shipbuilding business. Paul Johnson, Sr. and Al Jacobson, Sr. acquired the business in 1945 and their sons Paul Johnson, Jr. and Chuck Jacobson took over managment of the company from Archie Campbell in 1946. When the new US-31 came through Grand Haven in 1955 the business was moved to a much large facility on Robbins Road where it remains today in a business completely evolved from the old square piston engine days. Al Jacobson, Jr.'s son Nelson is in a managerial position with the Company today and therefore is the third generation of Jacobsons to have been in the business. In 1987 Paul Johnson, Jr. wrote an excellent history of Dake for the business's centennial. It is a paradigm more businesses would do well to follow.

Another historic business which contributed to Harbor activity, as did all lumber mills, was the Derk Bakker and Son saw mill. William Bakker had settled at Port Sheldon in 1851. His son Derk started his lumber mill in Grand Haven in 1871. It was located on the south channel at the foot of Third Street just west of the railroad bridge which had been built in 1869. Bakker was a relatively late comer to the lumber business but he must be given credit for having the insight to locate not only on the River but also near the railroad when he finally did set up shop; he undoubtedly sensed that rail was the wave of the future. And, of course, he was correct. The company is given mention because of all the names—and there were more than 35—associated with saw mills along the waterways during those halcyon years of lumbering in the Grand Haven, Spring Lake and Ferrysburg area only the name Bakker remains as the sole survivor in the lumber business. Derk's son John D. succeeded his father as manager of the company. The business was moved to its present site on

Pennoyer in 1912. In 1920, needing office help, John hired Martin Boon—Maurie and Marge Boon's uncle and uncle-in-law respectively. Ironically John died two weeks later. Derk came out of retirement to manage the business but then in 1925 he too died. Mart Boon ran the business from 1925 until 1945 at which time John D.'s son, John Douglas, Jr.—Doug—took over management of the firm. Mart—who served as mayor in 1948-51—remained until 1976, at which time he retired after 56 years with the business. He was 91. The Bakers have dropped a "k" through the years but today the fourth generation, Doug and Kathy's sons Bruce W. and John Dickinson (Dick), continue the business of D. Baker and Son at 720 Pennoyer Street, right next to—of course—the railroad track. Dick's son James Daniel—another J.D.—may some day be the fifth generation to manage the 119 year old business. Grand Haven's Tri-Cities Museum has on display the "D.B." log marker, the only one of many such log branders from this area which has survived the years.

Residents of Grand Haven in the 1860's must have had some concern the ship building business was able to keep pace with the ship wrecks. For, alas, even in those days the sensational news grabbed the headlines. In 1867 the sidewheeler *Milwaukee* was wrecked while attempting to enter the Grand Haven Harbor. She had been built at Buffalo in 1859, 8 years previous, and at the time of her demise she was serving as one of the Detroit and Milwaukee Railroad "Black Boats" on the Milwaukee run.

On October 16, 1870 the steamer *Orion* was wrecked on a sand bar while attempting a safe entry into the Harbor.

In 1865 Pfaff and Vanderhoef built the steam propeller *Phebe* to provide a ferry between Grand Haven and the Detroit and Milwaukee rail depot, thus supplementing service for the ferry which had sunk in 1859. The *Phebe* also served as a ferry between Grand Haven and Mill Point. Some years later she worked as a tug under the name *George Stickney* and became one of the oldest boats in local waters. On August 26, 1907 she was dismantled and taken to the local "bone pile" on the Grand River next to Kirby's Mechanics Dry Dock and Shipyard, there to rot next to another famous retiree, *Old Traider,* one of the first propellers on Lake Michigan when it plied out of Green Bay in the 1850's.

As mentioned previously, in 1869 the Detroit and Milwaukee Railroad contracted the Engleman Transportation Company to

Detroit, Grand Haven and Milwaukee Depot and Robbins office at the foot of Washington Street. Courtesy Grand Haven Area Historical Society.

operate the cross-Lake carferry service. George Stickney was the Line's local agent and the ships making the run were the *LaBell* and *Ironsides.*

The Goodrich Steamship Line's Grand Haven agent in 1871 was Zenos G. Winsor. As a 19 year old this same Zenos Winsor had been the agent at Rix Robinson's Trading Post and greeted William Ferry in 1834 when Ferry made his first canoe trip down the Grand River to Gabagouache—Grand Haven.

In 1868 the Muskegon and Ferrysburg Railroad was formed. The next year—1869—this railroad joined with the Grand Haven and Holland Railroad to form the Michigan Lake Shore Railroad. For years Grand Haven had pressured the Detroit and Milwaukee Railroad to move its depot over onto the Grand Haven side of the River. Formation of the Michigan Lake Shore Railroad was the catalyst needed, for now a railroad bridge across the Grand River between Ferrysburg and Grand Haven could become a joint venture between the two railroads. This accomplished, a new Detroit and Milwaukee depot was built at the foot of Washington Street which placed it directly opposite Dewey Hill where the original depot had been located since 1859. The new depot— today home of Grand Haven's Tri-Cities Museum—opened January 1, 1870.

Mineral baths and plunges were the rage in the latter half of the 19th century because of the amazing healing powers attributed to them. Spring Lake and Grand Haven both took advantage of the craze and the area's tourist industry was born. In 1870 the Spring Lake Salt Company was begun with Aloys Bilz, Hunter Savidge, Allan Adzit and Robert Haire as directors. Bilz owned a hardware business on Savidge Street in Spring Lake. In 1872 he built a home at 107 Division immediately behind his store. His son William joined him in the business which gradually expanded to include plumbing and heating. Aloys worked until his death in 1934 at which time he was 93. William's son Preston came into the business in 1940 after William's untimely death, April 9, 1940, and carried on Bilz Plumbing and Heating until his death on April 6, 1983. Isabel Bilz, Preston's widow, continues to live in the 118 year old home built by Aloys. Robert Cook, the present owner of Bilz Plumbing, operates the 120 year old business at the same Savidge Street address.

The Spring Lake Salt Company bored for salt where Barrett's boat storage buildings are located on Spring Lake today. They struck, instead, mineral water which possessed unusual magnetic qualities. Word "leaked" out and people flocked to Spring Lake to seek cures for all sorts of ailments. The superb 74 room 4 story Spring Lake House was built on the site and opened its doors in 1871 to accommodate the business. It remained one of the most popular summer hotels in the Michigan resort region until it was destroyed by fire June 16, 1916.

Meanwhile over in Grand Haven that same year—1871, W.C. Sheldon, not to be outdone, tried his hand at drilling for this magic elixir. He conveniently chose the main thoroughfare, the north west corner of Washington and Third Streets where the Old Kent Bank is located today, as the site for his "discovery". The well was dug and the mystical waters were found on schedule. A large, ornate sanitarium was erected on the site, set back far enough for grounds which accommodated croquet, archery, lawn bowling and, in general, promenading. It was called W.C. Sheldon's Magnetic Mineral Spring. Business was brisk and so Dwight Cutler, the recently retired City mayor, erected a magnificent 5 story, $200,000 hotel to accommodate the quests. The Cutler House opened July 4, 1872 and was located across from the Mineral Springs on the south west corner of Washington and Third Streets, today's location of the Oakes Agency. Its luxurious accommodations and beautiful decor

Cutler House. Courtesy Grand Haven Area Historical Society.

established a new standard of the day and it soon became the most popular hotel in the State. Wide spread advertising resulted in the whole operation—mineral springs and luxury hotel—to become known as "The Saratoga of the West". A Federal Building—more commonly referred to as the Post Office—was built on the Mineral Springs site in 1905 and the source of the magnetic mineral water was capped. Somewhere in the visceral depths of Grand Haven's Old Kent Bank lurks an asset not thoroughly appreciated by present day auditors or the Bank Directors.

This promotional activity in both communities initiated lake life on Spring Lake and beach life on Lake Michigan. Grand Haven's Lake Avenue was extended through to Lake Michigan in 1873 which spawned the growth of summer homes and resort development along Lake Michigan. Grand Haven's population jumped to 4,363 while in contrast Holland's remained steady at 2,469.

All of the above activity had a direct bearing on Harbor traffic because it was antecedent to the cruise ships which in the years to follow would be part of the Crosby and Goodrich Lines' fleets.

CHAPTER 9

CHANNEL MAINTENANCE

Harbor and channel dredging of the Grand River alluvium and Lake bars was ongoing business even after the piers were completed in 1894. Grand Haven was a natural harbor as the British sloop *Felicity* had reported back in 1776 but still silt and sand bars continually formed as a part of the natural flow of the River and Lake waters. In addition to the Harbor dredging there was also the inter-city River traffic which needed assistance. Grand River dredging and construction was begun in 1881 under the auspices of the U.S. Coast and Geodedic Service and in the ensuing years a 5 foot deep channel was dug from Grand Haven to Grand Rapids and wing dams built to control the current of the River to help keep the channel clean. The method of constructing these wing dams was the same system Lillie described as having been used by the Detroit and Milwaukee Railroad in building a south pier in 1859; i.e., rows of piling were driven, then a 10 inch thick mattresses of woven brush was wedged between the piling and weighted down with stone. (see Chapter 7) Appropriations for the Grand River work were as follows: State of Michigan $30,000 in 1838 and $25,000 in 1840; Congressional 1852-88 $50,000, 1897 $50,000, December 22, 1900 $125,000, June 13, 1902 $150,000 (signed by President Theodore Roosevelt) and March 4, 1905 $100,000.

The first mention of a Government dredge at Grand Haven Harbor or the Grand River was the vacuum dredge *Sandsucker.* In his small book "The Story of the Grand River" author Don Chrysler refers to one Chester Leavenworth who worked on the *Sandsucker* as a surveyor's assistant and helped in the construction of the wing dams. This undoubtedly referred to work done by the U.S. Coast and Geodedic Service in the 1880's and 1890's because Corps of Engineer dredges were named for former Generals and these are not mentioned as being in service

95

in the Grand Haven Harbor until 1901. In that year—1901—the dipper dredge *General Farquhar* under the command of Captain Patrick Butler, reported for duty. It is presumed the early dredges, such as the *Sandsucker,* were able to service the Harbor as well as the River channel but, as the sailing ships phased out at the turn of the century and deep draft steel hulled ships became larger, a deeper harbor was needed which required heavier equipment. For this the Corps of Engineers came in with its "General" series—*General Farquhar* being the first.

By 1905 there were two dredges in these waters; the suction dredge *General Ludlow*—built by Johnston Boiler in Ferrysburg—was on duty between Grand Haven and Grand Rapids and the new seagoing suction type hopper dredge *General Gillespie,* stationed in Grand Haven but doing the dredging at several other Lake ports as well. The last mention of a dredge on the Grand River was the *Saginaw* in 1915. In that year the *Saginaw* was on assignment between Grand Haven and Grand Rapids keeping the channel open for the last days of the side wheeler *May Graham* which made her final run in 1917 thus ending the steamboat days on the Grand River. (See Chapter 5)

The *General Gillespie* was built in Maryland in 1904 and arrived in Grand Haven June 24, 1905. This coal burner was 177 feet long with a 38 foot beam and carried a crew of 46 men. Her name was changed to *General George G. Meade* in 1909. In her 42 years of duty out of this Port she worked as far north as the Soo and as far east as Saginaw Bay under the capable command of the following Masters:

Captain D.A. McDonald	1904-1919
Captain D.A. French	1904-1906 Temporarily re-
Captain I.L. Evans	1906-1907 placed Mcdonald
Captain Charles H. Richter	1919-1924
Captain M. Rosie	1924-1940
Captain Otto C. Grimm	1940-1945
Captain Lester C. Brinkert	1945-1947

Les Brinkert started as a deck hand on the *General Meade* in 1922 at the age of 16, serving under his uncle, Captain Richter. Brinkert can remember, as an underling, shoveling coal from dock side piles to supply fuel for the *Meade*'s boilers. In 1931 a large coal silo was built at Government Pond which then did the work mechanically. The silo was removed in 1949, but according

Corps of Engineers' dredge "General George G. Meade" ex "General Gillespie" 1904-1947. Courtesy Grand Haven Area Historical Society.

to Perry DeLille, who lived near Government Pond as a youngster, the under-street tunnel that carried the coal from the Pere Marquette Railroad hoppers to the silos still exists in the basement of the present day Corps of Engineer Building as a fall-out shelter.

Captain Brinkert worked his way through the ranks and was the last to serve as the *Meade's* commander before she was decommissioned in June 1947. In that same year the *Meade* was replaced by her sister ship the *General Burton,* which had been converted to an oil burner before being transferred here from Buffalo. The *Burton,* under the command of Captain Brinkert from 1947 to 1949, was then replaced by the *General Peter Connover Haines.*

The *Haines* was a diesel-electric seagoing hopper dredge built in 1942 for war duty in the Pacific. This 215 foot long, beamy—40 feet—veteran had served at Philadelphia, in the Pacific for the Navy in WW II and Jacksonville before coming to Grand Haven in 1949. One of *Haines* assignments in World War II was Manila Bay in the Philippines. It was during this tour of duty she was attacked and hit by enemy aircraft, but during the skirmish she was able to shoot down 2 of the Japanese attackers. When the *Haines* arrived in Grand Haven she became the third dredge commanded by Captain Les Brinkert. The

Haines chronology of Masters during her 34 years of service in the Port of Grand Haven is as follows:

Captain Lester C. Brinkert	1949-1961
Captain Howard Reynolds	1961-1970
Captian Hughe Leroy	1970-1971
Captain Richard Behm	1971-1983

Dick Behm hired on the *Haines* as a deck hand in July 1946 when he was 16 years old and worked his way through the ranks until he was appointed its commander in 1971. Captain Behm was the last person to leave the ship when it was decommissioned November 25, 1983.

The *Meade* and *Burton* eventually found their way to the scrap heap. The *Haines* ended its career at the bottom of the Atlantic on July 14, 1987, having been taken to Puerto Rico to be fodder for Navy ship-to-ship gunnery training.

The one remaining vessel that must be included to complete this phase of the Harbor history is the bucket dredge *Tomkins* which arrived at this Port in the 1930's The *Tomkins* could affectionately be dubbed the ugly duckling of the fleet. She had no power of her own and therefore needed a tender to haul her to and from assignments. However, she was wily and had the distinct advantage of being small enough to work the smaller harbors—Pentwater, Saugatuck, South Haven, White Lake, Arcadia, Frankfort, North Port and the like—that the bigger dredges could not reach. The *Tomkins* made Government Pond her home base for nearly 50 years before being taken out of service in 1983. Her tenders during that tenure of duty were 45 footers in her early years, the 85 foot *Forney* and the 65 foot *Quintus* in her final years.

The United States Army Corps of Engineers has supervised all Grand Haven Harbor work since 1866 and has had an office here since 1881. In 1911, when attached to the Grand Rapids District, the Corps' Grand Haven base of operation was established at Government Pond were it has remained for 89 years. In that year—1911—the Government warehouse was moved from the shore end of the South Pier to Lot Number 1, Section 2 just south of Howard Street, which placed it on the exact opposite side of the street from the location of the warehouse Louis Campau had built at the "Lower Diggings" in 1835. On January 1, 1919 the Grand Rapids Corps of Engineer District was absorbed into the

Corps of Engineers' dredge "General Peter Connover Haines"—1942-83. Courtesy Richard Behm.

Milwaukee District with headquarters in Milwaukee.

A dwelling and an office building, which had been built in Wisconsin and delivered to Grand Haven by barge, were erected at Government Pond in 1921. They were added to and altered from time to time but these same prefabricated buildings served as the Corps' local offices for over 50 years. The Corps moved to its present Grand Haven offices on April 30, 1972. The Milwaukee District became a part of the Detroit District in 1954 and Detroit remains today the District headquarters to which our local Corps of Engineers office reports.

Let us conclude this chapter with an enlargement of the Coast Guard which occurred in 1942, the year the old Bureau of Marine Inspection and Navigation became part of the Service. Through the years this Bureau had grown with the needs of the time until it became fully fleshed. As has been mentioned earlier (see Chapter 3), the Steamboat-Inspection Service was established in 1838 in an effort to put a stop to the rash of detonating steamboats. The Bureau of Navigation was organized in 1884 to administer the laws of navigation. And then in 1910 the Motorboat Act was born as a means of halting the alarming number of exploding "naphtha launches". Although it may have seemed logical to have assigned the duty of enforcing the Motorboat Act to Steamboat Inspection it instead came under the

Revenue Cutter Service, as did the 1915 Seaman's Act, an Act passed to make ships safer for seamen and passengers.

So at that time the U.S. Government operated a host of maritime services: the Lighthouse Service, the Steamboat Inspection Service and the Bureau of Navigation, all units of the Department of Commerce and Labor; the Life Saving Service and the Revenue Cutter Service, units of the Department of the Treasury. A vessel on the high seas might have been safer but bureaucratically confused. Some of this bewilderment of duties was ended in 1915 when the Life Saving and Revenue Cutter Services were amalgamated to form the U.S. Coast Guard. The remainder of the tangle was gathered under one authority when the Lighthouse Service—in 1939—and the Bureau of Marine Inspection and Navigation—in 1946—became permanent units of the Coast Guard.

There were two Steamboat Inspection Service Districts located in the Great Lakes Region, Lake Michigan ports coming under the Eighth District headquartered in Detroit. An office was established in Grand Haven in 1876—the same year the Life Saving Service began on the Great Lakes. As just mentioned the Steamboat Inspection Service was under the authority of the Bureau of Navigation and Steamboat Inspection of the Department of Commerce. There were Inspectors of Hulls and Inspectors of Boilers, however the records are incomplete regarding who the inspectors were in Grand Haven and when they served. As was mentioned previously H.C. Pearson, a ship builder, was appointed Inspector of Hulls in 1872, which adds to the confusion because that was 4 years before an office was established here. Captain Jay McCluer's 1902 license to pilot the *Lizzie Walsh* was signed by Thomas Honner as Inspector of Hulls and Henry Bloeker as Inspector of Boilers. Captain Honner went down with his ship—the *Ira H. Owen*—during a Lake Superior storm November 28, 1905.

Historical records show that on April 8, 1903 the *U.S.S. Graham* arrived in Grand Haven from Detroit to be the Government inspection boat for the year. It is assumed that while in this port the *Graham* operated at the behest of the local Inspection Office. She was under the command of Captain John F. Cavanaugh, one of the better known sea captains from Grand Haven—a person we will learn more about later.

In 1905 two men—Swift and Collins—are listed as the boiler

Steamship License. Courtesy Grand Haven Area Historical Society.

inspectors while Captain George Pardee was the Inspector of Hulls. An Eckliff is also listed. Pardee was replaced because of poor health by Captain Robert Reid on September 20, 1909. Captain Pardee died September 30, 1912. Captain Reid continued his duties until he passed away January 13, 1922. There is brief mention of a Captain Martin Walle succeeding a Captain Samuel Thurston as Boiler Inspector in 1915. John F. Cavanaugh's 1932 license as a Steamship Master was signed by Bernard J. Gellick as the U.S. Inspector of Hulls and Hugh P. Mulligan as the U.S. Inspector of Boilers. Gellick's assistant was Captain Peter Thompson—Mulligan's was Edgar G. Ewing with an Elmer C. Huless listed as Clerk. And there the trail ends.

In these preceding pages the ships have been built, the piers constructed, the Harbor and adjoining channels dredged, the lighthouses and fog horns positioned. Now let us return to 1871 and learn the origins of the real heroes of those early pre-Coast Guard days—the legendary surfmen of the Life Saving Service.

CHAPTER 10

THE LIFE SAVING SERVICE COMES TO GRAND HAVEN

United States Life Saving Service Emblem. Courtesy USCG.

The schooner *Vermont* was owned and commanded by Captain A. Albee. On December 9, 1860 Captain Albee was running before a late fall storm on Lake Michigan and headed for safe harborage at Port Sheldon. However the heavy seas caused him to miss the channel opening and the *Vermont* was wrecked on the bars. The waves proceeded to pound the ship to pieces and the helpless crew headed for the rigging as their last means of survival. First Mate Richard Connell took his and his shipmates fate into his own hands, dove into the surf and swam ashore with a line. Secured on land this life line allowed all 18 of the crew to find their way safely ashore.

Richard Connell's bravery might have been unusual for a first mate but is was the sort of stuff common to the makeup of the fabled surfmen of the United States Life Saving Service. Between 1871 and 1941 the Service would be credited with 203,609 such rescues on the oceans and lakes. Eleven years after the *Vermont* incident Connell was to become the first Captain of the Grand Haven Lifesaving Crew.

As stated by T. Micheal O'Brien in "Guardians of the Eighth sea," "Despite the numerous accomplishments and sometimes daring exploits of both the Revenue Cutter and Lighthouse Services, the real makers of history among the Coast Guard's predecessors were the men of the U.S. Life Saving Service."

As related on page 25 the Life Saving Service was born out of public indignation over disasters which finally spurred Congress to positive legislation. As early as 1847 Michigan Representative Robert McClelland had convinced Congress that something should be done to protect the mariners who formed the country's mercantile lifeline. But the dribble of funds over the years was slightly more than lip service from Congress which took little or no interest in addressing the situation directly. For example a 1869 Bill calling for paid life saving crews was defeated. But the next winter—1870-71—was especially harsh resulting in numerous fatal disasters, 214 on the Great Lakes alone. And this time the public outrage got the attention of Congress. A Revenue Marine Bureau, which was to administer both the Cutters and the Life Saving Stations, was established February 1, 1871.

Three classes of life saving stations were recommended to Congress on January 29, 1874. The First Class stations would have full time crews and would be built at an estimated cost of $5,302. Third Class stations—unmanned houses of refuge—were used exclusively on the Florida coasts.

A majority of the stations along the Great Lakes were to be Second Class stations which would cost $4,790. These stations were to be equipped with a lifeboat and a few other pieces of essential apparatus and were to be located at the more active ports. Second Class stations were to have Keepers who were to be paid $200 a year and a volunteer crew who were to receive not more that $10 for a rescue which involved human life. Crewmen at First Class stations would receive not more than $40 a month while the Keepers would receive the same $200 a year.

Lake Erie was to have 1 complete lifesaving station and 4 lifeboat stations; 2 complete and 2 lifeboat stations on Lake Ontario; 4 complete and 1 lifeboat station for Lake Huron; 4 complete stations on Lake Superior; for Lake Michigan, 3 complete and 9 lifeboat stations.

The Great Lakes would make up 3 of the Life Saving Service's 12 districts; the Ninth headquartered at Buffalo, the Tenth reporting to Detroit and the Eleventh in Grand Haven. Some of the stations began operating on the Great Lakes in the Nation's centennial year, 1876, others followed in 1877. In his book "Guardians of the Eighth Sea", T. Michael O'Brien lists Eugene W. Watson as superintendent of the Eleventh District in 1877. However the official Annual Report of the United States Life Saving Service of 1878-79 lists William R. Loutit as the District Superintendent and other sources credit Loutit with having organized the Lake Michigan District. Therefore this work will consider William Loutit the superintendent of the 11th District when the Grand Haven Life Saving Station opened May 1, 1877. During 1876-77 28 stations began operating on the Great Lakes. At their apogee in 1914 there were 62. The locations and dates of opening of those original 28 stations is as follows:

Lakes Erie and Ontario
David P. Dobbins
Superintendent

STATION	LOCATION	DATE OPENED
Oswego NY Lake Ontario	Entrance to harbor	Sept. 28, 1876
Charlotte, NY Lake Ontario	Entrance to harbor	Oct. 2, 1876
Presque Isle, PA Lake Erie	Entrance to harbor	Oct. 6, 1876
Fairport, OH Lake Erie	Entrance to harbor	Oct. 10, 1876
Cleveland, OH Lake Erie	Entrance to harbor	Sept. 20, 1876

Point Marblehead   Near Quarry Docks   Sept. 20, 1876

Lakes Huron and Superior
Joseph Sawyer,
Superintendent

Point Aux Barques, MI Near
Lake Huron   lighthouse   Sept. 15, 1876

Ottawa Point (Tawas)   Near
Lake Huron   lighthouse   Oct. 6, 1876

Sturgeon Point, MI   Near
Lake Huron   lighthouse   Sept. 15, 1876

Thunder Bay Island   Near
Lake Huron   lighthouse   Sept. 30, 1876

The following are stations which were established in 1876 but did not begin actual operations until the opening of navigation the following year:

Lakes Ontario and Erie

Big Sandy Creek, NY   North side of
Lake Ontario   creek mouth   April 16, 1877

Salmon Creek, NY   East side of
Lake Ontario   creek mouth   April 1, 1877

Buffalo, NY   Entrance to
Lake Erie   harbor   April, 1877

Lakes Huron and Superior

Vermillion Pt., MI   10 miles west of
Lake Superior   White Fish Point   May 15, 1877

Crisps, MI   18 miles west of
Lake Superior   White Fish Point   May 15, 1877

Two Heart Rivers, MI Near mouth
Lake Superior   of river   May 15, 1877

Sucker River, MI   Near mouth
Lake Superior   of river   May 15, 1877

Captain William R. Loutit, first superintendent of the 11th Life Saving Service District—1876-1882. Courtesy Grand Haven Area Historical Society.

Lake Michigan
William R. Loutit,
Superintendent
North Manitou Island Near Packard's
Lake Michigan   Wharf   June 23, 1877

Point au Bec Scies   Near
Lake Michigan   lighthouse   April 23, 1877

Grand Point au Sable Lake Michigan	Near lighthouse	May 15, 1877
Grand Haven, MI Lake Michigan	Entrance to harbor	May 1, 1877
St. Joseph, MI Lake Michigan	In harbor	May 1, 1877
Old Chicago, IL Lake Michigan	In harbor	May 25, 1877
Racine, WI Lake Michigan	In harbor	June 2, 1877
Milwaukee, WI Lake Michigan	Near harbor entrance	May 7, 1877
Sheboygan, WI Lake Michigan	Entrance to harbor	May 4, 1877
Two Rivers, WI Lake Michigan	Entrance to harbor	May 1, 1877

William Robertson Loutit was born October 21, 1825 in the Orkney Islands, which are separated from Scotland by the Pentland Firth. He came to Grand Haven by way of Canada in 1854 and became a U.S. Citizen on October 11 that same year. He was a ship owner, captain and timber entrepreneur at a time when lumber was king. By 1891 the timber was exhausted so Loutit had a new ship, the propeller *Pentland*—named for his Scottish firth—built at the Duncan Robertson shipyard in 1894 and, at age 69, started a new business. In 1879 J.M. Bean and Judge A.C. May of Milwaukee started the Spring Lake Iron Works which was located on the west side of Spring Lake near Fruitport. Captain Loutit transported iron ore from Michigan's Upper Peninsula to the Iron Works where it was made into pig iron which was then shipped to eastern foundries.

Captain Loutit had one son, William Howlett Loutit, who in turn had three children, one of whom was William Robertson Loutit. Captain Loutit married for a second time in 1915 when

"Pentland" - built by Duncan Robertson in 1894 for Captain William R. Loutit. Courtesy Grand Haven Area Historical Society.

he was nearly 90 and then died July 9, 1921 at age 95. William H. was 82 when he died June 25, 1948 and William R. died November 29, 1961 at age 66.

In 1957 Bill Loutit established the Loutit Foundation and asked Paul A. Johnson, E.V. Erickson, Harvey L. Scholten and John H. Uhl to serve with him as trustees. Upon Loutit's death in 1961, his wife Kate was elected as trustee but she died the next year. Paul Johnson was elected President of the Foundation after Bill Loutit's death and continues to serve in that capacity. Gene Harbeck, Jr. was elected to the board in 1966 and Jon Eshleman in 1976. Each of the Loutits had been successful at their respective endeavors and today the Loutit legacy lives on through the philanthropic Loutit Foundation.

Through personal experience Captain Loutit was aware of the danger to mariners which could be meted out by Lake Michigan. He became vitally involved with the placement of lighthouses, construction of piers and the adequate dredging of harbors. By the time Congress got around to establishing a Life Saving Service—February 1, 1871—Loutit was already two steps ahead of them. He had also been an advocate of forming volunteer life saving crews at ports along Lake Michigan and therefore Grand Haven had a crew trained and ready by 1871. These were the men involved in the rescue of crew and passengers from the wreck of *Ironsides*; Captain Richard Connell and surfmen John DeYoung, John Wessel, C. Haffenback, John Fisher, C. VerMullen, James Barlow, R. Carmel and J.J. Glasson. These men were seamen and fishermen who had first hand experience in sea survival. In the tradition of American volunteerism which had preceded them—militiamen, firemen, the military—they unhesitatingly placed themselves in harms way when called upon to save human lives or property.

Grand Haven's first volunteer life saving group had no permanent base of operation, as later crews would enjoy, therefore records of their early exploits are sketchy. Their equipment probably consisted of a life boat, cork life vests, cork throwing rings and sticks, various lines but predominantly an abundance of courage and camaraderie. They served when needed but more importantly they were the first signal of hope for Lake mariners that someone ashore shared their plight.

The account of Captain Connell's crew aiding victims of the stricken *Ironsides* was told earlier. That same crew was called to duty on October 9, 1876 when the 87 ton *U.S. Grant* wrecked on the south pier. Another very sketchy account tells of *J.W. Whaling* of Chicago going aground off Grand Haven Harbor, Captain Connell's crew of volunteers saving all but one from the wreck. There were undoubtedly many other incidents because by the 1870's Grand Haven had become an extremely active port which actuarially would equate to an equally greater number of ship wrecks. However most of the accounts of the vaunted deeds of those early volunteer surfmen have been lost. Still it is not difficult to imagine how the citizens embraced these "Storm Warriors" as their heroes. As a port city, most townspeople in those days either made their living on the water or knew someone who did. An appreciation for the umbrella of safety provided by these surfmen led to a sincere bond between this port city and the Service. This phenomenon was not singular to any particular port but here in Grand Haven the relationship took on a uniqueness which is the genesis for our story.

The U.S. Life Saving Service opened the Grand Haven Station May 1, 1877. This date is of upmost significance because it marked the official beginning of Grand Haven's association with what would become the Coast Guard. The station was built on leased land on the north side of the River very close to the Harbor mouth but a little farther east, or up stream, from the Station which would replace it in 1922—the facility vacated June 5, 1989. The new base of operation for the 1877 volunteer Grand Haven Life Saving crew was a two story building with a two stall boat house and an observation tower. The architecture was quite typical of other stations built on the Lakes at that time. It was equipped with one 6 ton self-bailing, self-righting lifeboat, one 6 man surfboat and a life car. The picture on these pages dated July 18, 1883 shows the 6 man lifeboat with Keeper John DeYoung on the steering oar and was taken at a time of very high water. So high that the boat is floating at the back end of the building where the roof-top lookout is located. Viewing between the piling off the boat's bow one can see the revetments on the south side of the River. The other pictures, which reveal the roof-top lookout relocated to the south end of the building, were taken at the turn of the century, a time when the water was considerably lower.

The merits of the reorganized life saving stations were finally recognized by Congress on June 18, 1878. At that time the Life Saving Service was made a separate entity under the Department of the Treasury and President Hayes appointed Sumner Kimball as General Superintendent, a tenure which would extend to to the formation of the Coast Guard in 1915, thus making Kimball the only person to ever hold that position.

District Superintendents chose the Keepers for their District's stations. Keepers were required to be under 45 years of age, able-bodied, of reputable character and able to read and write. The Keepers in turn selected their crews using similar criteria. Keepers and crew were then examined by a board of inspectors comprised of an officer of Revenue Cutter Service, a surgeon of the Marine Hospital Service and an expert surfman to determine their character, health and knowledge of boating and surfing.

An appointed Keeper was required to reside at the station year round. He was not only responsible for the maintenance of the station and the performance of his crew, over which he had absolute authority, but was also an ex-officio customs inspector as well as custodian of all shipwrecked property until claimed by the owner or the agent. He manned the steering oar of the surf boats and directed the rescue operations. As with lighthouse Keepers the honorary appellation of Captain was part of the entitlement of being Keeper of a life saving station.

The size of the crew depended upon the number of oars of the largest boat at the station. And since Grand Haven's largest boat had 8 oars the Grand Haven Station had 8 man crews plus reserves. These men, a large percentage of whom came from fishing families, resided in the area, had thorough knowledge of the local waters and were required to live at the station during the active season, which was generally April 15 to December 15. During the 4 off months they fended for themselves as best they could, often working on the fishing boats.

The surfmen were ranked by skill and experience, the most proficient being Number 1. When the wearing of regular uniforms was begun—August 5, 1889—these numbers were worn on the left sleeve. In many of the posed group pictures of those early crews around the Great Lakes the surfmen of lesser rank were not inclined to show their number but the man who wore Number 1 invariably had his arm turned toward the camera so that his seniority could not be missed. One can only imagine the protocol which existed in the pecking order and the prevailing competition to bump up. Nepotism was not allowed.

Within a very short time the Life Saving Service gained legendary status. Considering that nationwide surfmen were saving 4,000 lives annually perhaps the position of honor was deserved. However, these "Heroes of the Surf", as the contemporary journalists immortalized them, were made to seem as "Clark Kents" of their day sitting around their stations patiently awaiting news of disaster so they could spring into action with their special skills which would be daringly displayed and the day won. This was, in fact, only partially true. Although the lifesavers did perform feats of unparalleled, inspiring heroism when called upon, their daily lives were far short of being valorous but rather could better be described as boring and tedious.

A publication entitled "For the Government of the Life Saving Service of the United States and the Laws Upon Which They Are Based" was the official manual which dictated the daily routine for the Keeper and surfmen. The title itself would indicate it was a no-nonsense handguide to proficiency and that is exactly what it was. It described in almost trivial detail the 24 hour, 6 day a

Life Car. Courtesy USCG.

week schedule of life at the station. The price for deviating from it could result in dismissal from the Service. Station decorum emphasized three things; discipline, discipline, discipline. It was a breeding ground for the development of an esprit de corps that resulted in exceptional mastery of drills and skills, all of which led to spirited rivalry from station to station.

The two major pieces of equipment at the station were the beach-apparatus cart for effecting shore to boat rescues and the life boat for water rescue. The apparatus on the beach cart consisted of a 200 pound brass Lyle gun (Invented by Colonel David A. Lyle, U.S. Army—two are on display in front of Grand Haven City Hall.), powder, projectiles, whip (or shot)lines laid up in a faking box, hawsers, various blocks with the necessary tackle and the breeches buoy. Another piece of equipment included in their armamentarium was the life-car, a water tight metal "coffin" into which distressed seamen would climb, seal the hatch and then be shuttled ashore through the surf along the same type of line used for the breeches buoy. Of the two the breeches buoy became the more popular.

During drills or an actual emergency the beach-apparatus cart was pulled into position by the surfmen, or by horse, or, later, by tractor. Drills consisted of positioning the cart, setting up the gear, attaching the whipline to the appropriate projectile and firing it to a superstructure, which simulated the mast of a wrecked ship, securing the hawser and operating the breeches buoy. A crew was expected to accomplish all of this in less than 5 minutes. Here again, competition from station to station was zestful.

The breeches buoy technique had been developed as a means of saving seamen from wrecks which were grounded so tantalizingly close to shore. A vessel disabled by storms could be driven aground or, in some cases, if caught in raging storm a captain might intentionally ground his ship as a means of saving it and the cargo. The crew would then take to the rigging to escape the seas which raked the hapless craft and there wait for the storm to subside or to be rescued. These grounded ships were often not more than 300 to 400 yards from shore but that meant 8 to 10 feet of water so everyone aboard was virtually stranded. Shooting a line to such a wreck and then establishing a ship to shore "suspension bridge" proved to be a very effective means of rescuing those in distress. The instructions that were sent out with the hawser on how and where to attach it to the disabled vessel were in English and French but the language of survival was universal and a seasoned seaman hanging on for life in the rigging caught on quite readily to the efforts those on shore were expending on his behalf regardless what language he or they spoke. The technique soon was used world wide. Mastery of this drill by the Life Saving crews was considered essential.

The steamer *Illinois* grounded off Charlevoix in 1910. That city's Life Saving station crew, under the direction of Keeper S. Bigwood, set some sort of a record when they got a line to the stranded vessel and by breeches buoy brought ashore safely all 500 crew and passengers without a single loss of life. One of the crewmen involved in this remarkable rescue was Ward W. Bennett who, as a Lt. Commander, served as the Coast Guard 10th District Commander at Grand Haven from 1933 until the headquarters were moved from this City in 1939.

Claude VerDuin witnessed the incident when the breeches buoy was used for the final time in a rescue on the Great Lakes. On December 7, 1939 the 537 foot *Sensibar* was being towed to Grand Haven by the tugs *Wisconsin* and *Montana,* to be refitted over the winter as a gravel hauler for Construction Materials (later Construction Aggregates). She had been used previously to make the fill area now known as Miggs Field for the Chicago World's Fair in 1933-34. There were heavy seas and as the flotilla approached Grand Haven an 8 inch hawser parted causing the *Sensibar* to be set adrift. Still she was able to set an anchor to stabilize herself while the two tugs headed into the Harbor for fuel and equipment. But in the interim northwest winds increased 45 mph and the tugs could not make it back out of the Harbor. As the intensity of the storm increased *Sensibar's* anchor chain broke and she began drifting south, finally being driven aground 2 1/2 miles south of the piers just 200 yards from shore in 7 feet of water. The Grand Haven Coast

The Breeches Buoy. Courtesy USCG.

Guard Station crew hauled the beach-apparatus to the sight, set up the Lyle gun and, as a gathered crowd looked on, fired a line to the stricken ship. Under the supervision of Keeper William Preston the hawser "suspension bridge" was set up and all crewmen slid to shore safely via the breeches buoy. There are no other recorded instances of a breeches buoy rescue on the Great Lakes after the *Sensibar* incident.

Like the beach-apparatus drills, mastery of the life-boat drills was also considered essential. And for good reason because the degree of proficiency with which a crew could handle their surf boat in heavy seas not only could be the determining factor for a successful rescue but also might mean the survival of the crew itself. "You have to go out but you don't have to come back" was never truer than with a life-boat rescue. Such was the case for the crew of the Life Saving Station at Point Aux Barques on Lake Huron. In October, 1880 they responded to a distress signal and launched their surf-boat into an unfriendly sea. The boat capsized, was righted, capsized again, righted and capsized yet again. The crew clung to the bottom of the craft but the cold and relentless pounding caused them to slip away one at a time. Only the Keeper was found, insensible, on the beach. He resigned his post immediately. His crew had been responsible for saving nearly 100 lives that same year. This true story points up the tenuousness of life for surfmen when they took their lifeboats into the breach. Needless to say, life-boat drills were performed with singular determination.

The life boat was launched from the boat ramp or taken to the surf on a boat cart. The type boats often used on the Lakes were self-bailing, self-righting, 700-1,000 pound vessels pulled by 6 or 8 surfmen with the Keeper on the steering oar. Drills consisted of launching into heavy surf, rowing, capsizing and righting. The adjoining drawing is from an 1884 manual which delineates in great detail the manner in which the gear was to be stored aboard the life boat for the most efficient readiness. Although operation of the breeches buoy was more dramatic it was the life boat that accounted for the most rescues.

The Life Saving Service manual described the weekly routine of drills and exercises as follows:

Monday—Practice with beach apparatus, overhaul and examine all apparatus and gear.

Tuesday—Practice with surf and life boat.

Wednesday—Practice with signals (semaphore, hand, colors etc.).

Thursday—Practice with beach apparatus.

Friday—Practice resuscitation.

Saturday—Clean the station and grounds.

Sunday was free from drills but the tour of duty in the observation tower and the schedule of night beach patrols continued 7 days a week.

After the first month of the season, practice with the beach apparatus on Mondays could be omitted.

The drills were conducted in near military style with commands and duties by the book. For example the following is taken from the 1884 regulations manual as to the governing of the "Beach-Apparatus Drill":

"When practicing, and before giving the command "Forward," the captain will muster his crew, and each man, upon his number being called, will salute by touching his hat, and answer as follows:

No. 1—Place gun in position; provide and load with shot; train the gun; bend the shot-line around the whip inside the block; tend the left part of the whip; hold the hawser for 2 to bend on the whip; overhaul back the whip, and if to leeward, unbend ends and bend outer end into traveller-block; if to windward, snap traveller-block onto hawser, and bend outer end of whip into traveller-block; man fall and left leg of (wooden support) crotch."

In this manner each in turn would recite his prescribed drill duties to the captain. Here, for example, would be the 5th ranking crewman's response after he saluted:

"No. 5—Unload and bury sand-anchor; man the weather part of whip when overhauling off the reel and sending off the hawser; haul in the slack of the hawser and make a cat's-paw in the end; man fall; belay fall, and am shifting man on the whip."

The recitations completed the captain would then conduct the drill giving the following words of command after which each surfman performed his prescribed part:

"Open boat-room doors—man the beach-wagon"
"Forward"
"Halt"
"Action"
"Man weather whip"
"Haul out"
"Man lee whip"
"Haul ashore"

Depending upon the day of the week, surf boat, signal and resuscitation drills followed the same disciplined format. All of these daily routines were conducted in full view of anyone who cared to watch and there is no doubt the bigger the audience the better was the show. Of course the real crowd pleasers were the firing of the cannon on beach-apparatus drill day and the capsizing drill on surf boat day.

Signal drill day was spent sharping skills receiving and sending semaphore flag code, distinguishing the definitions of 2, 3 and 4 flag or pennant hoists as well as memorizing and using the code book. The men of the Life Saving Service became so skilled in the use of this type of signal code that many were transferred to the Army Signal Corps during the Spanish-American War in 1898.

"Restoration of the apparently drowned" was practiced on resuscitation drill day. The "direct method" was the technique used in those early days; with victims on their stomachs water would be forced out of the chest cavity then they would be rolled over and their chests pumped to produce a bellows action until—hopefully—normal breathing was restored. Learning first aid was also part of the day's routine.

Although the drills changed from day to day the routine that never varied was the watch schedule. During the day watches were kept from sunrise to sunset, each surfman taking his turn in the lookout tower on the roof of the station. There were no seats in the tower which kept the watch-standers more alert besides which they were obliged to ring a bell each half hour to let the keeper know they were tending to business.

After sunset the watch took on the form of beach patrols with the first patrol being from sunset to 8 PM followed by three other patrols; 8-12, 12-4 and 4 until sunrise. A surfman would set out on beach patrol from the Grand Haven Station going north following along the beach as closely as the weather conditions would allow. Upon his return the next man would row across the River and patrol the south shore in the same manner. This was repeated through the night. Each "sand pounder" carried a lantern and Coston Signals, a self-igniting calcium carbide-calcium phosphide water flare used by the Service to warn vessels approaching too close to shore or to signal distressed mariners that help was on its way. The patrol distances were approximately 3 miles; Rosey Mound to the south and close to Hoffmaster Park to the north. Upon reaching the limits of his patrol the surfman would find a key concealed in a dugout portion of a post and this key made an impression on a special clock he carried to show the exact time he was at his post. These patrols along trackless sand in the black of night were performed under all—sometimes nearly impossible—weather conditions and were still part of Station duty as late as 1938.

The post used as the south limit for the Grand Haven Station beach patrol survived all of these years because it was being used as a corner support for a porch of a beach cottage built for the Holcomb family in 1937. When the beach patrols were discontinued in 1938, the post—an 8 inch diameter, 5 foot long hefty timber—was left on the beach and, having no further purpose, undoubtedly would have washed away or eventually used in a beach fire. Luckily the Holcombs salvaged it for a better purpose and, in effect, saved it. As is so often the case with vestiges, it took a few years for the post's historic worth to be appreciated. Mrs. Alice Danhof Storr acquired the Holcomb cottage and in 1968 made some repairs which included work on the porch. Mrs. Storr knew all along the significance of the timber, so, having a sense of history, she replaced the post and gave the relic of the old Life Saving Service days to Grand Haven's Tri-Cities Museum, where it is presently part of the Coast Guard display.

Bill Herbst and Glenn McGeorge, two local residents who served in the Coast Guard as surfman during the 1930's, can recall vividly the drills, watches, beach patrols and spit-and-polish Station life of those bygone days. According to Herbst, recruits were on a "Green Ticket", or probation, for 8 years, after which they went on a "White Ticket" and were then eligible for a pension. But "Green" or "White" ticket, everyone stood watch and everyone took his turn at beach patrol. Charlie Bugielski can remember how, as a young man, he was allowed to accompany the surfmen on their nightly rounds during the early 1930's. These gentlemen serve as an invaluable link to those bygone days of beach patrols which were common place 50 years ago but are now a bit of Coast Guard history which is nearly forgotten.

It was quite natural that a bonding between the station crew and the townspeople would develop, much in the manner towns tout their athletic teams today. This was true whether the station was in the Great Lakes or on the oceans because unlike other Services, the Life Saving Service was primarily a local affair. Surfmen had to be residents of the District in which they enlisted and could live no more than 5 miles from the station. In the evolution of command the No. 1 Surfman would eventually become the Keeper and one of the more experienced Keepers in the District would eventually become the Superintendent Thus, the Life Saving Service not only served the community in which they were located but they were also actually a part of those communities.

And with each rescue the station performed the pride and respect grew stronger. At Grand Haven the captain and crew responded by making the townspeople feel welcome at the station and even provided a ferry service across the River. They hung a bell on the south side of the Grand River channel near a small cut-out in the wooden pier designed to accommodate their life-boat and when the bell was rung by a local citizen a surfman would row over from the station in one of the station's boats, take the party aboard and row back to the north side of the River. Betty Olsen Hickey remembers the water taxi service and recounts how the surfmen would put the glasses on the bell ringers to verify they were bonafide hitch-hikers before launching

**Surfboat Launching show for visitors. Courtesy Grand
Haven Area Historical Society.**

their boat. Betty also remembers there was a token fee—25
cents—or a tip for the ride. But all remember with fondness the
mutual respect which was cultivated by the kindly gesture. There
were no roads to the north shore until 1928 so if a person wanted
to visit the Station, have a beach picnic or just a hike in the
endless north shore dunes the surfmen provided the water taxi
to do so. There is no record as to when the ferry service began
but there are those who can account for it as far back as the turn
of the century. It was discontinued some time before WW II.

The Life Saving Service also promoted safe boating and water
safety which included the teaching of swimming. Fern VerDuin
can recall renting a lifebelt at the Station for 50 cents an hour,
taking her first strokes in the Grand River while being tethered
by a watchful, helpful and patient surfman who served as the
instructor.

But for all the mundane day to day chores and drills, as well
as regular "white glove" inspections at the stations, these were
hardy men of great dedication. When duty called they performed
rescues of which novels and movies are made. All of this was
chronicled in great detail by the respective Keepers who in turn
reported to their District Superintendents. District
Superintendents reported annually to their superiors and then
the office of General Superintendent Sumner Kimball issued an
Annual Report of the Operations of the United States Life Saving

Service published by the Government Printing Office in Washington. The 1879 Annual Report, which is part of the Grand Haven Tri-Cities Museum Coast Guard collection, gives an invaluable account of the Service as it was over a century ago.

At that time there were 173 stations nation-wide, 30 on the Great Lakes, 12 of which were in Captain Loutit's 11th District, headquartered in Grand Haven. Stations at Manistee and Muskegon had been opened in the 1878-79 fiscal year and Ludington was nearing completion. The statistics reveal the Service responded to 219 disasters, 40 of which were on the Great Lakes, 17 of those being on Lake Michigan. Of those on Lake Michigan 10 of the disasters, or nearly 59%, came under the jurisdiction of District 11, Station No. 9—Grand Haven. That year Keeper Richard Connell's surfmen of the Grand Haven Station saved 56 lives while 5 were lost. These figures not only show Grand Haven to have been an unusually active port but also that the services of the Life Saving Service had come none to soon.

The Annual Report of 1879 shows that it was indeed an active year for Station No. 9, especially during the fall months. A treacherous fall storm raked Lake Michigan on October 11, with gale winds out of the northwest generating mountainous waves. The schooner *Alice M. Bears,* of Chicago, became stranded 50 yards north of the pier at 4:30 in the morning. Keeper Connell and his surfmen went out to her in a tug and took off the crew of 7 men on board. Then, to save her from being broken up, Connell scuttled the ship and when the seas subsided pumped her out and salvaged her.

That same day—October 11—the barge *C.O.D.,* of Grand Haven, with a crew of 4, sprung a leak and began to sink. Station No. 9 crew took off her deck load, pumped her out and towed her into port.

On October 28 the schooner *Presto* of Grand Haven, fighting a southwest gale and heavy seas, ran aground 50 yards north of the pier at 8:00 PM. Captain Connell and his surfmen got a line to her, worked her to the pier, took off her crew of 7 men and a passenger and then sank the vessel to save her.

That same night the surfmen went to the relief of the schooner *Persia,* which had stranded a half mile south of the pier, but upon arriving found that the crew had made it ashore safely.

The storm continued into the next day. October 29 at 7:00 PM the schooner *George W. Wescott* of Kenosha, Wisconsin was driven aground not far from the pier. Keeper Connell's men removed the crew of 7, took the vessel off the bar and towed it into the Harbor to safety.

That same evening at 9:00 PM the schooner *H.B. Moore* of South Haven stranded a half mile from the pier in a "baffled" effort to make the Grand Haven Harbor. Her crew of 8 men attempted to reach the beach by rowing their ship's life boat into the teeth of a violent shore break. Events were happening so rapidly the Grand Haven surfmen did not have time to launch their own life boat or get a line to the stricken vessel from the beach so instead rushed into the surf with lines and saved all of the schooner's crew.

October had provided enough action to last a season but November, with its "curse of the 11th month", would afford even more incredulities. At 11:00 AM on November 1, 1878 a telegraph was received at the Grand Haven Station requesting assistance in rescuing the crewmen of the *L.C. Woodruff* which was aground and awash in a raging storm on Lake Michigan a half mile north of White Lake. A special train was ordered but while Keeper Connell and four of his men were preparing to depart to the wreck of the *L.C. Woodruff,* the heavily laden lumber schooner *Australia,* of Muskegon, with 8 men aboard, seeking refuge from that same furious southwest gale, missed the channel to the Grand Haven Harbor and struck the north pier heavily, staving in her bow. Still under full sail she kept thumping the pier as torrents of water poured over her. During one of these collisions one of her crew jumped safely onto the pier, but another, in attempting to do the same, was swept overboard by a heavy sea and lost. The vessel continued to ram the pier but finally worked nearly alongside and grounded. At this point the Station crew got a line to her with their heaving stick and secured her to the pier thereby preventing her from swinging broadside to the beach and becoming a total wreck. The six remaining crewmen were taken off the *Australia* by noon.

The storm continued seething. Anticipating further problems at Grand Haven Keeper Connell left his No. 1 surfman John DeYoung at Station No. 9 in command of the remnant of the life-saving crew while Connell and the rest of the crew loaded their gear aboard the train headed for Whitehall.

The "1879 Annual Report of the Operations of the United

States Life Saving Service" devoted a paragraph to describe each of the 219 disasters which occurred nation-wide during that fiscal year. However the series of events which unfolded at District 11's Station No. 9 on November 1, 1878 were so noteworthy 4 pages of detailed description singled out Grand Haven's crew for its exceptional call to duty. So as not to miss the full flavor of the report we will quote directly:

Wreck of the Cleveland based *L.C. Woodruff*

The services often rendered by the volunteer life-boat crews upon the Lakes during the past year were in every respect admirable, as their record, contained in another part of this report, shows only too inadequately. More praiseworthy even than their feats in saving life and property at wrecks, was their voluntary assumption of patrol duty, under the most forbidding circumstances, at seasons when tempests menaced the shipping of those waters. It will be remembered that this guardianship is only required of regular life-saving crews, the volunteer life-boat crews appearing at call simply upon occasions for rescue. Nevertheless when storms gathered upon their coasts, these men, in a number of instances, without the slightest remuneration, assembled and kept vigilant watch night and day upon the beaches and piers, dividing their little bands into reliefs for the more thorough performance of the task so generously assumed.

Among these crews, credit is due the men of Life-Boat Station No. 9, Eleventh District, Grand Haven, Mich., who during a large part of October and November (1878), when the lake was swept by a succession of westerly gales, were on the alert, at one time patrolling beach and piers for two weeks without intermission, half the number alternating with the other half by night hourly. For most of this period, it was impossible to go upon the north pier at Grand Haven without being soaked to the skin by the spray and sea which constantly dashed over it. There was no fire in the boat-house, where for the whole fortnight the men were always in attendance, save when half their number were out on the tramp in the wind and rain, or the odd moments when the remainder could get a chance to run home for something to eat, or to change their wet clothing. Eleven disasters took place during this time at the port, nine of the vessels being driven ashore.

The heroic efforts of the station crew had their culmination on November 1, a day in which they gave aid and succor to five wrecks, and rescued 29 persons. One of these wrecks, unhappily the occasion for a series of untoward accidents in regard to life-saving endeavor, was that of the bark *L.C. Woodruff.*

On the 31st of October this vessel was at anchor in Lake Michigan, off White Lake, a body of water making inland therefrom. The evening previous all her sails, except her main staysail, had been carried away in a northwest blow, together with her jibboom, foretop-mast, and mizzen mast; the latter however, still held upright by the rigging. About midnight of the 31st, the wind began to blow from the southwest, and the vessel so dragged her anchors toward shore, that by four o'clock in the morning of November 1, her stern was in the outer breakers. Here she held until daylight, when she began to drag again, and by eight o'clock in the morning she fetched up on a bar in 13 feet of water, when her mizzen mast went over the side. At nine o'clock the gale had grown so violent, that the crew of the vessel were obliged to take to the for-rigging, the decks being swept by furious seas, and the situation had become alarming.

The position of the bark was half a mile north of the piers at the entrance to White Lake, and opposite a saw-mill, in front of which, protruding upon the water, was an ugly bank 12 feet high, consisting of slabs, edgings, and refuse stuff, the whole being covered with sawdust. The ends of the edgings bristled out all over the bank. Between the bank and the vessel was an old sunken wreck, an obstruction increased by an accumulation of refuse stuff from the saw-mill. Within a hundred yards was a beach of sand, on which and on the bank an excited crowd of spectators had gathered from the neighborhood, and from ten to twelve vessels windbound in White Lake. The captains and men of these vessels made repeated attempts to launch from the beach a yawl belonging to the schooner *Ellen Ellinwood,* and go out to the relief of the crew of the *Woodruff,* but the boat was swamped at every effort. Finally, at about nine o'clock in the morning, it was decided to telegraph from Whitehall, at the head of White Lake, to Grand Haven, for the assistance of the life-boat crew.

The telegram arrived about eleven o'clock, and by noon Keeper Connell, of Station No. 9, with a crew of four men, all that could be spared from wreck service then requisite at Grand Haven, started for the rescue by special train, taking with him the wreck ordnance and life car. The distance was 42 miles, the route taken being by the train to Whitehall, where the life-boat crew, with their apparatus, were transferred to a tugboat, which carried them across the inland waters of White Lake the scene of the wreck, at which they arrived by two o'clock in the afternoon.

The vessel lay within 150 yards of the shore, with a terrible running sea breaking over her, and her crew of ten men up in the fore-rigging under the eyes of the throng on land. Keeper Connell planted the wreck-gun on the bank, and at the first shot sent a line over the vessel just abaft of the main rigging. A tail block with a one and a half inch double line was next bent on the shot-dine, and the men on the wreck began hauling it off. An awful sea was then breaking against the bank and a strong current parallel with the shore was running rapidly. This current caused one part of the whip-line to sag to leeward, and when the tail-block at the end was about 40 yards from shore, the line unfortunately became entangled in the sunken wreck, while at the same time another part of it fouled in the jagged chevaux-de-frise of the protruding edgings. While an effort was made to clear the line, the hauling on the wreck continued, and the shot-line parted. In the midst of a scene of intense excitement and confusion on the part of the spectators, the whip-line was hauled in by the life-boat crew, and operations were recommenced.

The second shot fell short, the line being wet; but a third, carrying a dry line, was successful, and the line was seized by the men in the rigging. The keeper, in view of the experience of the former trial, judiciously determined to now send out the tail-block with a single part of the whip-line rove through it, having a bowline in the end, to which another shot-line was bent on for the purpose of hauling the end of the whip through the block back to shore after the block should be secured to the wreck. The tail-block reached the wreck, and was made fast, but unluckily in hauling the end of the whip-line ashore the shot-line fouled in a sunken obstruction. In the midst of an attempt to set it free, the excited crowd insisted, despite remonstrance, upon a volunteer attempt to reach the wreck by working out the yawl, attached by a painter to the whip-line suspended between the wreck and the shore, an attempt which resulted in the boat being capsized, and the five volunteers who had undertaken to haul themselves out in this way being thrown into the water, from whence they were rescued with great difficulty, but fortunately without loss.

The efforts of the keeper and crew, impeded by these accidents and interruptions, had up to this time resulted only in getting a single rope stretched between the wreck and the shore, and it was now beginning to grow dark. In his sworn testimony, obtained in the official investigation of this disaster, the keeper sustained by the testimony of his crew, states that at this point he proceeded to make ready the life-car, with the intention of having it hauled out to the wreck by the suspended whip-line in the hands of the men on board, arriving at which it could be drawn back by those on shore. Had this maneuver been executed, there is no doubt that all on board could have been quickly and easily landed. It appears, however, that the captain and some of the men on the wreck, despairing, in the growing darkness, of help from the shore, and unaware of any further attempts being made for their relief, had resolved, at this stage, to endeavor to work themselves along the whip-line to land, and the keeper while engaged, as he states, at the life-car, looking up as he heard a shout from the crowd, saw four of the men from the Woodruff in the water making their way along the rope. He at once rushed for the shore end of the whip-line, but at least fifty excited men had hold of it, and without listening or heeding, possessed with the one thought of dragging the sailors to land, they ran pell-mell up the bank, straining the line until it snapped near the tail-block on the wreck, thus severing the connection which had been affected with so much difficulty, and continued their headlong course, hauling the four sailors rapidly through and beneath the water until the capsized yawl, still attached to the whip-line, was reached, when boat and men came all together, over and under, in a terrible manner, to the shore. The captain when the yawl was reached, had contrived to seize and hold on to it, and came in unscathed. The three men were perfectly insensible when jerked up the bank from the sea, not only being nearly drowned by their sub-marine transit, but having suffered from the severe pounding of the boat, as it thrashed and tumbled with them through the water. The keeper at once went to work and succeeded in restoring them to consciousness by the practice of the method of resuscitation in use by the service, but one of them, the mate, died subsequently from his injuries.

The mainmast of the vessel now went over the side, and her stern began to break up. All connection with the shore being severed, the six men remaining on the wreck hastily made rafts of the floating deck planks, on which they endeavored to land. One sank and was drowned about 100 feet from the vessel. One came ashore safely a mile and a half up the beach, and another two miles and a half. Two others got to the bank abreast of the wreck. The sixth man perished obscurely, not having even been seen to leave the vessel. Thus of the ten men on board, two were drowned and one died of injuries incident to his rescue.

The result must be deeply regretted; yet it is difficult to see how it could have been otherwise. The recital of the disaster afforded by the evidence shows that the keeper and his men were victims of a series of adverse circumstances, which appear to have been incapable of master, and which baffled measures certainly well taken for the deliverance of those on board the vessel.

Meanwhile back at the Grand Haven Station the storm showed no signs of abating at midday so surfman John DeYoung, now in charge, had his men roll the surf-boat down to the beach in the event there may be further call to action. They did not have to wait long.

Shortly after noon the Schooner *America*, of Chicago, went aground north of the pier. DeYoung and his men launched the life-boat and, after a hard pull, reached the stricken vessel and brought her crew of 8 men safely ashore.

At 3:00 PM the schooner *Elvina,* of Oswego, New York, was driven onto the bar between the north pier and the *America,* her stern swinging against the latter's bow. The life saving crew waded out into the breakers as far as they could and succeeded in getting a line from her which they secured to the pier thus preventing the two schooners from destroying one another. The *Elvina's* captain was brought to shore at his request by the Station surf-boat.

But the day was not done for DeYoung and his charges. Shortly after the *Elvina* had been stabilized the schooner *Montpelier,* of Detroit, attempted to run into the Harbor but struck a bar, fell off to leeward and grounded on the abandoned wreck of the steamer *Orion*—sunk October 16, 1870. This stove a hole in her bottom and filling immediately the seas at once swept over her, the crew scampering up into the rigging. The life saving crew launched the surf-boat without delay and battled their way out to the sunken ship from which they rescued 7 men and 1 woman.

The 1879 Annual Report concluded its account of this remarkable day with following:

> The exploits of the life-saving crew at Grand Haven in effecting these rescues in the heavy sea that was that day running were the theme of general commendation in that region.

CHAPTER 11

FAMOUS SHIPS,
FAMOUS SHIP WRECKS AND
THE "HEROES OF PEACE"

As Gordon Lightfoot referred to her in his song "The Wreck of the Edmund Fitzgerald", ". . . the Witch of November came stealin" in the fall of 1879, once again living up to her reputation. On November 19, 1879 7 ships went aground at Grand Haven in one 24 hour period, a record never to be surpassed; the 87 ton scow *Maple Leaf,* the schooners *J.A. Holmes, Margaret Dall, C.O.D.* and *Mystic,* the 248 ton tug *General Payne* and the steamer *Amazon.* Keeper Connell and his crew saved the lives of all of those involved in these disasters as well as the crews of 2 other wrecks which occurred during the month—a total of 9 wrecks in the month of November, 1879 without the loss of a single life.

It is not hard to understand that the surfmen were viewed by the local citizens as heroes. And for good reason because many of the mariners saved by these "Wave Warriors" lived in the Grand Haven area so their daring rescues were viewed most personally. But that is not to say the life-savers were without their limitations; what they could not see or reach they could not assist. Such was the case for those aboard the *Alpena*—the first Lake disaster that struck close to the hearts of the residents of Grand Haven.

The 653 ton sidewheeler *Alpena* was built in Marine City, Michigan for Captain Albert Goodrich of Detroit at a cost of $80,000. She made regular runs between Grand Haven and Chicago and was the pride of the Goodrich Line. The evening of October 15, 1880 was unseasonably warm. Captain Nelson Napier loaded passengers and freight at Muskegon and steamed 12 miles south to Grand Haven to take on more passengers and cargo. It was 70 degree Indian Summer weather at 9:00 PM when the *Alpena* left Grand Haven bound for Chicago with a crew of 21 and 25 passengers. As she made her way through the night the temperature began to drop. Half way to Chicago she

"Alpena"—lost October 16, 1880. Courtesy Grand Haven Area Historical Society.

was sighted by the crew of the *Muskegon* and shortly after midnight—early October 16—Michigan City, Indiana logged her passing. Temperatures plummeted to 32 degrees and a violent storm developed accompanied by heavy snow. Many ships on the Lake that night experienced trouble and some were lost. The *Alpena* was not seen again and her whereabouts unknown until pieces of her wreckage began to wash ashore between Holland and Grand Haven. The ships log, which was recovered, gave an account of her last desperate hours. She had been blown from the Indiana shores to Kenosha, Wisconsin, up to Milwaukee and then to mid-lake where she sank after battling the storm for 18 hours. There were no survivors but the Grand Haven surfmen patroled the beaches for weeks looking for bodies and wreckage piecing together clues of the disaster.

Mr. and Mrs. W.J. Benham were included in the list of passengers, he having been the editor of the Grand Haven Herald at that time. However, there were 3 Grand Haven residents who were scheduled to make the trip that fateful night who, by some strange fortune, failed to make the departure. Dr. Arend Vanderveen, a well known physician who served the Grand Haven area for more than 50 years, had his unused *Alpena* ticket—now a part of Grand Haven's Tri-Cities Museum collection —hanging on the wall in their home at 508 Washington Street as a constant reminder of his good fortune. These words are written on the back of the ticket:

> Lost that night. None saved. Had Dr. Arend Vanderveen, wife and baby not been late in arriving at boat they would have shared the fate of drowning. They already had this ticket.

After the loss of the *Alpena,* Goodrich steamship service to Chicago was discontinued until 1882.

Surfman John DeYoung replaced Captain Richard Connell as Keeper of the Grand Haven Life Saving Station in 1881 and filled that post until 1885. Captain DeYoung's daughter, Helen DeYoung, resides in Grand Haven and can recall with some detail life at Station No. 9 in those early days. She is another civic treasure who affords us a direct link with those events which took place more that a century ago.

Captain Nathaniel Robbins succeeded Captain William Loutit in 1882 as the Superintendent of the Life Saving Service 11th District, a position he would hold for 16 years. District headquarters remained in Grand Haven. The 4th member of the seafaring Robbins family of Cape Cod, Massachusetts to bear the name Nathaniel, came to Michigan from the East in 1856 intending to set up a flour mill but instead became involved in the hauling of lumber. He sent his family on ahead to Benton Harbor, Michigan and then,

Nathaniel Robbins IV, superintendent of the 11th Life Saving District 1882-1898. Courtesy Grand Haven Area Historical Society.

with a complete flour mill loaded aboard, single handedly sailed his ship, the *Thomas Bradley,* up the St. Lawrence, through the Niagara canal and into the Great Lakes.

Having been told that the harbor entrance at St. Joseph was deceptive he headed for Chicago to pick up a pilot who could guide him safely into port at St. Joseph. The people in Chicago were astonished at his arrival because he was the first person to ever single handedly sail a salt water schooner from the east coast all the way through the Great Lakes.

With the pilot aboard Robbins set out for St. Joseph. But on their way a snow storm and an error on the part of the pilot caused the *Bradley* to run aground at New Buffalo. Robbins had traveled nearly 2,500 miles on his own without a mishap; he probably would have been better off following his own intuitive skills to reach his final destination. His cargo and ship were a total loss.

During the 1870-80's Captain Robbins operated a fleet of sailing ships which carried lumber from the mills of Grand Haven-Spring Lake to Benton Harbor and Chicago. The schooners were named for his sisters: the *Addie, Ora* and the *Cynthia.* The Robbins moved to Grand Haven June 24, 1884. Superintendent Robbins died August 3, 1898 aboard the Revenue Cutter *Fessenden* at Bailey's Harbor, Wisconsin during a routine inspection of the Life Saving stations in his district. He was brought back to Grand Haven aboard the sidewheeler *Fessenden* and was buried in Benton Harbor. This is the first record of a commissioned Revenue Cutter visiting the Port of Grand Haven.

There has been some confusion in the records about the ship which brought Captain Robbins' body back to Grand Haven. A 1934 Grand Haven Tribune article stated it was the Cutter *Andrew Johnson* and then a 1937 Tribune story reported it to be the Cutter *William P. Fessenden.* In the book "Guardians of the Eighth Sea" the *Andrew Johnson* is recorded as having been in the Great Lakes as early as 1865 but then leaving the Lakes in 1897. Since Robbins died in 1898 it undoubtedly was not the *Johnson* but rather the *Fessenden* that served as the Captain's water hearse from Bailey's Harbor to Grand Haven.

Captain Robbins' son, Nathaniel V, was born in Benton Harbor in 1866 and became the Grand Haven agent for the Goodrich Steamship Line in 1884 when he was just 18 years old. Three

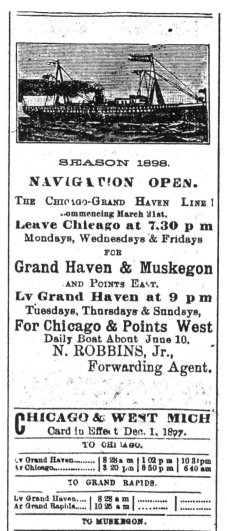

SEASON 1898.

NAVIGATION OPEN.

THE CHICAGO-GRAND HAVEN LINE !
..ommencing March 21st.

Leave Chicago at 7.30 p m
Mondays, Wednesdays & Fridays

FOR

Grand Haven & Muskegon
AND POINTS EAST.

Lv Grand Haven at 9 p m
Tuesdays, Thursdays & Sundays,

For Chicago & Points West
Daily Boat About June 10.

N. ROBBINS, Jr.,
Forwarding Agent.

CHICAGO & WEST MICH
Card in Effect Dec. 1, 1897.

TO CHICAGO.

Lv Grand Haven........	8 28 a m	1 02 p m	10 31 pm
Ar Chicago..............	3 20 p.m	6 50 p m	6 40 am

TO GRAND RAPIDS.

Lv Grand Haven....	8 28 a m	....	....
Ar Grand Rapids.....	10 25 a m	....	....

TO MUSKEGON.

Steamer Schedule

years later he purchased the coal, lime and cement business located at Washington and Harbor which was owned by H.L. Chamberlain and C.B. Winslow. The younger Robbins expanded the businesses into one of the more active docks on the Great Lakes for passenger and freight service. From there passengers through the years could board luxurious Goodrich Line steamers such as the *Atlanta, Alabama, Indiana* and *Arizona* for daily excursions on the Lakes. The Chicago bound steamers left at 9:00 PM and for Milwaukee at 10:00 PM. In 1925 "Nat" became a director of the Goodrich, Graham and Morton Steamship Line and then during the Great Depression operated the steamer *Grand Rapids* of the Goodrich Line for a trust company to transport passengers from Grand Haven and Milwaukee to Chicago for the Century of Progress World's Fair in 1933-34. For half a century area manufacturers and farmers shipped tons of industrial goods, produce and fruit across Robbins' dock. "Nat" Robbins died at his home June 24, 1940.

The Robbins dock area was used as a manufacturing site for Harbor Industry by Henry Parker from 1946 to 1969, at which time Harbor Industries moved its operation to 172nd Avenue where it remains today under the management of Henry's son,

Ted Parker. Meridian Corporation, started by Reno Offringa, occupied the buildings from 1970 to 1978. More recently the area has been remodeled as the Anderson-Bylsma Building by Len Anderson and Jay Bylsma. But through it all the continuity of the century old Robbins office has been retained and today serves as the office for Association of Commerce and Industry. This building and its neighbor on the other side of Ferry Landing—the old Detroit, Grand Haven and Milwaukee Railroad depot which is now home for Grand Haven's Tri-Cities Museum—straddle the River front where Rix Robinson had his first trading post and thus make a unique historic anchor for the beginning of Grand Haven's main street.

"Nat" Robbins had a daughter, who died at an early age, and two sons—Hunter and Nathaniel VI. Nathaniel VI married in 1919 and moved to Holland, Michigan. His son, Nathaniel Robbins VII, lives in Minneapolis. The grandson carries on the family name answering to Nathaniel Robbins VIII.

With a new keeper, DeYoung, and superintendent Robbins installed it was business as usual out on the Lakes. The *Jesse Martin* went ashore south of Grand Haven November 23, 1882. The old Grand Haven tug *Webster Balcheilu* pulled her off the next day but her seams had opened from the pounding and she began to fill with water. Keeper DeYoung dispatched his life-saving crew to the sight and began the rescue operation. As the ship filled with water it rolled to starboard and finally went over. The surfmen saved everyone except one crew member who had become entangled in the rigging and was pulled under. The November jinx continued when just two days later, on November 25, 1882, the 195 ton *Thomas Skinner* wrecked at Grand Haven.

The spring of 1883 produced a May storm which left Lake Michigan mariners reeling but because of the alertness of Life Saving Stations around the Lake there was little loss of life. The fall of 1883 was eventful as well. On October 30 the *Mary Nan* wrecked a half mile south of the Grand Haven pier. And one of Grand Haven's more famous sea stories occurred on November 13, 1883, a story which vividly portrays how seamen voluntarily assisted one another in times of mid-Lake tragedies. The drama involved two Grand Haven ships—the steambarge *H.C. Akeley* (see chapter 8) and the schooner *Driver.* However the complete story consisted of an extraordinary string of events

Captain John DeYoung and crew in the pond east of the station, c. 1880's. 1881 surfmen were: John Wessel, Cornelius VerMurlen, John Fisher, Andrew VanHoef, Peter Fisher, Martin VanderNoot, William Anderson and Tony VanToll. Courtesy Grand Haven Area Historical Society.

which began a week earlier.

On November 7, 1883 the schooner *Arab* was driven aground at St. Joseph, Michigan by a furious fall storm that wreaked havoc across the Lakes. Both the crew and cargo were saved by the surfmen of the St. Joseph Life Saving Station. When the seas had calmed they started to pump her out to refloat her but found the pump inadequate for the job, so another pump was brought to the site aboard the tug *Protection*. The *Arab* was brought off the bottom, temporarily patched and then at 7:00 PM, in calm seas, the *Protection* set out for Milwaukee with the *Arab* in tow. But the seas did not remain calm. About thirty miles from Racine another November storm lashed the Lake that proved too much for the beleagured *Arab* and around 4:00 in the morning she rolled over and sank. *Protection* put out a small boat which saved all the crew but one. However in maneuvering to retrieve the rescue boat *Protection* wrapped the towing line around her propeller shaft and became disabled which left the 15 men aboard the *Protection* at the mercy of the mounting seas. About

9:30 the next morning, November 12, the 230 foot steambarge *H.C. Akeley,*—one of the largest ships on the Lakes at that time—bound from Chicago to Buffalo with a cargo of grain, appeared on the scene and Captain Stretch responded to the tug's plea for help. By 11:00 AM the *Akeley* had *Protection* in tow and began laboring toward safe harborage. However the gales intensity proved too much and at 4:00 PM *Akeley's* rudder gave way. Now all the crews could do was hold on while the seas battered the two vessels. *Akeley's* cargo shifted and by 7:00 that evening she had taken on a frightful list so the tow line was cast off allowing the angry seas to drive the crafts aimlessly through the night on their seperate courses toward the Michigan shore. *Protection* grounded off Saugatuck the morning of November 13 with her crew still in peril. A call for help went out to the Life Saving Station at Grand Haven, but their crew was out on another rescue, leaving the St. Joseph Station—53 miles to the south—as the only hope for the beaten and wrecked tug. The St. Joseph surfmen promptly loaded their boat and beach apparatus aboard a train bound for Richmond, 40 miles to the north, where, upon arriving, they transferred their gear to the tug *Ganges* which took them the remaining 13 miles, reaching Saugatuck at 5:00 PM. All the crew aboard the *Protection* were rescued by the breeches buoy with the exception of one man who was lost while attempting to swim ashore on his own. However the *H.C. Akeley* was to suffer another fate.

During the night *Akeley* lost her smoke stack as well as her main and mizzen sails. By morning she had been blown to a point just off Saugatuck and Captain Stretch dropped an anchor in an attempt to stabilize the ship. But the ill-fated *Akeley*, leaking badly, was in her death throes as the raging seas slowly demolished her and by 1:30 PM November 13, 1883 she foundered stern first.

The schooner *Driver*, bound from Chicago to Grand Haven, had come upon the scene about noon and stood by the *Akeley* in an attempt at rescue. When the *Akeley* sank Captain David Miller—born in Eastmanville in 1843, died August 27, 1902— Master of the *Driver*, immediately headed his ship to the area where the steamer had disappeared and at first found nothing but debris from the wreck. The fury of the storm went unabated but the search continued until finally a yawl was sighted with survivors and *Driver* put a boat over the side to attempt getting a line to the yawl to effect a rescue. Daniel Miller, mate of the little schooner as well as brother of the captain, and crewman Pat Daley volunteered for the job. They left the *Driver* knowing their chances of returning were slim. They entered the boat and began rowing in the direction they had last seen the yawl, not even knowing if it was still afloat. Within minutes the mountainous waves covered all traces of Miller and Daley's whereabouts. They rowed on hoping by luck they would remain upright and by serendipity they would stumble onto the *Akeley* survivors. The odds of either were incredible. Remarkably they sighted the yawl, got a line to it and eventually found their way back to the *Driver* where all 12 drenched castaways were taken aboard. These 12 lived to tell the story but 6, including Captain Stretch, had gone down with the *H.C. Akeley*. For their acts of heroism Congress awarded gold medals to First Mate Daniel Miller and Seaman Pat Daley and a silver medal to David Miller, as Master of the *Driver*.

Just two days later, November 15, 1883, another famous rescue was performed by the crew Grand Haven's Station No. 9. The *Clara Parker*, under the command of Captain Andrew Lewis, went aground 10 miles south of Grand Haven in the same gale which had sunk the *Akeley*. Keeper DeYoung responded to the order from Superintendent Robbins, his surfmen hauling the beach apparatus to the site with the use of four horses. The Lyle gun was used to fire a line to the stranded vessel and all 9 men aboard were brought ashore safely. The beach cart used in this rescue was displayed at Grand Haven's first Water Fete in 1937. (see chapter 20)

In 1884, at the height of the lumbering era in the Grand River Valley, there were 62 ships registered in Grand Haven. By 1926 only 5 would name Grand Haven as their home port. And these 62 made up only part of the number of vessels which visited this port regularly in the 1880's to haul away the some 200,000,000 board feet of lumber which the mills in Spring Lake and Grand Haven were producing annually. In addition, at that time Grand Haven maintained one of the more extensive fishing fleets in the State. Disasters were a part of sea life but the ceaseless vigil and timely rescues by the surfmen of the Grand Haven Life Saving Station kept the loss of lives in these waters far lower than if their services had not been present.

Captain John DeYoung retired as keeper of Station No. 9 in

Grand Haven Life Saving Station Crew, c. 1903. (Front, left to right) Charles Robinson, Jacob VanWeelden, Charles Peterson, Herman Castle. (Rear, left to right) Peter Deneau, John Lysaght, John Walsh, Frank Vogel and William Walker. Courtesy Grand Haven Area Historical Society.

1885. He had been a volunteer surfman for 10 years—1871-80—and Keeper of the Grand Haven Station since 1881—a total of 15 years of service. Although there is no accurate count, records which are available credit him with having been involved saving in excess of 60 lives during his tour of duty.

Keeper DeYoung was replaced by Captain Thomas Beavais in 1885 who was in turn succeeded on July 19, 1888 by Captain John Lysaught. Lysaught held the position as Keeper until 1910—22 years—a tenure which was to be longer than anyone before him or after him.

At that time Keeper's received $75 a month while the surfman were being paid $65 a month. There were no pensions for Keepers of the Life Saving or Lighthouse Services, officers of cutters, surfmen nor cuttermen in those early days. Army and Navy men were pensioned based on the argument that it was a reward for their valor and hence proper. Cuttermen and Keepers, on the other hand, belonged to the Treasury Department, a civilian agency, and pensions for civilians was heresy. Inroads were made in 1894 when the facilities of the Marine Hospitals were extended to keepers of Life Saving Stations and all Revenue Cuttermen. And then in 1902, after having been refused retirement for more than a century, the officers of the Revenue

Grand Haven Life Saving Station Surfmen and Keeper, c. 1903. Courtesy Grand Haven Area Historical Society.

Cutter Service were at last put on an equal status with their Army and Navy counterparts; enlisted cuttermen would not receive parity until 1915. The Life Saving Service, on the other hand, had been brought under the rules of the Civil Service on May 6, 1896 and so they too—keepers as well as surfmen—would have to wait until 1915 to receive retirement. Prior to that time keepers were forced to stay on long past normal retirement age just to support themselves.

Captain John Lysaught opened the Grand Haven Station in March, 1910 but then, because of ill health, resigned his post on May 4. He died 12 days later. His first command had been at the Big Sauble Station, then Racine, Wisconsin before transferring to Grand Haven in 1888. On July 1, 1910 William Walker, who had been Keeper Lysaught's No.1 surfman in 1892, transferred from the Sleeping Bear Station, where he had been keeper since 1902, to become keeper of Station No. 9. It is of interest to ponder why Walker would have left his home town with a relatively stable job as No. 1 surfman to go to such a remote location as Sleeping Bear. Had he remained at the Grand Haven Station he undoubtedly would have been elevated to keeper because that was the practice. But then the pay of a surfman was seasonal at $65 a month, or $585 a year, whereas the keeper's position was permanent at $75 a month, or $900 a year. That in itself was probably enough to move a man but just as likely was the opportunity to assume a command. For whatever reason he left, Captain "Billy" Walker was back home where he served as keeper until 1922, which made him the Keeper of record when Life Saving and Revenue Cutter Services were combined in 1915 to form the Coast Guard.

Uniforms were not required in the Life Saving Service until August 5, 1889, 5 years after the Lighthouse Service received its authorization for uniforms. Regulations prescribed that a keepers uniform would consist of a dark indigo-blue, doubled-breasted coat of either jersey or flannel with matching vest and trousers. The cap was to be dark blue cloth with a visor and chin strap with the Service's symbol, a life buoy, crossed and interlocked oar and boathook, of gold embroidery worn on center with the letters "U.S." above and "L.S.S." below. Buttons were to be gold gilt with the symbol embossed.

Surfmen's uniforms were similar to those of keepers but were single-breasted and had no vest. They wore the Service emblem on the right sleeve and their seniority rating number on the left sleeve. Buttons were plain and black. Surfmen's caps had no chin strap and on a 1 1/2 inch band "U.S. LIFE SAVING SERVICE" was printed in gold.

Members paid for their own uniforms. A Keeper's cost about $20 with an optional overcoat for $17. Surfmen's were about $15. In the early 1900's Peter VanLopik of Grand Haven was a manufacturer of "U.S. Surfman's Supplies and Naval Blouses."

In 1893 the original 28 Life Saving stations along the Great Lakes had increased to 47. There were 60 stations by 1900. New facilities in the 11th District included those at Charlevoix, South Manitou Island, Sleeping Bear Point, Frankfort, Manistee, Ludington, Pentwater, White Lake, Muskegon, Holland and South Haven in Michigan, Michigan City in Indiana, South Chicago and Jackson Park in Illinois, Kenosha, Kewaunee, Sturgeon Bay, Bailey Harbor and Plum Island in Wisconsin.

Up in Marquette in 1899 Keeper Henry Cleary and his surfmen began to experiment with motorized lifeboats. It was the dawn of a technological revolution for the U.S. Life Saving Service which eventually led to the use of telephones, telegraphs and ultimately radios. Steam engines were never a practical solution

Grand Haven Life Saving Station Crew, c. 1903. Courtesy Grand Haven Area Historical Society.

to lifeboat propulsion because of weight, start-up time, bulkiness and the overriding fact that they could be easily extinguished in heavy weather. However, the development of the internal combustion engine in the latter part of the nineteenth century gave some promise and Keeper Cleary saw it as the possible answer to the surfman's needs. He and his crew worked with Lieutenant C.H. McLellan, a Revenue Cutter officer and experience marine equipment researcher, and the Lake Shore Engine Works to outfit and test the first motor lifeboat. The prototype was a 34 foot lifeboat in which a 2 cyclinder, 12 horsepower Superior engine had been installed. The trials in September 1899 were successful enough that the Secretary of the Treasury turned the project over to M.I.T.—The Massachusetts Institute to Technology. By 1905 12 motorized lifeboats were in operation. The motorized lifeboats allowed sations to respond more quickly to calls for assistance besides greatly extending their range of operation.

Ice during the winter months and early spring presented its own unique problems for shipping on the Great Lakes. Ships

"Naomi" in ice, c. 1905. At this time the 52 foot tower was on the end of the pier. Courtesy Grand Haven Area Historical Society.

trapped in ice were not often in peril and yet there was always the nagging concern that the ship—particularly the wooden ones—could be crushed if the ice began to move. Even then few lives were lost because in many cases it was simply a matter of walking ashore or over to another ship. If stranded long enough, however, the concern for fuel and food supplies was ever present.

The Goodrich Line passenger ship *Wisconsin* was stuck in the ice from March 12 to April 12, 1885 while in command of Captain W.P. McGregor. Although she received a warped keel for her ordeal she managed to live on for many years. The complete story of the *Wisconsin* is a fascinating one and her pedigree is given at this time, although out of context, so the reader will have a better chance of recognizing her true identity as the story continues. The 203 foot *Wisconsin* was built in 1881 at the Wyandott Shipyards and provided the Goodrich Streamship Lines with one of the fastest passenger ships on the Great Lakes. The Goodrich Line sold her to the Crosby Line in 1898 which had her refitted, in 1899, as a luxury liner—the work done by Johnston Bros. in Ferrysburg under the supervision of Duncan Robertson—after which she was renamed *Naomi*. *Naomi* sailed out of Grand Haven on May 21, 1907 and burned in Mid-Lake. (see Chapter 13.) Her remains were rebuilt as the *E.G. Crosby*. During World War I she was used by the Government and sailed under the name *General R.M. O'Reilly*. After the war she once again became the property of the Goodrich Line sailing this time as the passenger liner *Pilgrim* on the Grand Haven to Chicago run. And then in 1922 she was given back her original name *Wisconsin* which she kept unit her demise in 1929. A convoluted but interesting genealogy.

The propeller *Michigan* was lost in the ice 30 miles off South Haven on March 19, 1885. All aboard were saved by the tuge *Artic.*

As was often the case at Grand Haven, 2 or 3 ships at a time could be stuck in the same ice pack trying to enter port. On February 11, 1899 the *John V. Moran, Naomi, Nyack* and *Mary H. Boyce,* all owned by the Crosby Line, were stuck in the ice 15 miles out with temperatures hovering at 30 degrees below zero. The 214 foot *Moran*, built in Bay City in 1888, was crushed and sank but Captain McLeod and all others aboard escaped to the *Naomi*. The report listed the *Moran* as carrying a cargo of freight cars—the first indication that carferries were used in this area.

Because of the lack of ice in the early months of 1900 the Crosby Line passenger ships *Nyack* and *Naomi* were able to carry on their business out of Grand Haven but then winter finally caught up with them and on March 22, 1900 *Naomi* was again stalled in the ice. Some passengers became impatient and walked ashore. The next week both the *Naomi* and *Nyack* were marooned in the ice and had to be freed by the tug *Fields.*

Radios were not yet available so if a ship was ice bound those ashore might have no way of knowing of its plight. The Pere Marquette solved this problem, during the winter of 1900, by supplying all of its ships with carrier pigeons.

The Goodrich Line passenger ship *Iowa* was lost in the ice in 1914. This is not recorded as a great disaster so it is assumed the vessel is the only thing which suffered in the incident.

The winter of 1917-18 produced some of the worst ice conditions in 25 years. Because of the cold and wind the ice was packed 55 feet deep along the shore at Grand Haven. The Goodrich Line passenger ship *Alabama* and the carferries *Grand Haven* and *Milwaukee* were stranded in the deep freeze for 10 days. Supplies were taken to them over the ice.

Ice conditions similar to those of 1917-18 were experienced in 1924. The *Grand Haven* and *Milwaukee* were unable to move in the Harbor ice for 4 days while the *Alabama* and *H.J. Dornbos* were locked in the freeze for 5 days.

In March, 1925 late winter ice trapped the *Alabama, Milwaukee, Grand Haven* and *United States* for 5 days at the Grand Haven Harbor mouth.

Walking on the ice was sometimes a chancy thing. Claude VerDuin tells the story of he and two friends taking food out to his father's fishing tug *C.J. Bos* which was stuck in the ice off shore in 1927. Upon arriving at the boat he was told they had better head back for shore because the wind had shifted and the pancake ice had begun to move. On their return trip the trio's leisurely stroll turned into a sprint as the ice began to break-up under foot. They made it safely to shore winded and wet.

Grand Haven's port history abounds with interesting sea yarns but none is more remarkable than the tale of the schooner *Porcupine.* As is true of any war, for success in the War of 1812 convenient routes for supplies and communications were essential. In the Northwest Territory where the early stages of the war were fought, the most expeditious routes were the rivers and lakes—particularly the Great Lakes. The September 10, 1813 historic Battle of Lake Erie between the British fleet of 6 ships, carrying 63 guns commanded by Robert Barclay, and the American fleet of 9 smaller vessels, bearing 54 cannons commanded by Oliver Perry, gave the Americans a decisive naval victory that resulted in two significant developments which were pivotal in the outcome of the war. Perry's victory not only crushed British naval strength in the Old Northwest, thus enabling the Federal army and its supplies to be transported simply and efficiently to the Canadian mainland, but also ultimately resulted in defeat of an outnumbered, demoralized British and Indian force at the Thames River less than a month after the transfer of naval supremacy. Perry's mastery of the British fleet on that day is a story in itself. His victory was accomplished with fewer guns and smaller ships, one of those being the one gun schooner *Porcupine.*

In September, 1891 parts of a sunken ship were unearthed near the Johnston Boiler plant in Ferrysburg which were later identified as being those of the *Porcupine.* How was it the *Porcupine* found its final resting place in Grand Haven waters? Research reveals two separate stories regarding her career after surviving the Battle of Lake Erie.

In Orlie Bennett's account the *Porcupine* was taken to Detroit in 1830 where her upper decks were rebuilt, thereafter sailing under the new name *Caroline*. She was eventually brought to Grand Haven by a Captain Harry Miller who sailed her for a number of years and then sometime in the early 1850's— apparently deciding that her useful days were done—set the *Caroline* (ex-*Porcupine*) adrift near the mouth of the Grand River. The current carried her out into Lake Michigan but some days later a west wind blew the ghost ship back to Grand Haven. Someone salvaged the durable derelict, refitted her and the former *Porcupine* sailed again for a couple more seasons. At this point if she had been a horse they would have shot her but instead the ex-*Porcupine* was tied up near Johnston Boiler and left to rot. In all fairness one must assume that by then no one was aware of the true indentity of the ship or if they did it was not far enough removed timewise from the historic naval battle for the *Porcupine* to be considered a national treasure. Whatever the reason she was left uncared for and about 1855 she sank.

After the discovery of her true indentity in 1891, what was left of the *Porcupine* was taken off the bottom of Spring Lake and hauled to the barn of Charles C. Bolthouse where her carcass was cleaned as best it could after laying in the silt for 40 years. Her remains were taken to Detroit then placed aboard the steamer *Frank E. Kirby* to be transported to Put-In-Bay for display at the 1913 Perry Centennial. Half way across Lake Erie, at the site of that momentous 1813 naval encounter, as part of a ceremony a piece of *Porcupine's* stem was attached to an anchor and thrown over-board with these words spoken: "In honor of Commodore Oliver Hazard Perry and his brave sailors, I consecrate the old relic of the schooner *Porcupine* to the waters of Lake Erie. May his memory be ever cherished by patriotic and liberty loving American people."

A second version of *Porcupine's* story comes from "The Great Lakes Historical Society" in Vermilion, Ohio which has in its collection a series of articles that appeared in the Muskegon Chronicle on September 10th, 13th and 22nd of 1938. According to these articles the *Porcupine* stayed in Government service until 1842 at which time she was purchased by Thomas W. Ferry of Ferrysburg who used her as a lumber freighter until 1847. Her useful days done she was tied up near Johnston Brothers, left unattended and finally sank. In 1898 Charles C. Bolthouse—a Johnston Brothers' employee—and B.J. Reenders—a former

Cleveland teacher, native of Ferrysburg and cousin of Bolthouse—raised *Porcupine,s* carcass off the bottom of Spring Lake and on June 29, 1913 the remains were taken to Put-In-Bay for display during the Perry Centennial. According to J.F. Johnston, President of Johnston Boiler Works at that time, the wooden ribs and keel were made into yardsticks and rulers and the hand forged iron spikes into paper weights for sale at the Centennial. In 1938 Mary Bolthouse, then widow of Charles, still had a card signed by B.J. Reenders upon which was printed "This is a souvenir of the old *Porcupine.*"

Which ever version one cares to believe, both stories agree that the old wooden hull which was pulled out of the ooze of Spring Lake at the turn of the century was that of the historic warship *Porcupine.*

But not all of the *Porcupine* left the area in 1913, for a section of the historic vessel remains as part of the Coast Guard display in Grand Haven's Tri-Cities Museum.

The steamer *Roanoke,* built in Cleveland in 1867, went aground 300 yards south of the Grand Haven piers on February 4, 1893 and remained stranded in 12 feet of water. Captain Lysaught and his surfmen stood by as the tug *E.G. Crosby* released her the next day.

That next fall on November 23, 1893 the schooner *Wanderer,* commanded by Captain Waltman, wrecked on the beach at Two Sisters about 5 miles south of Grand Haven.

By 1893 the number of steam powered ships on the Lakes was steadily increasing while the construction of large sailing ships had declined sharply. The schooner's days as commercial vessels on the Lakes were numbered. On November 7, 1893 the Lake Carrier's Association shipping office at Chicago announced that seaman's wages were raised to $1.75 a day for schooners and $1.50 a day for steambarges trading on Lake Michigan. Either the work on a schooner was considered more skilled or the supply of able bodied rigging climbers had dwindled to such a point that they commanded a higher price on the labor market. Which ever the case these schoonermen—along with their ships—were fast disappearing from the scene. By 1899 some of the schooners listed as still serving Grand Haven were the *Indian Bill, Una, Jesse Winters, City of Grand Haven* and the Spring Lake Ice Company's *Robert Howlett.* In 1909 760 steam vessels visited the Port of Grand Haven but only 7 sailing ships. By 1921 there were

"Indiana Bill"—last of the sailing schooners. Courtesy Winifred VanZantwick Album.

just three of the old sailing vessels left on the Lake, two of them on the registry of the Grand Haven Customs—the *Rosa Belle* and *Stafford.* The third, although not registered in Grand Haven, was the *City of Grand Haven.*

The *Rosa Belle* was built in 1863 and wrecked October 21, 1921. She was owned by the Great Waters Transportation Company, part of the House of David in Benton Harbor. Her hull, laying on its side with the bow blown out, was sighted by the crew of Ann Arbor Railroad carferry No. 4 while on a cross-Lake trip to Grand Haven. None of the *Rosa Belle* crew was found. It was presumed that gasoline stored in the bow figured into the disaster.

The *Stafford,* built in 1868 at Tonawanda, New York, was last used as a lighter at Charlevoix. With the passing of these two schooners from the Grand Haven Custom House registry in 1921, the last of the "wind jammers"—and a romantic, nostalgic era—faded into history at the Port of Grand Haven.

Directly or indirectly every ship wreck figured into the country's economy. This concerned the Government and in 1892 studies were begun to provide a better understanding of the cause of the great number of disasters which occurred annually on the Great Lakes. A series of five sets of maps were produced between 1892 and 1898 by the Lake Marine Service, a division of the Weather Bureau of the Department of Agriculture. Produced under the direction of Norman B. Conger, head of the Lake Marine Service at Detroit, these maps were based on the assumption that many of the Great Lakes' ship wrecks were attributable to bad weather. The "Wreck and Casualty Chart of the Great Lakes, 1894" was the only map showing the effects of a single season on the navigation of the Great Lakes. When released in February, 1895 only 6,000 copies were produced with only a few surviving. The Historical Society of Michigan has made available reprints from an original which is kept permanently in the State Archives. It is a remarkable document with detail so fine that reproduction on these pages would not do it justice. A copy may be seen in the Loutit Library or purchased at Grand Haven's Tri-Cities Museum or from the Historical Society of Michigan, 2117 Washtenaw, Ann Arbor, 48104.

This casualty chart compiled a description and location of each disaster which happened in one shipping season. It lists 111 wrecks for all the 5 Great Lakes with 62 wrecks, or 55%, of them, occurring on Lake Michigan. Of the 111 casualties, 44 were total wrecks with the loss of 68 lives, 37 of those lives in Lake Michigan waters. The worst storm of that season occurred on May 18, 1894 which wrecked or badly damaged 26 vessels, 25 of those on Lake Michigan. Interestingly, dense fog from forest fires during the year is credited for causing several of the mishaps in Lakes Michigan, Superior and Huron.

The author of the chart views the tabulations for 1894 as an improvement over 1893 in that the losses for 1894 showed a 47% savings on vessel property and 28% on lives over 1893, which would indicate 94 lives were lost during the 1893 shipping season.

If the number of disasters at a given harbor can be used as a measure of that harbor's activity—although a rather macabre method of evaluating a port's popularity, it may have some actuarial basis—Grand Haven was the most active port on the Michigan side of Lake Michigan in 1894 but was behind Chicago, Manitowoc and Milwaukee when considering all of the Lake. The casualty chart records 13 wrecks at Chicago, 4 at Manitowac, 3 at Milwaukee and 2 at Grand Haven.

The two listed at Grand Haven both occurred in the fall of 1894. The schooner *Agnes L. Potter* struck the south pier on September 23 during a 60 mile gale resulting in an estimated $100 damage to the vessel. And then the last casualty reported on Lake Michigan for the 1894 season was the old schooner *Antelope* which capsized and foundered off Grand Haven in a heavy southwest gale on November 15 with the loss of the entire crew of 3. The *Antelope* had formerly—1878-1883—sailed under the name *Ellen G. Cocharen* when she was first registered at Grand Haven on August 22, 1878. Her name was changed to *Antelope* at Chicago, March 15, 1883

During construction of a water intake at Grand Haven's State Park in the fall of 1989 part of an old wooden rudder was uncovered that is believed to be from the wreck of the 32 ton schooner *Antelope*. The unearthing of this relic quite naturally raised renewed interest in the disaster. On Wednesday, May 16, 1990, in a weather-shorted ceremony attended by the State's Chief Historian, Secretary of State Richard Austin, the rudder was reburied at a marked sight so that its wood would remain preserved.

The 1895 "Annual Report of the Operations of the United States Life Saving Service" devoted 2 pages to the *Antelope*. According to the 1895 report the crew was made up of Captain Christopher Johnson, John Hanson and a sailor named John Larsen. The schooner was bound from Chicago to Whitehall, Michigan without cargo on the night of November 14-15, 1895 when she was caught in a heavy southwest gale off Grand Haven and the captain headed for the safety of this Port. Witnesses testified later that the seas breaking over the bars during that storm were as powerful and violent as ever seen here. Surfman VanWeelden was on lookout from 12-2:00 AM at the Grand Haven Life Saving Station and just before watch change sighted the *Antelope* heading for the piers about 2 miles out. His relief, Surfman Clevering, continued to watch while VanWeelden went down to arouse Keeper Lysaght and the rest of the crew. The *Antelope* was being driven by a following sea and as the crew hauled her up to make it between the pier heads she was caught broadside to both the wind and the seas, when she instantly rolled over and disappeared from view. Clevering sounded the alarm gong and ran down the steps to join the rescue.

The wagon was hauled to the beach, the lifeboat launched and Keeper Lysaght steered the vessel toward the masts of a ship running for the Harbor thinking that it might be the *Antelope.* When they reached the ends of the piers the vessel turned out to be the schooner *Alert,* stranded, with two men on board who were rescued and taken ashore. No wreckage was sighted and the captain of *Alert* said he had seen no other vessel. Convinced that another ship had sunk, Keeper Lysaght sent out beach patrols. The surfmen located wreckage strewn along the shore including a fragment that bore the words "Antelope of Chicago," which confirmed the *Antelope* had foundered. No bodies were found until 10 days later when that of John Hanson washed ashore 9 miles north of Grand Haven. The report from which this information was taken was published June 30, 1895, 7 months after the *Antelope* disaster, and at that time no other bodies had yet been recovered.

The Mansfield 1899 "History of the Great Lakes" has an interesting tabulation compiled from reports of the Life Saving Service concerning the Lake disasters which occurred between 1882 and 1897. Although Mansfield's 1894 figures do not agree with those of the 1894 "Wreck and Casualty" chart, Manfield's list is printed here as it appeared in 1899 with no attempt on the part of this author to justify either of the two:

Year	Disasters	Lives Imperiled	Lives Saved	Vessels Lost
1882	140	1,082	1,080	12
1883	187	1,508	1,496	11
1884	157	1,072	1,071	15
1885	138	902	900	7
1886	161	1,091	1,087	11
1887	186	865	865	12
1888	234	1,253	1,252	8
1889	213	1,320	1,313	9
1890	188	1,388	1,380	11
1891	205	1,121	1,109	11
1892	217	1,157	1,149	5
1893	228	1,752	1,744	15
1894	265	1,509	1,508	26
1895	232	2,489	2,479	11
1896	248	2,093	2,092	11
1897	276	1,530	1,525	7

Captain Charles Morton succeeded Captain Robbins as Superintendent of the 11th Life Saving District in 1898, Robbins having served since 1882. Morton was Superintendent until 1911. As has been mentioned the appellation "Captain" was a title of honor that went with the job, however Morton and the two Superintendents who preceded him—Loutit and Robbins—had been seamen and had earned the rank as Captain in their own right before becoming involved in the Life Saving Service. All three were Lake men.

The Crosby Line purchased the *Wisconsin* from the Goodrich Line in 1898, refitted her in 1899 and renamed her *Naomi*—a story related previously. In 1899 the Crosby Line was operating with the *Mary H. Boyce, Nyack* and *Naomi.*

At the turn of the century the responsibilities, daily drills, watch duty, night patrols and inspections for Station No. 9 remained as they had been for nearly 25 years. The season began April 15 and ended December 15 and one of the final duties Captain Lysaught's surfmen would perform for the year was to assist the barge *S.H. Foster* on December 5, 1900. She had broken away from the steambarge *Oregon* and the Life Saving Station crew rowed out to her and was able to set anchors to keep her from going onto the beach.

There were still those in 1901 who were convinced Grand Haven to Grand Rapids transportation by River could compete successfully with the railroad, even though the *Valley City,* just 5 years previous, had proven it would not work. The Government dredges still maintained a 5 foot channel and early in the year the newly formed Grand River Transportation Company announced its schedule for the 1901 season which was to include stops at Ferrysburg, Spring Lake, Robinson, Bass River, Eastmanville, Lamont, Sand Creek, Plaster Creek, Jennison, Grandville and Grand Rapids. The stern-wheel steamer *Evelyn,* 124 feet long, 29 foot beam with a 22 inch draft, had been built in Oshkosh, Wisconsin in 1883 for the Fox River to Green Bay run. She was purchased by the Grand River Transportation Company and arrived in Grand Haven ready for service on May 23, 1901. It took Captain Fish 8 hours for the first trip from Grand Haven to Grand Rapids because there were no channel markers. The return trip required only 5 hours. On July 22 the *Heath,* a smaller side-wheeler from Saugatuck, joined the *Evelyn* but the venture did not last long after that. By August 26 both boats were

Steamer Grand on Grand River, Grand Rapids, Mich.

Steamboat "Grand". Courtesy Grand Haven Area Historical Society.

tied up at Grand Rapids with a court order under complaints filed by a coal company and a meat dealer. On September 14, 1901 the Grand River Transportation Company was declared defunct.

But the railroad's dominating presence did not dissuade the Corps of Engineers from its River assignment. At 2:00 PM on December 17, 1903 the hydraulic dredge *General William Ludlow* was launched at Johnston Brothers in Ferrsburg and was placed on channel maintenance duty between Grand Haven and Grand Rapids.

This 44 mile 5 foot channel maintained by the Corps kept luring would-be entrepreneurs because it was like a free highway and it just seemed to make sense that transportation on a cost free thoroughfare ought to be able to beat the pants off a competitive mode that had to maintain its own roadbed. And if that was all that had to be considered they were probably right, but what the riverboats could never match was time and convenience; it took the boats 4-6 hours to make the trip and the trains could cover the distance in 1/3 that time. Even that obvious fact did not stop the prospectors so the riverboat speculators kept coming. In 1905 the newly organized Grand Rapids and Lake Michigan Transportation Company launched the 134 foot, twin stacked sternwheeler *Grand* in August and its sister ship *Rapids* in September. As can be seen in the photograph, these were river-

THE "FANNY H. ROSE" FROM SPRING LAKE LANDING AT GRAND HAVEN, MICH.

**Packet Steamer "Fanny M. Rose" arriving at Grand Haven.
Courtesy Grand Haven Area Historical Society.**

boats of the classic design and style. The company's endeavor had been prompted by high Grand Trunk Railroad freight rates—tariffs which the boat owners hoped would drive the Grand Haven and Grand Rapids business their way. In 1906 three weekly trips were offered between the two cities, the trip downriver taking 4 1/2 hours while the return trip required 6 hours. A one-way fare was 50 cents. The business barely survived for 2 years. In 1908 the riverboats were sold in bankruptcy and taken to the Ohio and Mississippi Rivers.

Through all of this grandiose speculation one little steamer—the *Allendale*—just kept puffing along. At the turn of the century the only remaining sawmill in Ottawa County was at Allendale and on December 10, 1900 the steamer *Allendale* arrived at Grand Haven with a scow of lumber from that mill for the Corn Planter Factory. In 1903 both the *Allendale* and the *Antelope* were in service on the River and as late as 1905 the *Allendale* was doing duty as a freighter hauling baskets from Grand Haven to Grand Rapids.

Water transportation—passenger as well as freight—from Grand Haven to Fruitport, with 28 dock stops along the Spring Lake section of the route, had its glory days but was to eventually suffer the same fate as its counterpart on the Grand River. This seasonal service was provided by picturesque small steam propellers which were making as many as 4 round trips daily

Boat Landing, Arbutus Banks,   Spring Lake, Mich.

Shuttle Boat "Helen B" stopping at Arbutus Banks Dock on Spring Lake. Courtesy Grand Haven Area Historical Society.

from Fruitport to the Grand Haven docks around the turn of the century. Between 1893 and 1904 at one time or another the following boats were making the run: the *Lizzie Walsh*—built and operated by Jay McCluer and then later his son Marshall, the *Antelope* and *Nellie* operated by Captain Rush Cobb, the *Fanny M. Rose*—launched August 12, 1893, the *Helen, Hazel* and *Ottawa*. Docks which were stops along the Spring Lake part of the route displayed a large red ball suspended from a rope that was hoisted up the a mast if the occupants wanted one of the shuttle boats to stop. The little steamers had no competition because the railroads did not provide better service for the customers on that circuit. But with the coming of the Grand Rapids, Grand Haven and Muskegon Interurban railway—arriving in Spring Lake March 5, 1902 and then in Grand Haven July 13, 1903—the days of the small shuttle steamers were numbered. Unable to compete with 5 cent rail fare, the quaint little packet steamers soon passed into the abyss of nostalgia. (the "Dummy Line", a small steam train that provided seasonal service between Grand Haven and Highland Park, began April 30, 1895 but it in no way competed with the packet steamers.)

In 1910 the Grand Haven-Spring Lake-Fruitport shuttle service had a revival. That year Captain G.L. Boswell brought the *Helen B* here from St. Joseph for use between Grand Haven and

Fruitport and then in 1914 he added the *Hazel B,* a new boat powered by a 35 hp gasoline engine. Business must have been good because in 1914 the packet boat *Ensign* joined the fleet. The *Hazel B* was still in service as late as 1919.

On June 12, 1901 Johnston Bros. launched the *H.J. Dornbos* and thus began the illustrious career of a vessel, the saga of which continues even today. As was the custom at that time she was named for Henry J. Dornbos, the largest smoker of white fish chubs in the Uniteds States, in return for which he furnished the tug's compass, life preservers, whistle, life boat and other miscellaneous required items. This steel fish tug was 72 feet long, had a 15 foot beam with a 7 1/2 foot draft and was fitted with a 16x16 Montaque steam engine with a 6x6 foot Johnston boiler for power. She was built for William VerDuin and Company and joined the *C.J. Bos*—launched at Johnstons 3 years previously— as part of the VerDuin fishing fleet. Captain Caleb VerDuin— Claude VerDuin's father and Captain William VerDuin's brother—went into the fishing business with William in 1902, the brothers sharing commands between the *Dornbos* and *Bos.* The other tugs in the Grand Haven fishing fleet at that time were the *Alice, J.W. Collister* and the *C.H. Augur.* These were powerful tugs and figured significantly in the growing mutual respect which was developing between the Life Saving Service and Grand Haven. The life-savers still had only pulling boats to do their rescue work and although they did not hesitate to "go out" when a call for help came, it was apparent that propellers could extend their effectiveness in reaching and aiding those in distress. For that reason Keeper Lysaght, and Walker after him, began to call upon these sturdy, seaworthy tugs to assist them in their life-saving work. Claude VerDuin can remember when, as a youngster, he would be sent with a message for his father Caleb—on one occasion during evening church choir practice— to fire up the fishing tug to assist the life-savers or to aid in moving a hapless side-wheeler railroad ferry away from the Goodrich Line docks.

On one such occasion in 1908 Keeper Lysaght and his surfmen had gone out in their pulling boat to assist the tug *Leathem* out of Sturgeon Bay, which had lost her rudder in heavy seas, but the life-savers were unable to tow the heavy tug through the mountainous waves. The *Leathem* sounded her distress signal again which brought out the *Dornbos* and with the surfmen handling the lines between the two tugs the *Dornbos* was able to bring the *Leathem* safely into port. Captain Lysaght and his crew had a narrow escape when a huge comber threw their boat against the pierhead on their return trip, but they too made it back safely. These tugs were durable work-horses and rapidly became honored members of this Port's marine team. Besides assisting the life-savers with rescue work they were called upon for a variety of other duties such as towing, freeing stranded boats, ice breaking and in one situation even as a "war ship". Commercial fishing had its rules of conduct but not everyone chose to live by them. In 1906 the State of Michigan Conservation Department was having a problem with Indiana and Illinois fishermen coming into Michigan waters and carrying on illegal netting. The *H.J. Dornbos* with her crew of 5 was commandeered by State Conservation officer Brewster and she became the flagship for "Brewster's Navy" which went down into the southern Lake Michigan waters to put a stop to the poaching.

By 1919 fishing on the Lake was not good and the *H.J. Dornbos* was sold to the Heywerth Company of Chicago for $9,000 to be used by the recently formed Michigan Materials Company (later renamed Construction Materials and today Construction Aggregates) to tow gravel scows from the Bass River pits which were located just off the Grand River in Robinson Township. She was renamed the *Urger* and joined by two other former fishing tugs, the *Robert E. Johnston* and *Liberty.*

The *Urger*'s venue of operation was eventually switched from Lake Michigan waters. In 1921 she was purchased by the New York Transportation Department for use on the New York Barge Canal System and thus became part of the "Empire State Navy".

Nothing more was heard of *Urger* until the VerDuins received a letter on January 10, 1989 from a Thomas Brindle of the Waterways Maintenance Division for the State of New York. Brindle was tracing the history of an old but still operable tug they had in their fleet that New York intended to honor with New York State and National Registry historical status and asked the VerDuins if they could shed any light on this venerable vessel. Well of course Brindle had hit an archivist's jack pot because the VerDuins could recite verse and chapter of the *Urger*—ex-*H.J. Dornbos*—chronology since the boat's history was actually a part of their family history. Although she had been converted from

Fishing Tug "H.J. Dornbos" pulling "Gunderson" off the ice in the Grand River, February 1, 1907. Courtesy Grand Haven Area Historical Society.

steam to diesel in 1948 the *H.J. Dornbos* remains today ostensibly as she was when she came down the ways 89 years ago. And what makes the story even more remarkable, Brindle was able to trace the boat's origins back to Grand Haven because of parts on her, which remain part of her running gear today, that were manufactured by Johnston Boiler and Dake Engine back at the turn of the century. That speaks quite well for the quality of the products which were coming out of the Grand Haven Area at that time.

Driver, another of Grand Haven's historic boats, capsized and sank at Frankfort on August 29, 1901. This had been Captain Kirby's first boat in his great fleet and one of the last he sailed. He then sold the schooner to David and Daniel Miller who used *Driver* to make the heroic rescue of the crew of *H.C. Akeley* in 1883. *Driver* was 103 feet long with a 26 foot beam and had been built in Milwaukee. Prior to commanding *Driver* David Miller had been First Mate on the 240 foot passenger ship *Charles H. Hackley,* which was owned and operated by the Muskegon lumber firm of Hackley & Hume. The 80 state room *Hackley* was acquired by the Goodrich Line in 1906 and sailed for many years under the name *Carolina.*

John Walsh was the No. 2 surfman for Keeper Lysaught in 1905. He is recognized here for his contribution of the pictures

Grand Haven Life Saving Service Ensemble, c. 1905. John Walsh first on left in white. Courtesy Grand Haven Area Historical Society.

1905 Surfmen Frank Fisher on left, Ole Melkild on right. Courtesy Grand Haven Area Historical Society.

on these pages. Ole Melkild and Frank Fisher were also members of those turn-of-the-century crews and their picture gives us some insight into the pride these surfmen had for their roles as members of the Life Saving Service. When photographs were taken in those days the print was delivered to the customer in the form of a post card. Melkild sent this card written in Dutch.

CHAPTER 12

THE CARFERRIES

Until the turn of the century the goods which arrived in Grand Haven by rail were transported across the Lake as break freight, i.e., the freight was taken off the railroad cars in Grand Haven, loaded aboard a ship for cross-Lake cartage and when the freighters reached the opposite shore the cargo was placed aboard waiting rail cars for the continuation of the journey to its western destination. Break freight was handled in the same manner from Wisconsin and Illinois ports to Grand Haven. The Detroit, Grand Haven and Milwaukee Railroad had previously leased the rail ferry business to other shipping companies, namely the Engleman Transportation-1869, Northwestern Transportation-1876, the Grand Haven and Milwaukee Transportation Company-June 5, 1883, and the Goodrich Steamship Line. Under an agreement dated April 14, 1901, between the Detroit, Grand Haven and Milwaukee Railroad, the Grand Trunk Railway, Edward G. Crosby of Milwaukee and Robert B. Rice of Muskegon—the last 2 gentlemen doing business as the Crosby Transportation Company—the Crosby Line steamers began providing the passenger and broken bulk freight service between Grand Haven and Milwaukee.

A year later, on May 30, 1902, the "Grand Trunk Car Ferry Line" was established and a contract signed between the railroads and the Crosby Transportation Company. The plan was for Crosby to place ships on the cross-Lake route which were large enough to handle the rail cars themselves, thus affording much more efficiency over the break freight system.

The 306 foot *Grand Haven* was christened with a bottle of champagne by Miss Harriet Crosby, daughter of E.G. Crosby, and launched at 3:00 PM on June 22, 1903 at the Craig Shipyard near Toledo, Ohio. *Grand Haven* was equipped with 8 boilers, each 12 1/2 feet in diameter, that fed steam to triple expansion engines

Carferry "Grand Haven" on Grand Haven to Milwaukee run 1903-1933. Courtesy Grand Haven Area Historical Society.

which pushed her along at a top speed of 18 knots when fully loaded with 26 rail cars, each 40 in length, and a full compliment of passengers. She arrived at Grand Haven in all her magnificence at 7:00 PM September 27, 1903 with her search lights sweeping the hills in a welcoming salute.

The Grand Trunk Railroad—parent company of the Detroit, Grand Haven and Milwaukee Railway—bought the *Grand Haven* in November of 1905 and took over the carferry and passenger operations, adding large ice houses for refrigerated rail service. Carferry service was expanded in 1908 with the addition of the 338 foot ill-fated *Milwaukee.* Built for the Manistique, Marguette and Northern Railroad she came down the ways in December of 1902 and sailed as the *Manistique, Marquette and Northern No. 1* between Northport and Manistique until she was purchased by the Grand Trunk in 1908, thereafter sailing under her new name *Milwaukee.* Three others joined the fleet in later years, each 347 feet in length; the *Grand Rapids* and *Madison* in 1926 and 1927 respectively then the *City of Milwaukee* in 1931. The *City of Milwaukee* cost $721,609 to build, $396,000 of which came from the insurance settlement after the loss of the *Milwaukee.* Not only was Grand Haven a busy port but it also became a major rail terminus. At the height of carferry service as many as 90 trains arrived or departed from Grand Haven each day. That in itself

CAR FERRY at DOCK,
Grand Haven, Mich.

Landing a carferry at the Grand Haven Terminal near the South Channel. Grain elevator at left. Courtesy Grand Haven Area Historical Society.

is an astounding statistic but equally amazing is the fact that in the waterfront area from the Farmers Market to the Municipal Marina there was a turn table, a 6 stall engine repair house, 15 sets of tracks to accommodate all the rail traffic, a huge 7 story grain elevator and the carferry terminal. Standing there today it is difficult to visualize how all of that could fit into the space. Only the restored #1223 steam engine gives any hint of those halcyon days that were.

In 1933 the Grand Trunk transferred the carferries to Muskegon for a larger port and hoping to find more local traffic. The *City of Milwaukee* made her final departure from the port of Grand Haven at 2:00 PM, July 16, 1933. The *Grand Rapids* left the same evening at 11:30 PM and finally the *Madison* was the last to leave the next morning, July 17, at 4:30 AM. The sounds and sight of the coming and going of these giant vessels had become a way of life for a generation of Grand Havenites. But this was the end of an era for the Port of Grand Haven. The finality of it was all too clear to the townspeople when they heard the long feared last farewell—"3 long and 3 short".

The dowager *Grand Haven* served as a car ferry until the service out of Grand Haven was discontinued in 1933. In 1946 she was sold to the West Indies Fruit and Steamship Company, Norfolk, Virginia and used as a "banana boat" between Havana

"City of Grand Haven"—1872-1923. Last of the schooners on the Lakes. Courtesy Grand Haven Area Historical Society.

and Florida. She was brought back to Lake Erie in the early 1950's and moored at Cleveland where she sank at her dock September 19, 1969. Raised on November 29, *Grand Haven* was towed to Hamilton, Ontario were she was scrapped.

During the years the carferry *Grand Haven* was in service there was another Grand Haven in Lake Michigan waters—the old schooner *City of Grand Haven*—which had been built in 1872 and sailed on the Lakes until 1923. It was quite anachronistic when the two passed. Such a passing did occur in Milwaukee Harbor on September 25, 1905. Although nothing remains of the carferry *Grand Haven,* recently a rotting hull in a bog near Marinette, Wisconsin was identified as the remains of the archaic sailer *City of Grand Haven.* Molly Perry, director of Grand Haven's Tri-Cities Museum, is currently assisting the Great Lakes Visual/Research from Holland, Ohio in producing a video on the history and adventures of this Coast Guard City namesake.

Ships by the same name can cause some confusion, seen side by side, each has its own distinguishing characteristics, but reading about them is another matter. The *Milwaukees* are a good example. We have now made mention of four of them which perhaps has presented some puzzlement to the reader so let us take a moment to untangle their history. The first was the sidewheel steamer *Milwaukee* built in 1859 which sank at Grand Haven in 1867. The second was the side-wheeler *City of Milwaukee,* renamed the *Holland* then *Muskegon,* which sank in Muskegon in 1919. Next—and the one which plays the most important role in our monograph—the carferry *Milwaukee,* built in 1903 and sank, as we will learn later, in 1929. And lastly another *City of Milwaukee*, a carferry built in 1931, which continued to operate into the 1950's.

CHAPTER 13

COUNTDOWN TO CONSOLIDATION

The evaluation of the research which had begun in 1892 by the U.S. Department of Agriculture Weather Bureau concerning ship disasters on the Great Lakes apparently led to a Government reassessment of the deployment of its agencies which dealt maritime safety. The 30 year old sidewheel Cutter *Andrew Johnson* was assigned to the Port of Milwaukee in 1895, thus making her the first Cutter of record to be assigned to Lake Michigan waters which were in that close proximity to Grand Haven. The Cutter *Morrill,* a salt-water Revenue Cutter, was ordered to Milwaukee in 1898 to replace the *Johnson.* There is no record of *Morrill* coming to the Port of Grand Haven but since she served in these waters until 1903 it is reasonable to assume she did.

The Revenue Cutter Service was still in the business of enforcing customs laws and providing assistance to distressed mariners. However with the arrival of the *Morrill* in Milwaukee, Revenue Cutters on Lake Michigan were to display another facet of their personality. In addition to her regular responsibilities the *Morrill's* duties included patroling regattas and attending ceremonial events. Even when she left Milwaukee in 1903 her new found samaritanism followed her to Lake Erie.

The sidewheel Cutter *Fessenden*—not assigned to these waters but the first Cutter to visit Grand Haven when it returned the body of Captain Robbins from Bailey's Harbor, Wisconsin to Grand Haven in 1898—was equally as popular an attraction at yacht races, celebrations and ceremonies throughout the Great Lakes during a career which spanned 43 years—1865-1908.

Morrill's replacement was the 178 foot U.S. Revenue Cutter *Tuscarora,* which was commissioned at Baltimore, Maryland on December 27, 1902. Assigned to the Port of Milwaukee, she arrived there October 5, 1903, and, except for a leave of absence during WW I, this would remain her duty station until she left the Lakes in 1925. The *Tuscarora* became the third Revenue Cutter assigned in this vacinity of Lake Michigan and it too undoubtedly made visits to Grand Haven, although no record has been found to confirm this. In his documents "Shipping in the Port of Grand Haven—1820-1940" Orlie Bennett states that in 1909 *Tuscurora* was the "Revenue Cutter in service", which implies she visited Grand Haven but this is not verified with specific dates.

The official record, supplied by the Coast Guard historians office in Washington D.C. with the assistance of Commander Larry Mizell, commander of Group Grand Haven, reveals more conclusively that Cutters at that time, although primarily concerned with enforcing customs, were beginning to perform some of the ceremonial and humanitarian functions with which we associate the Coast Guard today. During its 19 year tenure on Lake Michigan *Tuscarora* was on patrol at 30 yacht races or regattas, 2 speed boat races and 1 hydro-aeroplane aviation meet. In addition, on 14 other occasions she was present to sprinkle flowers for Memorial Day ceremonies, to commemorate the 4th of July, the 100th anniversary of Perry's victory, the 50th anniversary of the Soo locks, the Star Spangled Banner as well as officiating at fountain dedications, Naval parades and water fetes. Nowhere in the official record is there a report of rescue work or law enforcement but it has to be assumed this too was part of *Tuscarora*'s day to day duty.

Even though the stated purpose of the these three Cutters at the regattas and ceremonial functions was to enforce the rules of navigation and promote safety, quite clearly the Revenue Cutter Service had at this time begun to take on the "family" demeanor which had always been a part of the personality of the Life Saving Service. The gap was closing.

The little schooner *Swan* of St. Joseph, under the command of Captain Gelain, went on the beach 3 miles south of Grand Haven at Rosey Mound on October 16, 1903. She was salvaged by Captain Lysaught's crew and the fish tug *H.J. Dornbos* at 4:00 PM October 21.

The surfmen of the Life Saving Service were to make history in yet another rather unusual way at the turn of the century. The Wright brothers were looking for a good place to test their theory of flight and chose the treeless sand dunes called Kill Devil Hills which were located along the ocean shore near Kitty Hawk, North Carolina. The Kill Devil Life Saving Station was also located on that beach. The Wrights set up camp in 1900 and from that time until their famous flight in 1903 the surfmen became well acquainted with Orville, Wilbur and their older brother Lorin. Hauling their winged contraption up the sand dunes for test flights was laborious so the Wrights would hoist a signal flag up on their hanger on test days, which was the prearranged method of letting the surfmen know they could use some help. On Thursday morning December 17, 1903 the signal flag went up and 5 surfmen from the Kill Devil Station arrived to assist in yet another series of attempts at getting the Wright flying machine into the air. But on that day it was not just another try—it worked. The winged creature was taken up a dune, placed on its single launching track and released. As Wilbur ran along to steady the wing the biplane lifted into the air for man's first controlled fight. One of the 5 surfmen that were witnesses was John Daniels who manned the camera and captured the moment in what was to become one of the world's most famous pictures—the soles of Orville Wright's shoes. When the excited witnesses came down off the dunes they headed for the Kitty Hawk post office and one of the surfmen shouted the news to the world in a rather salty way: "They have done it! Damned if they ain't flew!"

We have spoken previously of the monotony and boredom which filled much of the daily life of the surfmen. Since it is more interesting to review the rescues performed by the lifesaving crews one tends to forget that the largest share of their time was involved in repetitious, dull tedium. And 1904 was a year to test the mettle of a "combat" ready surfman at the Grand Haven Life Saving Station. Station No. 9 opened the season in April at the usual time but then closed early—November 30, 1904—without one call of significant importance to be recorded in the log book having been received for the entire season.

Naomi's lineage was given earlier in Chapter 11. Built in 1881, she sailed as the *Wisconsin* until 1899 at which time she was rebuilt at the Johnston Boiler Works in Ferrysburg and took her new name *Naomi*. *Naomi* was a true luxury liner of her day, one of the fastest ships on the Lakes and the pride of the Crosby Line. She left Grand Haven at 11:00 PM May 21, 1907 with a light load of crates, an automobile, a car load of beams and a complement

"Naomi" steaming out past small tug inside revetment—today's site of Escanaba Park. Courtesy Grand Haven Area Historical Society.

of 82 people—31 crewmen under the command of Captain Thomas Traill and 51 passengers. It was a calm, moonlit spring night and after the gaiety of the departure from the docks and the exhilaration of clearing the Harbor the passengers retired to their staterooms. At 1:15 AM May 22 *Naomi* was in mid-Lake, about 35-40 miles from Grand Haven, when fire was discovered aboard. First Mate Robert McKay—a man we will learn more of later as captain of the ill-fated *Milwaukee*—was in the pilot house when the alarm was sounded.

Fire aboard ship had been an uncommon occurrence in the days of the sailing schooners but it was a constant threat for the early coal fired steamships, a fear which was not easily put aside by crew or passengers. Most of the steamers after the turn of the century had metal hulls but even those generally had interiors and superstructers which were wood, a construction material readily available coupled with a pool of skilled artisans left over from the wooden boat building days who were exceptionally competent at applying it. Such was the structure of the *Naomi*.

The crew began running from stateroom to stateroom to arouse

the sleeping passengers and soon the dreaded words "Fire! Fire!" were heard everywhere. The odor of smoke was seeping up from below decks and in a matter of minutes flames could be seen in the forward section. Three Grand Haven men—First Mate McKay, Purser William Hanrahan and Steward Phillip Rosbach, were later singled out as heroes of the ordeal for the way they calmly awoke passengers, helped people with life vests and assisted lowering and loading the life boats. This was all done with a composed assurance that kept down the panic which could have easily swept over the confused passengers resulting in pandemonium that would have been catastrophic.

Four life boats were lowered with only women and children loaded into the first 3 as well as 2 crewmen in each boat for rowing power. The last boat off contained 14 men and 3 women. The fireman, who had been battling the blaze below deck, came through a port hole and was taken into one of the boats. A calm sea accounted for an uncomplicated deployment of the life boats to a safe distance from the inferno which was about to erupt.

Signal flares had been fired from *Naomi* immediately after the

**"Kansas" towing burned remains of sister ship "Naomi"
into Grand Haven—May 22, 1907. Courtesy Grand Haven
Area Historical Society.**

discovery of the fire but within a short time the burning ship
could be seen for miles in the clear, cool night. Soon the freighters
Kerr and *Saxonia* and *Naomi*'s sister ship *Kansas* were racing
to the scene. A fourth vessel, perhaps the *S.S. Curry* it was
decided later, came past the burning ship but stayed her distance.
Captain Traill turned *Naomi* away from what little wind there
was in an attempt to confine the fire to the forward part of the
stricken vessel but it was in vain as the flames raced through the
upper works. *Naomi* had been doomed from the moment the
fire broke out but now its demise was obvious. The only concern
was saving the lives of the passengers and crew—and some of
the crew were still trapped below.

    Kansas was wooden so had to stay her distance but the steel
hull *Kerr* put her bow into the side of the burning *Naomi* thereby
allowing the remaining passengers and crew above deck to
escape. Captain Traill was the last to leave the burning decks with
the moon shining down on the surreal scene. J. Flynn, a deck
hand, reported that he had talked to 4 men who were hopelessly
trapped below deck shortly after the fire began. Their crys for
help could be heard but there was nothing anyone could do for
them. *Naomi* burned to the water line.

    As morning dawned *Kerr* and *Saxonia* took the burning hull
in tow. When 3 miles off Grand Haven the *Kansas,* which now
had *Naomi's* passengers and crew aboard, took over and ferried

Burned hull of "Naomi" at Goodrich Dock—flags at half staff. Courtesy Grand Haven Area Historical Society.

the charred remains into Port, arriving at the Crosby dock at 10:30 AM with a crowd of 3,000 looking on. The name *Naomi* was still visible on the bow and her stack still stood as a mute sentinel to the disaster. The fire department had been called to the docks to extinquish the smoldering ruins—the last time the old fire engine "Rix Robinson" would see duty. Purchased as Grand Haven's first engine in 1869, it was decommissioned July 11, 1907.

A passenger, J.M. Rhodes, a traveling salesman from Detroit, representing, ironically, the Diamond Match Company, had been badly burned. He was placed aboard a Grand Trunk train and transferred to a Grand Rapids hospital where he died later that same day.

The 4 bodies were removed from the ruins and identified by coroner Walkley as wanderers and adventurers who had no known relatives. They were "Muskegon Dutch" or Richard Nesberg, a Jackson from London and C. Miner and S. Gordon, homes unknown. Grand Haven's Lake Forest Cemetery records reveal Jackson and Gordon were buried in Potter's Field—a section of public burial places reserved for paupers and unknown persons.

Ship inspectors Pardee and Eckliff examined the hull and concluded that some of the ship's port holes were too small for any adult to have escaped. Following this tragedy it became a regulation that henceforth all future port holes would be the

1907 view of Government Pond with Lighthouse Tender, grain elevator at South Channel, telegraph lines along interurban tracks. Courtesy Grand Haven Area Historical Society.

width of a man's shoulders.

On July 25 the fishtugs *Dornbos* and the *Bos* towed *Naomi's* remains over to Johnston Boiler in Ferrysburg and there the whole incident took a bizarre twist. When the charred debris was being removed from the hull another body was discovered. It was thought to be that of a stowaway whose name, perhaps, was Harrington. The passengers were questioned and one of them, Dr. Hake, said he had talked to a man by the name of Harrington who had confided in him that he—Harrington, that is—had envisioned a fire aboard ship. Clairvoyance? Arson? No one will ever know.

Grand Haven continued to be one of the more active ports along the Lakes. In 1909 760 steamships were logged at Grand Haven Harbor but only 7 sailing vessels, a statistic given earlier but repeated here in its proper time sequence. Sails had had no peer on the Lakes since LaSalle launched the square rigger *Griffin* in 1679 and although the 1909 numbers may not be totally accurate their relativity emphasizes how steam had phased out the sail to the point of near extinction. Grand Haven had been quite a ship building center during the wooden windjammer days and when one considers that no metal hulls were produced here until 1898—the year the *C.J. Bos* went down the ways at Johnston Brothers in Ferrysburg—the dominace of the new

Last Grand Haven Life Saving Service Crew-1914. (Front, left to right) Harry Vanden Berg, Charles Peterson, Herman Castle, William Fisher. (Back, left to right) John Janssens, unidentified person, Keeper Bill Walker, Peter Olsen, Ernie Wasco. Courtesy Grand Haven Area Historical Society.

technology in such a short time is quite remarkable. Of course some of the steam vessels in 1909 had wooden hulls but these were carry-overs from another era and very soon would be complete anomalies.

A 1911 *Tribune* article reported that the lighthouse tender *Hyacinth* had been in Grand Haven. The 1907 photograph of Government Pond—or "Navy Yard" as the picture labels it—shows a white vessel which, because of the ship's boom arrangement, Coast Guard personnel concure is most likely a lighthouse tender. Although the ship is not identified in the photograph it is representative of what a lighthouse tender, such as the *Hyacinth,* looked like at that time.

Captain Charles Morton had served as Superintendent of the 11th Life Saving District since 1898. He resigned that position in 1911 after a remarkable career. Born in Ireland July 12, 1853, he was one of the few who fought with Colonel George Custer and survived the Battle of the Little Bighorn July 25-26, 1876. He was in the Life Saving Service for 31 years. He died on July 7, 1913.

The next man to assume the superintendency had a rank rather than a title which was a portent of things to come; no longer were the superintendents to be addressed by the honorary title "Captain", but rather by their Service rank. Formally that is. Around home, such as in Grand Haven, these Revenue Cutter officers were still affectionately addressed as "Captain" regardless of their rank. Traditions like that die hard.

Lt. Commander G.B. Lofberg—another Lake man—served as Superintendent of the llth Life Saving District from 1911 to 1915 and then, when the Revenue Cutter and Life Saving Services merged to form the Coast Guard in 1915, Captain "Gus" Lofberg served as Commander of the newly organized Tenth Coast Guard District until 1921—headquarters still in Grand Haven. The following is the list of the 11th District Superintendents and the Tenth District Commanders while the headquarters office was in Grand Haven:

Life Saving Service 11th District Superintendents
1877-81   Captain William R. Loutit
1882-98   Captain Nathaniel Robbins
1898-1911 Captain Charles Morton
1911-14   Lieutenant Commander G.B. Lofberg

Coast Guard Tenth District Commanders
1915-21   Lieutenant Commander G.B. Lofberg
1922-26   Lieutenant Commander Chester Lippincott
1927-29   Lieutenant William Wolff
1930-33   Lieutenant Commander John Kelly
1934-39   Lieutenant Ward W. Bennett

In 1939 the 10th District Headquarters were moved from Grand Haven to Chicago and then in 1942 they were moved from Chicago to Cleveland, with Captain Ralph W. Dempwolf as the commanding officer.

Grand Haven shipping was touched by history in an unusual way in 1912. Edward G. Crosby of Milwaukee had begun his transportation company in the 1880's and for over 2 decades the Crosby Line offered passage between Grand Haven and Milwaukee aboard luxury steamships. In 1912 a round trip fare to Milwaukee aboard the *Nyack* and *E.G. Crosby* was $3.50 while the round fare between Grand Haven and Chicago on the Goodrich Line's *Alabama* and *Virginia* was $3.75. Grand Haven

Steamship promotion, c. 1914. Courtesy Grand Haven Area Historical Society.

citizens had the availability of luxury cruising on Lake Michigan at very affordable prices.

In April of 1912 Edward Crosby, his wife and daughter Harriet boarded the *Titanic* in England, along with 2,200 others of the world's privileged class, for the unsinkable ship's maiden voyage to America. On the night of April 14-15, 1912 the *Titanic* struck an iceberg and sank. Mrs. Crosby and Harriet made it to safety in a lifeboat but Edward went down with the ship along with 1,500 other passengers. Memorial services for Edward G. Crosby were held on April 28, 1912 aboard *Nyack,* which had been Queen of the Crosby Line fleet since Crosby purchased her in

Real Sport

How to Reach Spring Lake

Steamship promotion, c. 1914. Courtesy Grand Haven Area Historical Society.

1894. The *Nyack* was built in Buffalo in 1878 and had carried passengers to Chicago's Columbia Exposition in 1893. She burned and was lost on December 30, 1915 while being refitted in Muskegon. The cause of *Nyack's* demise was never determined.

Following the death of Edward Crosby the Crosby Transportation Company continued operating under the management of Fred G. Crosby but then discontinued all service in the spring of 1925.

The sinking of the *Titanic* also affected the Revenue Cutter Service—and later the Coast Guard—in that *Titanic's* loss instigated the formation of the International Iceberg Patrol.

Fishing tug "Fisher". Courtesy Grand Haven Area Historical Society.

Bringing in the catch to the Grand Haven fish shanties. Courtesy Grand Haven Area Historical Society.

Ships burning while tied at a dock, such as the case with *Nyack,* apparently was not entirely uncommon. The 32 year old, 202 foot *Manistee—*ex-*Lora,* ex-*Alice Stafford—*had been completely refurbished for the Northern Michigan Transportation Company by Johnston Brothers in Ferrysburg over the 1913-14 winter and was ready for the season's passenger service. The crew came aboard Saturday, June 27, 1914 in preparation for the next days departure for Chicago. However, between 3:00 and 4:00

Fishing tug "Meister". Courtesy Grand Haven Area Historical Society.

o'clock Sunday morning, June 28, fire broke out and although everyone made it off the boat safely, the flames swept over *Manistee* so rapidly that most made it to the dock with just the night clothes they were wearing. The mooring lines burned and the wind took *Manistee* on her final voyage, in a mass of flames, across Spring Lake to Savidge Point—today Barrett's Marina— where the fire finished devouring her and she sank. Pathe News captured the spectacular night scene on newsreel film. Cause of the fire was never determined.

Grand Haven had an active fishing community in 1914. The fleet was made up of the *Robbins III*—owned by Nat Robbins, the *Anna, Alice* and *C.A. Meister*—owned by E.P. Kinkema and operated by Captain Noantay, the *C.J. Bos* and *H.J. Dornbos*— owned and commanded by William and Caleb Verduin and the *Johanna*—owned and operated by the O'Beck brothers, Roger and Martin. In 1916 the *Anna* and *Meister* were sold by Kinkema to companies in Northport and Cheboygan.

The *Johanna,* the newest fishing tug in the fleet, was launched in 1912. She had been designed by Klaus Katt of Ferrysburg who was also the superintendent of the Gile Shipyard in Ludington where the boat was built. The *Johanna* was the last fishing tug to operate out of Grand Haven. Bill and Walter Fritz, *Johanna's* last owners, tied her up for the final time at the close of the 1971 season.

Our country entered the 20th Century with public insistance that there be an end to corruption and public waste. An editorial in the April 5, 1912 Washington, D.C. "Evening Star" called for the application of business principles to Government agencies as a means of eliminating waste caused by the duplication and dispersion of duties. Those in the agencies concerned with maritime safety felt the finger was being pointed straight in their direction because the bureaucratic jumble under which their services functioned was a classic example of just this sort of dissipation. The Lighthouse Service, Steamboat Inspection Service and Bureau of Navigation were units of the Department of Commerce and Labor; the Life Saving and Revenue Cutter Services, both collectors of customs, operated under the Department of the Treasury—yet all had interrelated and, in many cases, identical duties to those of the other services.

President William Howard Taft, a stalwart proponent of consolidation and organization, appointed the Honorable F.A. Cleveland to head a "Presidents Commission on Economy and Efficiency." The Cleveland Commission, among other things, recommended the merger of the Lighthouse Service with the Life Saving Service and that the Revenue Cutter Service be absorbed into the Navy. The Commission claimed that these moves would save over $1 million a year. The Commission's arguments impressed President Taft who sent the report to Congress with a request he be given authority to carry out the proposed reorganization. Understandably the Commandant of the Revenue Cutter Service, Captain Ellsworth P. Bertholf, was of a different opinion. Bertholf not only questioned the $1 million a year savings but contended that if the Revenue Cutter Service was disbanded the agencies which took over its duties would need at least as many men and as much equipment, which might result in the services costing more not less. The press and some Congressmen agreed with Captain Bertholf's arguments.

A second proposal came from Charles Nagel, Secretary of Commerce and Labor, which called for the consolidation of all the Services under his department. Secretary of the Treasury, Franklin McVeigh, offered the least radical approach, which was quite simply the merger of the Services already under his authority—those being the Revenue Cutter and Life Saving Services—into one amalgamated Service. A recent and well publicized ship fire supported exactly the cooperation between the two Services which McVeigh was advocating. In April 1912 the burning ship *S.S. Ontario* was discovered off Long Island by the Cutters *Mohawk* and *Acushnet* which shepherded the *Ontario* toward shore so that the surfmen of the Ditch Plain Life Saving Station could help battle the fire. When the captain of the *Ontario* decided the ship had to be abandoned, the lifesaving crew used the breeches buoy and their lifeboats to take off all those aboard.

McVeigh was so confident of his logic of the two Services complimenting each other that he appointed Sumner Kimball, Superintendent of the Life Saving Service and Captain Commandant Bertholf to draw up a bill to that effect. Secretary McVeigh's proposal was introduced to the Senate June 5, 1912 as S #2337 by U.S. Senator Charles E. Townsend of Jackson, Michigan. However, the Taft supporters sensed an end-run attempt by McVeigh and were successful in stalling the bill's progress, so it received no real action until the Taft administration left power.

Hearings on the merger were held in early 1914 and by March the Senate had approved the bill. President Woodrow Wilson lent his support to the proposal. The bill was guided through the House by Representative William C. Adamson of Georgia who made the argument that the cuttermen would provide a trained Naval Reserve when needed and, with the clouds of war rolling over Europe, the point was a good one. The "Act to Create the Coast Guard" was approved in the House January 28, 1915. President Wilson quickly signed it into law.

Thus, on January 30, 1915, 125 years after Alexander Hamilton received authorization for a fleet of cutters, the United States Coast Guard was born. The new Service had 255 officers—13 of whom were the former Life Saving Service superintendents— 3,900 enlisted men and warrant officers, 17 regions, an academy, 25 cruising Cutters, 20 harbor Cutters, 280 equipped lifeboat stations all under the command of Captain Commandant Ellsworth P. Bertholf. Sumner Kimball was retired after 45 years of service. A special board was appointed to administer the transition. However reorganizing all of this was no easy matter.

The new Coast Guard, although now "a military service", was still under the authority of the Department of the Treasury but would transfer to the Navy in time of war or as the President might direct. For that reason the Navy classification system was used and under these classifications district superintendents became commissioned officers, keepers became warrant officers, No. 1 Surfmen were made petty officers and the remaining surfmen were considered regular enlisteds. However, it would not be until 1920 that all enlisted grades would draw equal pay with their Navy counterparts.

On January 29, 1915, from his headquarters in Grand Haven, District Commander Lofberg announced that the Life Saving and Revenue Cutter Services would be renamed the Coast Guard, which would become functional Monday, August 2, 1915. After that both Services would operate year round. From this time on, surfmen would not sign on for a year at a time but instead would enlist for a multi-year hitch.

Military discipline, longevity pay, uniform allowance and retirement were now applicable to everyone in the new Coast Guard. The latter—retirement—was the plum that had been long sought by all of those in the service of maritime safety, something the officers of the Revenue Cutter Service had been granted in 1902. One can only imagine the lobbying which took place between 1912 and 1915—the period during which it was questionable which of the Services would be joined with which—on behalf of those in the Lighthouse Service, Steamboat Inspection Service, Bureau of Navigation, Life Saving Service and enlisteds of the Revenue Cutter Service. With the passage of this new law those of the Life Saving Service and the Cuttermen could now enjoy the privileges as well as the obligations of the military. The rest of the Services would have to wait until 1918 for parity.

The Lighthouse Service was at least given some recognition. On August 28, 1916 the privileges of the Marine Hospital were extended to members of the Lighthouse Service. It in a sense was a trade off because the very next day—August 29—the Lighthouse Service was put on notice that it too would be under control of the Navy in time of war.

CHAPTER 14

THE COAST GUARD
IN THE "GREAT WAR"

The Coast Guard was barely 2 years old when, on the morning of April 6, 1917, all Coast Guard units received the following dispatch: "PLAN 1, ACKNOWLEDGE." This was the code which meant the United States was at war with Germany and that all Coast Guard facilities, equipment and personal were now assigned to the Navy where they would remain for the duration. In August of 1914 the *Tuscarora* had received orders to observe and enforce the neutrality laws on Lake Michigan; 3 years later—April 6, 1917—she was transferred to the Navy and by September she left Milwaukee for war duty in the Atlantic, not to return to these waters until 1920.

During the World War the Coast Guard was given the duty of guarding all ports and waterfronts. This grant of authority was part of the Espionage Act of 1917 which was passed by Congress following an explosion of questionable origins at a military munitions depot on Black Tom's Island, New Jersey earlier that same year. The Coast Guard functioned in the same capacity in WW II under the Dangerous Cargo Act and during the Korean conflict under the Magnuson Act.

On the Great Lakes during the "Great War"—as the First World War was labeled—the Government took control of all wireless stations operated by the Marconi Wireless Company. The Grand Haven station was in the structure which is today the State Park Beach concession building; the Marconi manager was Ferdinand Boaeker. The carferries *Grand Haven* and *Milwaukee* were equipped with radios and operated under Government control as the Lake Michigan Carferry Association. As mentioned earlier, the winter of 1917-18 produced some of the worst ice in 25 years on the Lake. High winds and severely cold temperatures built up ice that measured 55 feet thick, a barrier which trapped the *Grand Haven, Milwaukee* and *Alabama* for 10 days in January and then another 8 days in March. Food had to be taken out to the marooned vessels over the ice and it can only be imagined how suddenly necessary and useful the new radio equipment was for the stranded ship captains. War accelerates technology and these ship-to-shore radios were a far cry from the carrier pigeons used aboard the Pere Marquette ferries during the winter of 1900.

The Crosby Transportation Company was very busy shipping Reo, Oldsmobile Hamilton, Buick, Ford, Dodge and Oakland automobiles from Grand Haven to Wisconsin in 1917, in the months immediately preceding this country's entry into the World War. Crosby purchased the 293 foot *America* to facilitate the auto shipping—the new vessel arriving in Grand Haven April 16, 1917 just 10 days after the United States had entered the war. Her officers were Captain Thomas McCambridge, First Mate Thomas Fagan and Chief Engineer Harry Robinson. In order to move men and equipment to the European war zone the Government needed all the ships it could get and confiscation of private vessels was the quickest means of accomplishing that. The *America* was cut in half in Cleveland, taken through the Welland Canal, reassembled and was then ready for war duty. On November 20 she was followed by the *E.G. Crosby,* whose Navy name became *General R.M. O'Reilly.*

Five of the six tugs conscripted for Government service had been made at Johnston Brothers, which spoke well for the product turned out by this Ferrysburg company. The tugs were the *Williams, Mayer, McCarty, Stewart* and another *America.*

A rather historically poignant event occurred at this Port in 1918 which harked back to another war at another time and was insignificant enough to go unnoticed by most—which, because of its subtleness, is quite understanding. But viewed 70 years later this historic coincidence seems more significant in that, if only tangentially, it does add an interesting facet to our story. In 1898, during the Battle of Manila Bay in the Philippines—the most important Naval encounter of the Spanish-American War—Admiral George Dewey directed a spectacular defeat over the Spanish fleet. Dewey became an instantaneous National hero. Not long after the completion of that war the citizens of Grand Haven, in a gesture of patriotism, named their major Riverfront landmark Dewey Hill—which each August turns into "Coast

Guard" Hill. One of the prizes of war taken by Dewey at Manila Bay was the Spanish ship *Isla-DeLuzon*. On July 19, 1918 a Navy ship which was on the Lakes under special assignment as a Coast Guard Inspection vessel arrived at the Port of Grand Haven. It was the *Isla-DeLuzon*. And what is of even more historic coincidence, the *Isla-DeLuzon* was under the command of Commander McMont who had been at Manila Bay when she was captured. One has to wonder if the moment was grasped—did the captain salute as the old war ship *Isla-DeLuzon* passed Admiral Dewey's namesake?

Most of the Atlantic naval action during the World War involved undersea warfare. The first American ship to be sunk was Lightship #71 at Diamond Shoals Station off the North Carolina coast. On August 6, 1918 a German submarine surfaced by Lightship #71 to politely request that the crew evacuate the vessel. Having no means of defense the keeper accepted the invitation and as the lightship crew rowed ashore to safety the submarine blew the lightship out of the water. No one was lost in this encounter with an enemy submarine but the cover supplied by the Coast Guard in its duty of convoying American cargo ships across the Atlantic as well as from England to Gibralter exposed the Cutters to the constant threat of U-boat attack. By the end of the war the Coast Guard had lost more men in proportion to its strength than any of the other U.S. Armed Forces.

As a part of the war effort Congress authorized the electrification of all lighthouses in 1918, which included telephones and radios. It was another giant step toward the modernization and mechanization of the facilities used for maritime safety. No record can be found to verify the date that the Grand Haven light switched from flame to electricity but since the City generated its own power there is reason to believe the change came before 1918. The 1907 picture of the Government Pond shows overhead lines and poles paralleling the interurban tracks running out toward the beach, however these do not appear to be electric lines but rather telegraph lines which served the lighthouse.

Flying machines had captured the imagination of the entire country just before the World War and although for most the first "aeroplanes" were viewed simply as good entertainment at local fairgrounds on a Saturday afternoon, the possibilities of their military application did not escape the Army and Navy. The Army had an "air force" of sorts during the Civil War and even though these were merely observation balloons, the great advantage they afforded the crew in the hanging basket for scrutinizing enemy positions had proven to be effective. In 1915 two young Coast Guard officers, 2nd Lieutenant Norman Hall and 3rd Lieutenant Elmer F. Stone, on the Cutter *Onondaga,* were convinced that aviation could facilitate their search for derelict vessels as well as being very useful in Coast Guard beach patrol and rescue work. Their commanding officer, Captain B.M. Chiswell, was captivated by the reasoning of these two officers and relayed their ideas to headquarters in Washington. This resulted in Stone and 2nd Lieutenant Charles E. Sugden being assigned to the Navy's newly established air station at Pensacola, Florida.

In 1916 Congress authorized a Coast Guard Aviation Corps, an aviation school and 10 air stations, but failed to fund the program. However, 16 more men were sent to Pensacola and the Coast Guard set up an office for an "Inspector of Aviation." During the war these new Coast Guard flyers served with Naval units and one of them commanded the Naval Air Station at Ille Tudy, France. After the war these air pioneers returned to a Coast Guard which still had not received the means to fund the 10 air stations and aviation school authorized by the 1916 Congress.

The escalation of aviation technology and airplane design during the World War was nothing short of phenomenal. When one compares the flimsy, wire-braced, under-powered contraptions available to aviators at the beginning of the war in 1914 to the clean designed, multi-horsepowered, swift airplanes—such as Germany's Fokker D-VII—at the end of the conflict in 1918, you begin to see what a quantum leap it actually was. With man's mind bent on destruction the world was vaulted into the air age in just 4 short years.

Although most of the usual routines of civilian life were curtailed during the World War, the Port of Grand Haven was considered essential enough that harbor maintenance continued through the duration. A pile driver owned by the Robert Love Company of Muskegon had completed its work in Grand Haven on October 18, 1918 and was being towed back to Muskegon by the tug *Ida M. Stevens* when it was caught in a fall storm. Both the tug and the pile driver were driven aground and all made it ashore safely except John King, Engineer of the pile driver, who was drowned when the pile driver capsized. His body was found on the beach November 9.

In November of 1918 an armistice was signed which brought the First World War to an end at 11:00 AM, November 11, 1918—the 11th hour of the 11th day of the 11th month. By Executive Order the Coast Guard was returned to the Department of the Treasury on August 28, 1919.

By the end of the conflict the Navy was equipped with some large flying boats which, the Navy brass was convinced, were capable of doing what no other airplane had yet accomplished—to cross the Atlantic. The 3 huge Curtis flying boats—each with a wing span of 126 feet and powered by four 400 horsepower Liberty engines—weighed 14 tons apiece and carried the crisp military designation of NC-1, NC-3 and NC-4. The plan was to fly from Newfoundland to Portugal using 41 U.S. destroyers as navigational aids along the way. Coast Guard aviator Lieutenant Elmer Stone was chosen co-pilot for the NC-4, along with Navy Lieutenant Commander A.C. Reade as the other co-pilot. The 3 planes left Canada on the evening of May 16, 1919 headed for Europe, with a refueling stop scheduled in the Azores. The NC-1 and NC-3 were both forced down in the Atlantic, their 5 men crews rescued by the destroyers. The NC-4, with Coast Guardsman Stone at the controls, made the refueling stop in the Azores and then arrived in Lisbon May 27, 1919, thus becoming the first airplane to fly the Atlantic.

Riding on the enthusiasm and publicity of the NC-4 flight, in 1920 the Coast Guard set up an Air Station at Moorehead City, North Carolina using 6 old H-S Navy Curtis flying boats and a tent for a hanger. The Service was only 5 years old and it was already getting used to castoffs and tight budgets. Nevertheless, the Coast Guard air-arm was off and running.

The Crosby Line had discontinued regular service to Grand Haven during the war but resumed business on May 28, 1919 with the 230 foot sidewheeler *Holland*—ex-*City of Milwaukee,* which used the Robbins dock along with the Goodrich Line ships. The sidewheeler *City of Milwaukee* had been built for Captain Albert E. Goodrich in 1880 as a cross-Lake ferry for the Detroit, Grand Haven and Milwaukee Railroad. In 1896 the ship was charted to the Graham and Morton Transportation Company for their Benton Harbor-Chicago run. In 1904 Graham and Morton transferred the *City of Milwaukee* to the Holland-

Carferry "Grand Haven" served from 1903-1933. Courtesy Grand Haven Area Historical Society.

Chicago run and renamed her *Holland.* The Goodrich Line reacquired her in 1915 to replace the *Iowa,* which had been lost in the ice and then in 1917 she was obtained by Crosby to replace *Nyack,* which burned December 30, 1915.

During the 1919 shipping season *Holland* had mechanical problems and was towed into Racine for repairs. She returned to the Lake with yet another name—this time *Muskegon.* And then on October 28, 1919 she met her end.

The *Muskegon* left Milwaukee at 10:00 PM, October 27, 1919 bound for Muskegon on calm seas with 37 passengers and a crew of 35. As she made her way across the Lake a storm developed which festered into a full blown 46 mph gale by the time Captain Edward Miller sighted the Muskegon light. Captain Miller manuevered the sidewheeler into position for a run at the harbor but missed the entrance. Consequently the *Muskegon* was thrown onto the south pier. In that precarious straddled position the waves poured over her and she began to break up. Within 20-30 minutes the *Muskegon* was totally demolished by the raging seas. That was time enough for 39 of the 72 people aboard to scramble off the ship to the wave swept pier and then to safety. Twenty-three were lost.

The crew of the Muskegon Life Saving Station got to the scene but events happened so rapidly they did not have time to assist those aboard prior to *Muskegon* being pounded to pieces. The surfmen were, however, able to rescue several who were clinging to the pilot house which was floating in the harbor. Crewmen that escaped from the stricken vessel who were from the Grand Haven area were Albert Hallman, First Mate from Grand Haven and Grant Johnson, Chief Engineer from Ferrysburg. Johnson's mother, Mrs. Kate Johnson, was one of the victims. One body from the *Muskegon* disaster was found April 26, 1920 at Macatawa Beach in Holland which is 30 miles south of Muskegon. Kate Johnson's body washed ashore at the Ottawa-Muskegon county line a year later.

CHAPTER 15

PROHIBITION DAYS

In 1920 the Grand Haven Lifeboat Station—with the new designation of Station No. 270—was in the 10th Coast Guard District. In that year the Coast Guard reorganized its Field Service into 3 major groups: Cruising, Lifesaving and Patrol. Patrol dealt with deep-sea cruising and therefore did not involve any units on the Great Lakes.

Lifesaving was, in essence, the same as the old Life Saving Service and was composed of 3 distrcits. The Ninth District with Headquarters in Buffalo, New York, included 20 stations along the coasts of Lakes Ontario, Erie and Huron up to Hammond Bay—which is located on the northern tip of Michigan's Lower Peninsula between Rogers City and Cheboygan. The Tenth District with Headquarters in Grand Haven was comprised of 21 stations along Lake Huron west of Hammond Bay, the East coast of Lake Michigan, Beaver Island, Mackinac Island and Louisville, Kentucky. The Eleventh District, consisting of 21 stations along Lake Michigan's west coast and Lake Superior, was headquartered in Green Bay, Wisconsin—62 Great Lakes stations.

The Tenth District stations which reported to Grand Haven were Bois Blanc, Mackinac Island, Beaver Island, Charlevoix, North Manitou, South Manitou, Sleeping Bear Point, Point Betsie, Frankfort, Manistee, Big Sable Point, Ludington, Pentwater, White River, Muskegon, Grand Haven, Holland, South Haven and St. Joseph, Michigan, Michigan City, Indiana and Louisville, Kentucky.

The Cruising Service consisted of 7 divisions and the Bering Straits. The 5th Cruising Service Division, which was Headquartered at Sault Ste. Marie, Michigan, served all the Great Lakes except Lake Ontario and was responsible for rendering assistance to vessels in distress and enforcement of maritime laws.

Coast Guard vessels which are over 65 feet are considered

Cutters. The original 10 Cutters in 1790 did not fit that definition because of size. In fact some of those original 10 were not even rigged as Cutters in the true sense because some were sloops— i.e., a single mast—and the proper definition of a Cutter was a vessel with a fore-and-aft rig—i.e., 2 masts—with a running bowsprit, a mainsail and 2 or more flying headsails—yet all of the original 10 ships were referred to as Cutters. Today a cutter is the same as a sloop—i.e. 1 mast—except the mast is stepped 40% of the distance from the bow to the stern instead of 30%, as with a conventional sloop, and a jib is hoisted to the top of the mast with a second jib usually carried.

Early Cutters were named for notable persons, such as the secretaries of the Treasury or statesmen. Later they were named for qualities, such as "Alert" or "Active" or for the states where they were stationed. Between 1900-21 all Cutters were given Native American names. In 1920 the Great Lakes 5th Cruising Service Division received vessels which filled all of these catagories: 1 second-class cruising Cutter, the *Kankakee,* the harbor Cutter *Chippewa,* the *AB-1*—formerly *Advance, AB-12*—formerly *Search, AB-13*—formerly *Sentinel, AB-17*—formerly *Vigilant, AB-18*—formerly *Voyager,* patrol boats *Cook* and *Crawford* and several picket boats.

Congress passed Prohibition—the Eighteenth Amendment or The Volstead Act, named for its sponsor Congressman Andrew Volstead of Minnesota—on January 17, 1920 and for the next 14 years the Coast Guard would be charged with the responsibilty of ensuring that no unlawful liquor entered the country through its seacoasts, which included the Great Lakes. All of the Great Lakes except Lake Michigan share their waters with Canada and so the Coast Guard's Cruising Service on the Great Lakes was exceptionally busy—and very unpopular—during prohibition. Smuggling prevention had given birth to the Coast Guard and it seemed at first that a little extra vigilance was all that would be needed to enforce this new law, but no one had estimated the voracious taste the usually law-abiding citizens would soon develop for illicit booze. The drinking public's defiance of prohibition was contagious. One measure of the growing National thirst was that in the first five "dry" years Federal "Revenuers" closed down 696,933 stills. But for every "Moon Shine" site that was dried up another water delivery route was developed. The annual import of foreign liquor onto our shores jumped from 50,000 quarts to 10 million quarts.

Coast Guard boats were slow so the answer for the "Rum Runners" was simple—build faster and faster boats to carry the whiskey across the waters to the waiting trucks on shore. The bottles whizzed past the Coast Guard everywhere: two thirds of them across the narrow waters from Canada, one third off the Atlantic Coast. In 1924 the territorial waters were extended from 3 miles to 12 miles, but finally the coastal limit for boarding vessels was extended to the speed of the vessel; e.g., if a boat traveled 40 mph it could be tracked down and boarded 40 miles from shore. The Coast Guard added these speedy "blacks"—as contraband crafts were called—to their own fleet if and when they could catch them. Before it all ended the Coast Guard had transferred 649 captured craft to its own registry.

It was during this period of National exposure that the Coast Guard made the final alteration to its ensign. As described in Chapter 1, the original ensign authorized in 1899 consisted of 16 vertical stripes, alternating red and white, a stripe for each of the original 13 States and 1 for each of the next 3 States admitted to the Union—Vermont, Kentucky and Tennessee, in that order. In 1927 the official Coast Guard emblem was adopted—a shield within 2 concentric circles superimposed upon 2 crossed anchors—and added to the ensign in the middle of the 7th red stripe. This, then, is the famous Coast Guard ensign we see today. Another addition which helped build esprit de corps during these trying times was the finest marching song of all branches of military service—"Semper Paratus", written by Coast Guardsman Captain Francis S. VanBoskerck, Jr. in 1928.

It did not take long for the Coast Guard Commandant, Rear Admiral Fredrick Billard, to learn that policing prohibition was a no-win situation; the Service was reprimanded by the indignant "Drys" for allowing anything through and tongue lashed by the "Wets" for being so heavy-handed at cutting off the flow of spirits which sustained what had become their fashionable national sport—frequenting the "Speak Easy". The Service estimated that it was catching only 5% of the bottles driven shoreward by speeding propellers. And this underworld tryst was not just fun and games. Several Coast Guardsmen lost their lives attempting to enforce this unpopular law.

Congress' answer was to shovel out more money—the expected procedure in any kind of war. They appropriated

$13,853,980 to expand the Coast Guard fleet in 1924. The Lakes' patrol boats were increased to 20 and picket boats to 75 with the additional crew to man them. A machine shop was set up in Buffalo to keep the boats running and a radio station was also established at Buffalo in a vain attempt to keep pace with the advanced technology of the Rum Runners. Soon the Coast Guard found itself emersed in cryptology devising its own system of covert language and, at the same time, cracking the underworld's codes. Smuggling on the Great Lakes reached its peak between the fall of 1927 and the spring of 1928. Since Lake Michigan did not have an international boundary it would not be involved in this "war."

The Coast Guard's use of a Navy Vought UO-1 seaplane flying from Ten Pound Island near Glouchester, Massachusetts was so successful in curtailing the Rum Runners' activity that the 1924 Congress authorized $152,000 to purchase 5 new planes. By 1926 the Service took delivery of a more advanced design aircraft—the first airplanes ever ordered strictly for Coast Guard duty. The Loening OL-5 bi-wing amphibian cruised at 75 MPH and had a range of 415 miles. Three were purchased—the 101, 102 and 103. The 101 and 103 eventually crashed and were irreparable, but the 102 served until 1935.

When Congress passed the Volstead Act no one doubted that it would be a bone-dry success. As it turned out the law caused more corruption, crime and bloodshed than any other in the country's history. It also introduced millions—for better or for worse—to the Coast Guard. But between 1920 and 1932 the Coast Guard's job was done well because it provided an obstacle which proffered the notice to those shuttling illicit booze into this Country that although, it might be a profitable enterprise, it was more practical not to be involved in it because of the consequences.

Congress finally recognized the insanity before the Nation was totally eviscerated. The madness ended when prohibition was repealed on December 5, 1933 with the passage of the Twenty-first Amendment. But the Nation and Coast Guard were to bear the scars for many years to follow.

CHAPTER 16

ORIGINS OF A TRADITION

Captain William "Billy" Walker retired as keeper of the Grand Haven Lifeboat Station on June 10, 1922. He had attained the rank of boatswain and was the first person from the Grand Haven Station to avail himself of the Coast Guard pension plan. As mentioned earlier, Walker had begun his Service career in 1889 as a surfman at the Grand Haven Life Saving Station under Keeper John Lysaght, in 1902 became keeper of the Sleeping Bear Station and then moved back to the Grand Haven Station to assume the position of keeper when Captain Lysaght resigned in 1910. Captain Walker was replaced by Captain William E. Preston—alias "Stormy", alias "Barnacle Bill"—whose last command had been the Michigan City Station. Preston was to command Grand Haven Lifeboat Station No. 270 until 1939.

This was a year of transition for the Grand Haven Lifeboat Station in other ways. On January 20, 1922 the Government purchased the Lifeboat Station property on the north shore from Charles E. Soule and William N. Angell in preparation of a replacement for the old facility. The Government had leased the Life Saving Station property since it was built in 1876. Bids for a new station to be erected just west of the 1876 buildings were requested on January 23, 1922. Alvin Morrison of Port Huron was awarded the contract and construction was begun immediately. The new station—the one still standing today—was completed on schedule and the crew moved in December 22, 1922. The 4 stall boat house, with inclined rails for launching, was opened August 12, 1927.

It was mentioned earlier that the Grand Haven Life Saving Station, which had no power boats at the turn of the century, from time to time would call upon the local steam fish tugs to assist in a rescue. Following the World War Lifeboat Station No. 270 had its own power boat and on at least one occasion had

Grand Haven Lifeboat Station No. 270. December 22, 1922-June 5, 1989. Photograph by David K. Seibold.

the opportunity to repay the favors shown by those fish tugs in earlier years. On October 6, 1921 Caleb Verduin's fish houses, which were located at the foot of Dewey Hill opposite Howard Street, caught fire. Fish oil was a natural byproduct of the fish business, so over a period of time the docks and work areas in and around the buildings became saturated with the stuff. It did not take long for the Verduin operation to be completely engulfed in flames. The fish tugs tied at the docks were steam powered and it took time to fire the boilers to move them. But there was no time. Captain Walker went to the rescue with his boat, which was powered by internal combustion engine, and pulled the tugs away from the conflagration to safety. The docks and buildings were totally destroyed. It was not one of the more daring rescues performed by the Coast Guard but it once again demonstrated the mutual cooperation shared between the townspeople and Service.

George VanHall's fish houses, which were located at the foot of Dewey Hill opposite Washington Street, were destroyed by fire on the night of March 17, 1922. Captain Walker and his crew once again moved their lifeboat into position ready to tow the fish boat

Jensen and DeYoung's fishing tug "J.W. Callister" and crew. Courtesy Grand Haven Area Historical Society.

to safety, but luckily on this occasion the tug *Theresa D.* had been tied up on the east side of the River.

On September 8, 1923 Captain G.B. "Gus" Lofberg, Commander of the Tenth Coast Guard District in Grand Haven, was transferred to the Twelveth District at San Francisco and was replaced here by Captain Chester A. Lippincott from the Fifth District at Bay Shore, New York. Lippincott had started as a surfman in the Life Saving Service at Little Beach, New Jersey in 1894.

These types of transfers, which had not been commonplace prior to 1915, were to become a way of life for officers and, to a lesser extent, line personnel as well. The "home grown" officers and crews of the old Life Saving Service days were now a thing of the past. In those early days troop morale was a minor consideration because the whole operation was a hometown affair. But with the new Coast Guard, rotation of duty assignments became the modus operandi. An enlisted man could request Cutter or Lifeboat station duty and a choice of venue, but there was no assurance that he would get his wishes. Officers knew from the start that their assignments would change more frequently. Because of this, troop morale did become more of a consideration. The Service now found that the "family" would have to be built within its ranks. It was not that the bond between the towns and the Service no longer existed. A bond did exist but it was not the same as it had been when the station crews and townspeople were likely to be blood relations.

It was about this time the Tenth District began to make plans for some sort of an annual outing so that the men and their families from the several stations could get to know one another. Among those on Commander Lippincott's staff was a Warrant Officer by the name of Sigval B. "Sig" Johnson. If the idea of a district picnic was not Johnson's, he certainly must be given credit for seeing that it materialized and developed. The plan was to have a "company" picnic each August at a different station within the District to help build esprit de corps among the servicemen, retirees and their families. All evidence points to 1924 as the year the picnics began but the location of that first event cannot be documented.

The District Headquarter Office in 1924 was on the second floor of the Masonic Building above Beaudry's Dry Goods Store—today the Oakes Agency. The clerk in the Coast Guard office was Irene Boomgaard. Also located on the second floor were the Weather Bureau and the law office of Louis H. Osterhous, the City attorney. Irene Boomgaard's good friend, Elizabeth Fisher, worked for Osterhous so quite naturally Irene would visit the Osterhous office and Elizabeth would visit the Coast Guard office and it was in this way Elizabeth became acquainted with Service personnel. Irene was soon to leave as clerk of District Headquarters and suggested to Elizabeth that she apply for the job. Elizabeth had become quite familiar with the Coast Guard during her school days, having graduated from high school with Captain Lofberg's son Ted, so she took the Civil Service examination and applied for the position. Irene also invited Elizabeth to attend the 1925 District picnic which was to be held at the White River Station—it certainly could not harm Elizabeth's chances of getting the job. Elizabeth attended the picnic, enjoyed herself and went to work for the Coast Guard in 1926 where she remained until 1942.

Due to the efforts of "Sig" Johnson the District picnics became a very popular annual event and Elizabeth attended all of them. Her brother Ray Fisher—later to become a newspaper reporter— attended the 1927 picnic with his father. Chief Johnson transferred to the Ninth District at Buffalo in 1929 and then on May 2, 1931 he became Commander of the Eleventh District in Green Bay. But the momentum he had established kept the

1926 District Picnic at Pentwater. (Sitting on grass, left to right) George Wessel, Genevieve "Sis" Wessel and Don Wessel being held by his mother, Lillian. (Kneeling, left to right) Mary Van Lopik, Mrs. Lippincott, Mrs. Robinson, Elizabeth Fisher, Ann Garfield, Mrs. Benson and Dorothy Robinson. (Standing, left to right) Mrs. Pierson, Mrs. Pierson, Mrs. Palmer, Billy Preston, Abraham Wessel, Billy Walker, Nels Palmer, Chester A. Lippincott and George Robinson. (Back row, left to right) Jim Wessel, Evan Van Lopik, Fred Marsh, Heaman, Mrs. Rapin, Berger Benson, Harold Peterson and Ward W. Bennett.

picnics going here. In fact the idea had been so well received in the Tenth District that Johnson took the concept with him to the other two Great Lakes districts. The following is the chronology of the event in the Tenth District:

1924	Unknown
1925	White River (White Lake)
1926	Pentwater
1927	Manistee
1928	South Haven
1929	Ludington
1930	Grand Haven
1931	East Tawas
1932	Frankfort
1933	Sleeping Bear

Commander Lippincott saw an opportunity for these gatherings to be productive so in addition to building esprit de corps and renewing friendships they became briefing sessions during which there was an exchange of ideas on improving water safety and rescue techniques.

Lieutenant William Wolff replaced Lieutenant Commander Lippincott as Commander of the Tenth District in 1927 and then in 1930 Wolff was replaced by Lieutenant Commander John Kelly. Commander Kelly died unexpectedly on November 11, 1933.

In 1929 Chief Warrant Officer Abram J. "Bram" Wessel, who had been commander of the Point Betsie Lifeboat Station, was assigned to Tenth District Headquarters to replace Chief "Sig" Johnson. Wessel brought with him his wife, 1 daughter and 6 sons. His daughter, Genevieve Madsen, and 1 son, Don, still live in Grand Haven. Following the untimely death of Commander Kelly, Chief Wessel assumed the position of chief administrator of the Tenth District until Lieutenant Ward W. Bennett took command in April 1934.

Through all of these changes in personnel Elizabeth Fisher remained and she was the person who provided the continuity to hold the operation together—especially the picnics.

Tenth District Headquarters was moved across the street to the Federal Building—Post Office—in 1929 where it shared the second floor with the Office of Steamboat Inspection. The inspector of hulls was Captain Bernard Gellick, assisted by Captain Peter Thompson and the inspector of boilers was Hugh Mulligan, assisted by Edgar Ewing. The clerk was Elmer Huless. Elizabeth Fisher was the only female among all of those Government employees.

Before we continue with further evolvement of the Coast Guard picnics we must take time to review the Harbor activities in the decade of the 1920's which ultimately led to the nucleus of our story—the arrival of Grand Haven's first Coast Guard Cutter.

CHAPTER 17

THE SHIP DISASTERS OF 1929

I

Following the Great War post-bellum exuberance brought changes to Grand Haven as well as the Coast Guard. America was beginning to put itself on wheels so in 1922 the City extended Water Street—today Harbor Avenue—from the Government Pond to Highland Park. A new power operated swing bridge across the Grand River between Grand Haven and Ferrysburg was dedicated November 11, 1924—Armistice Day— which for years to come would remain a popular date for such auspicious occasions. The new bridge, which cost $250,000, replaced the 1866 toll bridge —later referred to as the "Interurban" bridge due to the fact that the Interurban tracks were placed on this bridge when the Interurban service was extended to Grand Haven in 1903. The 1924 swing bridge, which accommodated 2 lanes of traffic, was replaced by today's 4 lane lift bridge—dedicated July 9, 1959.

In 1928 the North Shore Road was extended from Ferrysburg to the Coast Guard Lifeboat Station. Townspeople could then drive their automobiles to the beaches in Grand Haven or the North Shore. The North Shore Road provided the surfmen with passage to town which, since 1877, had been accessible to them only by boat in the open months, or by ice via the Sag to the railroad bridge in the winter. Concrete for the North Shore Road was conveyed to the construction site by a railway which was built parallel to the road bed and then the tracks removed at the conclusion of the job. Completion of the North Shore Road led to the development of the property around the Lifeboat Station. One of the first streets laid out was immediately behind the Station and was named Main Street—which gave the Station a prominent address. It remains today what is probably the shortest Main Street in the country—a scant 1 block long. Grand Haven's Main Street was unpaved until 1984.

U.S.-31 Swing Bridge over Grand River, November 11, 1924-July 9, 1959. Courtesy Ron Baker, County Road Commission.

The Port of Grand Haven was to set national legal precedence in 1923. During that year Orrie Foppen, a fisherman, was lost overboard from the fish tug *Alice*. Until that time the courts had not decided what jurisdiction should prevail on these inland seas. The Foppen case went all they way to the U.S. Supreme Court, which handed down the decision that the rules of the Federal Admiralty and Maritime Jurisdiction would be used in cases involving legal matters arising from incidents which occurred on the waters of the Great Lakes.

In 1925 Construction Materials—today's Construction Aggregates—had the *Baystate* and *Andaste* on the run between Grand Haven and Chicago as well as the dredge *Sandcraft* mining torpedo sand offshore.

Flooding in the southern states in June 1927 was critical enough that additional rescue boats were needed so several lifeboats from the Great Lakes Coast Guard stations were sent. Captain Preston and 3 of his crew from the Grand Haven Station spent 6 weeks in the New Orleans area, returning in time for the opening of the Station's new 4 stall boat house on August 12.

Grand Haven's 1928 fishing fleet was composed of the *H.J. Dornbos II* and *A.W. Dutch* operated by Peter Fase and Sons, the *Neptune* owned by A. Abbinga, the *C.J. Bos* commanded by William VerDuin and the *Hazel G* run by the VanHall Brothers.

Pay scales, which had escalated during the war, carried over to those post-war days. Aboard the Goodrich Line's *Alabama* and *Indiana* in 1923, Able Seamen were making a whopping $95 a month while Deck Hands were drawing an equally ambitious $70 a month. The economics of the steamship business played a role in the Crosby Line's decision to discontinue service in the Spring of 1925. That is not to say the Grand Haven shipping was declining. On the contrary, it was yet to reach its peak.

In 1925 the *E.G. Crosby* was being operated by the newly organized Wisconsin-Michigan Transportation Company. In addition to the *Alabama,* the Goodrich Line had the 315 foot *City of Grand Rapids* and then on July 2, 1926 put into service the newly acquired 275 foot *Theodore Roosevelt.*

The 420 foot *Sultana,* owned by the Nicholson Steamship Company of Detroit, started hauling automobiles to Wisconsin on September 9, 1926 with a load of 35 Oldsmobiles. She used the Barn dock 4 times a week and was the largest ship to operate out of Grand Haven up to that time. On September 14 *Sultana*'s companion ship, the 500 foot *City of Bangor* began auto-mobile transportation service to Duluth, Minnesota, but on November 30 she wrecked on the rocks off Michigan's Keewenaw Peninsula in Lake Superior.

The Grand Trunk had the *Grand Haven,* commanded by Owen Gallager, and *Milwaukee,* captained by John Cavanaugh, in regular carferry service between Grand Haven and Milwaukee in 1925. On October 23, 1926 Grand Trunk launched the 360 foot *Grand Rapids* at Manitowoc and at that time Captain John Cavanaugh left his command on the *Milwaukee* to assume command of this new ship. When *Grand Rapids* made her maiden voyage to Grand Haven on December 10, 1926, 3,000 townspeople were on hand to welcome her.

On January 19, 1927 the *Madison* was christened with Wisconsin milk and the Grand Truck had its fourth carferry. The *Madison* was under the command of Captain Edward Martin and made her first trip to Grand Haven on March 3, 1927, arriving at 3:30 AM with a load of Nash automobiles, many boxed for foreign delivery. The Grand Trunk's schedule called for 6 carferries in and out of Grand Haven every 24 hours.

By 1928 there were 3,310 steam vessels entering or leaving the Port of Grand Haven annually, which made it the most active harbor on Michigan's west coast. In that year the carferry *Grand Rapids* alone made 850 trips—which totaled 82,000 miles.—

Automobiles on Washington Street waiting shipment, c. 1920's. Courtesy Grand Haven Area Historical Society.

carrying 20,100 rail cars on the cross-Lake circuit.

This brings us to 1929, one of the most tragic years for those on Lake Michigan waters between Grand Haven and the Wisconsin shore. The majority of Lake catastrophies occured during the fall of any given year, which would prove to be true of 1929. However, this fateful year had an early start when, on July 4, the unusually heavy surf claimed the lives of 10 persons at Grand Haven's State Park. That incredible number of drownings in a single day has never come close to being equaled at this or any other beach park on the Great Lakes. More tragedies were to follow.

II

Clarence Snock, assistant foreman at Construction Materials in Ferrysburg, signed the bill of lading allowing the ship to leave port. She was bound for the Construction Material Yard on Chicago's Calumet River with a load of 2 inch stone. Lake Michigan had only a rolling sea as Captain A.L. Anderson cleared Grand Haven Harbor at 9:30 PM, Monday, September 9, 1929—but there were reports of a storm coming. Captain Anderson had called the Coast Guard for weather information before leaving and they had advised him to stay in port, but he had stubbornly remarked that he "had run it in the past and will in the future." And run it he had—4 times a week for the past

2 seasons.

The semi-whaleback *Andaste* had been built in 1892 as a 290 foot vessel but was cut down to 266 feet in 1920-21 so she could negotiate the Welland Canal. Aboard *Andaste* on that night of September 9 was a crew of 24 and a 14 year old young man from Grand Haven by the name of Earl Zietlow, who was taking his first trip on the Lakes as a guest of the First Mate Charles Brown, also of Grand Haven. The *Andaste* left Grand Haven and disappeared into history. No contact was ever made with the ship—radio or sighting—and none of the 25 aboard was ever seen alive again.

When *Andaste* was reported overdue on Wednesday, September 11 search boats from Chicago's harbors and training planes from the Chicago Naval Training Station searched for her in vain. The first evidence that she had wrecked came from Grand Haven fisherman George VanHall who was operating his fish tug *Bertha G* 14 miles south of Holland on September 13 when he sighted boat wreckage. Vernon King and Henry Swatosh, who were also aboard VanHall's tug, reported sailing through the wreckage for 15 minutes and, although they saw no bodies, they did take some of the debris back to the Holland Coast Guard for indentification.

The *Alabama* had left Grand Haven bound for Milwaukee the same night as *Andaste* and at a Maritime Court inquest in Cleveland later that month—also attended by Clarence Snock and Ed Morse, Superintendent of Construction Materials—Captain S. Crawford, *Alabama*'s master, testified that at 1:12 AM September 10 the sudden storm had created seas so large his ship went through 4 bad rolls so he headed *Alabama* into the 60 mph wind. This led to speculation that perhaps a "rogue" wave had swamped *Andaste*, or that her cargo had shifted in a sudden emergency turn causing her to capsize. But the answer went to the bottom with *Andaste*.

Wreckage washed ashore between the Getz farm—south of Grand Haven—and Castle Park—south of Holland—and then the bodies began to appear on the beaches 2-3 miles south of Grand Haven, that of Engineer Ralph Wiley of Benton Harbor the first to be indentified. Captain Anderson's body came ashore at Stickney Ridge on September 15; his clothing contained the ship's payroll—$479. Clarence Snock and other Construction Materials employees used a horse and wagon as a hearse to remove the bodies scattered along the shore between Grand Haven and Holland to Govert VanZantwick's funeral home in Grand Haven. VanZantwick, who had opened his mortuary in 1926, was also the coroner for North Ottawa County. Five morticians were brought in to assist embalming the 14 victims.

Of the 14 bodies recovered, 11 were wearing life jackets—one crewman wearing 3. This evidence indicated the crew had some forewarning of the impending doom as the small underpowered ship fought for her life. *Andaste*'s sister ship *Clifton* had sunk September 22, 1924, with 28 aboard, under similar conditions.

On September 17 a piece of wreckage was found at Holland's Macatawa Park carrying a message which read, "Worse storm I have ever been in. Can't stay up much longer. Hope to God we're saved", and it was signed "A.L.A."—Captain A.L. Anderson. Inspectors said later it was a hoax because it was written in paint on a new board. However, in his papers Orlie Bennett—a man who spent a lifetime studying shipping in the Port of Grand Haven—expressed the opinion that the message was not a fraud.

Debris from the *Andaste* was displayed in the window of the Tribune, which at that time was located at 120 Washington Street, today Russ Meengs' Office Supply store. Curiosity seekers flocked to the Tribune to view in awe a cork life jacket, 2 life rings, a pilot house step and a lifeboat rudder with "*Andaste*" inscribed on it. Morbid interest ran high but reached a point of impropriety when a local theatre owner persuaded Pathe and Universal News to come to town and film a re-enactment of the tragedy's aftermath—wreckage which the local publicity seeker artistically laid out on the beach for the cameras.

Most of the crewmen were from Michigan but others were from North Carolina, Ohio, Wisconsin and 2 from Australia. Grand Haven's Lake Forest Cemetery records show that on September 18, 1929 George Watts of Grand Haven and 3 wandering adventurers—Thomas Godas, George Rathcliff and William Joslin—were buried side by side in Block 32, Lots 100, 101, 102 and 103 respectively, which are located just off the driveway near the Grand Avenue entrance.

Within a week the *Andaste* disaster was no longer front page news. But then the City was jerked back to the horror of the tragedy when on October 15 and 16 the bodies of 2 more crewmen washed ashore—those of Harry Lutes and H. Raymond. The repercussions of this sudden reminder of an event people were trying to forget were felt all the way to the Nation's capitol. Senator Arthur Vandenberg, of Grand Rapids, pressured President Hoover to reopen the *Andaste* inquiry, which Hoover did, giving Secretary of Commerce Lamont full responsibility for the new investigation. But no new evidence surfaced with the bodies and the cause of the loss of *Andaste* remains a mystery to this day. Even the hull was never found.

Many stories of coincidences and fate, which usually can be drawn from such tragedies, were attendant with the loss of the *Andaste* as Grand Haven groped with the shock of the incident. It was learned and then told and retold how Albert Boyink had luckily turned down a free trip to Chicago. George Evans, Joe Collins and William Johnson were men whom the community suddenly viewed as having a charmed aura about them because they had all quit their jobs as crewmen just 2 weeks before Lake Michigan claimed *Andaste*. Johnson was so elated over his deliverance he accepted too much hero worship in the form of complimentary rounds and was given a free night's lodging in the Grand Haven hoosegow after his arrest in a local tavern. A dog Queenie, the ship's faithful airedale mascot, stood vigil for weeks at the Chicago dock waiting for Captain Anderson. However, it took a year to play out the final act of the drama; the body of young Earl Zietlow finally found its way to shore in October of 1930—more than a year after the *Andaste* went down.

But the strangest kismet involved a crewman who had grown up in Ferrysburg. All of the *Andaste* victims bodies had come ashore south of Grand Haven—all, that is, except one, which is the basis for this final poignant twist to the episode. The body of Fred Nienhouse washed ashore north of the piers on September 16, 1929, coming to rest just a few hundred feet from his parent's Ferrysburg farm. Fred had come home.

In all 17 bodies were recovered from the wreck, which left 11 of the crew unaccounted for and assumed trapped in *Andaste* when she went down. The 5 Grand Haven victims were Charles Brown—First Mate, Frank Kasperson—cook and watchman, Fred Nienhouse—crane operator, George Watts—cook, Harry Lutes—deckhand and Earl Zietlow—cabinboy.

The 4th of July State Park and *Andaste* tragedies had accounted for 35 water deaths in 1929—but these disasters were to be merely a preview as Mother Nature and Lake Michigan got ready for the October main show.

III

If ever there was a man fit for the challenge it was Captain Robert "Heavy Weather Bob" McKay., a veteran seaman who had coped with every form of adversity the Inland Seas had sent his way in 51 years on the Lakes. McKay had been one of the heros of the *Naomi* burning in 1907, when, as First Mate, he made certain everyone was in lifeboats, then went back and broke out stateroom windows with his bare fists to check for anyone left behind. He had become Captain of the carferry *Milwaukee* in 1927. McKay lived in Grand Haven as did his good friends and forward officers on the *Milwaukee*, First Mate William Vaxter and Third Mate James Pett. All three had sailed together since their days on the old *Pentland* years ago.

To recap the geneology of *Milwaukee* as given earlier, the carferry *Manistique, Marquette and Northern No. 1* had been built in Cleveland in 1903 for the Manistique, Marquette and Northern Railroad. She was 338 feet long and was capable of carrying 30 rail cars spread over 4 sets of tracks. She was purchased by the Grand Trunk on September 21, 1908, renamed *Milwaukee* and had served out of Grand Haven since 1909.

Storm warnings were up on the Lake on October 21, 1929 but the Grand Trunk carferries sailed on schedule just before the full force of the northeast winds lashed Lake Michigan—the *Grand Rapids*, with Captain John Cavanaugh in command, and the *Milwaukee* made it safely from Grand Haven to Milwaukee, as did the *Madison* and *Grand Haven*, commanded by Captain Owen Gallagher, making the stormy crossing in the opposite direction. However, when it was time for the return trip on Tuesday, October 22, the full force of the gale was on the Lake and a decision had to be made.

The *Milwaukee* had no passengers but a well seasoned crew of 52—9 of whom lived in Grand Haven—and a cargo of 25 eastbound railroad cars loaded with lumber, Nash automobiles, salt, butter, barley and bathtubs. She was due to leave Milwaukee at 2:15 PM Grand Haven time, but was delayed while company officials debated if it was safe for the boat to attempt the crossing back to Grand Haven. Captain McKay cast the deciding vote and at 2:30 PM the seasoned captain ordered the seagate lowered, the lines were released, "Slow ahead" rang in the engine room.

Car Ferry "Milwaukee" built in 1903 - sank October 22, 1929. Courtesy Grand Haven Area Historical Society.

Surprised sailors on the Pere Marquette carferries—whose ships were being held in all harbors for 2 days— and hardened dock workers watched in wonder as *Milwaukee* entered the frothing sea lanes. Her deep throated whistle sounded her departure, but the haunting tones were lost in the wind.

Katherine Cavanaugh remembered her father, Captain John Cavanaugh, telling her another version of the story. Captain Cavanaugh, commander of the *Grand Rapids*, had preceeded the *Milwaukee* on the Grand Haven to Milwaukee crossing on October 22 and was himself scheduled to leave Milwaukee for the return trip later that same day. When Cavanaugh saw *Milwaukee* leaving port at 2:30 PM, heading straight into the teeth of the tempest, he called to Captain McKay through the megaphone, "Bob, pull in back of the breakwater", to which McKay replied, "That's what I'm going to do. I'm not going out." According to Cavanaugh, McKay was a very accomplished mariner and would not have lost his ship ". . .except for the shore captain." The shore captain was from Long Island with salt water experience and, as Cavanaugh told it, "Oceans were altogether different. He ordered the *Milwaukee* out."

The last person to see the *Milwaukee* was the captain of Lightship #95 anchored 3 miles east of Milwaukee Harbor. He logged her out then watched the carferry churn into the fearsome gale until his view was obscured by rain and snow squalls. The barometric reading was 28.49 inches!

Captain Cavanaugh left Milwaukee with *Grand Rapids* at 6:30 PM, Tuesday, October 22—just 4 hours after the *Milwaukee*— for the usual 5 hour crossing to Grand Haven. He arrived in Grand Haven at 8:30 AM, October 23—7 hours overdue—and reported monstrous seas at mid-Lake. It was the same throughout the Lakes. The *Lake Frugality* was feared lost in Lake Superior with all hands. The *Pilfey* was aground, awash and in danger at Detour. The *Maple Court* was hard on Magnetic Reef in Lake Huron with the crew awaiting rescue. *Nesson* and *Cadwell* were both ashore and breaking up on Lake Erie. Lake St. Clare had become the safe haven for 40 large freighters, but even there one dragged her anchor and went aground. Three steamers were ashore at Detroit and many others sought shelter there. It took the steamer *Puritan* 31 hours to make the trip from Chicago to Ludington—12 hours more than usual. The crew said it was the worst storm they had ever witnessed. At Chicago Navy Pier was awash for the first time ever and the outer drive was flooded and being undermined. Similar shoreline damage was being reported all around the Great Lakes. Locally, shore erosion along Stickney Ridge and Holcomb Hills was severe enough to require later removal of several homes. The force of the storm was horrendous.

When the *Grand Rapids* arrived in Grand Haven the morning of October 23, *Milwaukee* was already 17 hours overdue but Captain McLaren of the Grand Trunk office expressed no apprehension and reminded the public that Bob McKay, the most experienced Captain of the Grand Trunk Line, was in command of the *Milwaukee*. The Grand Trunk ships did not carry wireless because it was thought unnecessary for such a short run. Even so, a late report had placed the big boat safe in the Manitous.

However, the Coast Guard was less certain of McLaren's optimism and, stung by criticism of slow action in the *Andaste* search, surfmen were out from South Haven to Manistee. But with only small powercraft their efforts were limited. On the Wisconsin side an all out surface and air search was mounted. Grand Haven feared that it had suffered its second terrible loss in 6 weeks and now only hoped the "all hands lost" verdict of the *Andaste* would not be repeated.

It was remembered that *Milwaukee*'s twin, *Pere Marguette #18*, had sunk September 8, 1910 with the loss of 29 of the crew of 64. It was also remembered *Pere Marquette* #18 had wireless and the S.O.S. which it sent out had brought rescue ships to the scene; the heroic wireless operator was still at the keyboard when his ship went down.

By 2:30 AM Thursday, October 24 *Milwaukee* was 36 hours overdue. Then on that day—October 24—the steamer *Colonel* found a field of wreckage off Racine, Wisconsin, which was the first grim evidence of a disaster. In the next days and weeks to follow, lifeboats and bodies would be found but the whereabouts of the *Milwaukee* would remain a mystery for 43 years.

The bodies of Captain McKay and Purser Richard Sadon came ashore at Milwaukee. Both had life belts. An empty lifeboat, with all safety equipment in tact, came ashore at Douglas. A lifeboat, with 4 bodies lashed to the boat, was found by the Coast Guard at St. Joseph. It was determined their deaths had been due to exposure. The freighter *Steel Chemist* recovered 2 bodies off Kenosha, Wisconsin, each wearing the familiar *Milwaukee* life preserver. All bodies recovered wore life gear. The watch of one victim had stopped at 9:45, which set the time of the sinking at 6 1/2 hours after the *Milwaukee* had cleared the Milwaukee harbor and headed directly into the worst October storm in memory. There were no survivors.

Grand Haven residents who had been aboard, besides the officers McKay, Vaxter and Pett, were Harry Owen—1st Chief Engineer, Kenneth Martin—3rd Chief Engineer, Richard Sadon—Purser, Stuart Fox—Assistant Purser, Ossie Jackson—Lookout and Phillip McNello—Coal Passer.

Although the bodies did not litter Grand Haven's beaches as had been the case with the *Andaste* disaster, the grim reality of the loss was reflected in the coffins and funerals, as well as the fact that friends, neighbors, acquaintances and loved ones were gone from the circle in Grand Haven.

The usual tales of "misses", "near misses"", coincidences and fate surfaced almost immediately. This was to have been 68 year old Captain McKay's final trip before retirement. First Mate William Vaxter, a former Great Lakes captain himself, had quit the Lakes at his wife's request to become commander of a gravel barge on the Grand River for Construction Materials. But he became bored and longed for the sea so he signed on the *Milwaukee* with his old friend Bob McKay. Nine men had missed the Tuesday morning departure from Grand Haven: Fireman J. "Bozo" Merica stayed ashore because of a "hunch" and 2nd Mate

Goodrich Line steamboat "Alabama" served from 1912-32. Her hull is still used today as a barge on the Saginaw River. Courtesy Grand Haven Area Historical Society.

Elmer Hahn was honeymooning. At least one crewman was late for the departure from the Milwaukee side. The significance in the pair of lucky numbers "77"—the total of those lost in the *Andaste* and *Milwaukee* disasters—was analyzed for a possible message.

The loss of the *Milwaukee* marked the beginning of the end of Grand Haven as Michigan's preeminent carferry port. The Great Depression lowered traffic from a pre-Depression high in 1928 of 3,310 arrivals and departures to 2,630 in 1931, which was the beginning of the Depression. More than that, the figures pointed to the beginning of the end for shipping out of Grand Haven. But even in 1931 the Port of Grand Haven was doing a good automobile shipping business. In January alone 650 Hudson, Essex, Dodge, Plymouth, Buick, Oakland, Pontiac, Reo and Oldsmobile automobiles left the Harbor. In 1932 the *Missouri* and *Alabama* were still serving Grand Haven, but then on March 15, 1932 foreclosure was announced against the Goodrich Line. The *Alabama* was laid-up November 7, 1932, which marked the first time she had been off the Chicago-Grand Haven-Muskegon run in 22 years. The last Goodrich Line boat to serve Grand Haven left December 22, 1932.

At the depths of the Depression in 1933 the carferry traffic had declined to a point that the operation was moved to Muskegon in an effort to rejuvenate the business. The *Milwaukee* was finally located by scuba divers in April of 1972, upright on the bottom, heading north as if pushing the storm which sank her. Her pilot house was nearly blown off by the force of the air trapped in the hull when she went down. The sea gate at her stern was badly twisted but most of the railcars were still secured to the tracks. *Milwaukee*'s final port of call was 120 feet below the surface of the Lake, 7 miles north of Milwaukee and 3 1/2 miles off Fox Point, Wisconsin.

Scuba gear—credited to Jacque Cousteau, "scuba" is an acronym for "self contained underwater breathing apparatus"— has made it possible for more and more amateur divers to enjoy searching for the hundreds of ships on the bottom of the Great Lakes. As some means was needed to control the sanctity of these public treasurers, the 1987 Abandoned Shipwrecks Act was passed. Until then the Admiralty Courts could grant title to shipwreck artifacts to private salvors without requiring that the salvagers protect the artifacts or the wrecks. The Abandoned Shipwreck Act supersedes the Admiralty Law and gives states title to historic vessels because states are uniquely qualified to manage these resources in the public interest.

The answer to the sinking of *Milwaukee* will never be known because, as with *Andaste*, the key to the mystery went to the bottom with her. However, an official Grand Trunk brass message cylinder, which was found by a South Haven Lifeboat Station surfman while on his regular beach patrol October 27, contained a final note—later authenticated—written by Purser Richard Sadon on that terrible Tuesday night. Its chilling words were the last contact with anyone aboard the stricken vessel in its last desperate moments:

S.S. Milwaukee October 22 8:30 PM

The ship is making water fast. Have turned around and headed for Milwaukee. Pumps are working but seagate is bent and can't keep water out. Flicker is flooded. Seas tremendous. Things look bad. Crew roll is about the same as last payday.

Grand Haven did not celebrate Halloween that year.

IV

October still had 2 more surprises in store, neither of which involved Grand Haven directly but certainly played a roll in the destiny of this Port.

The *Wisconsin*, formerly *Naomi* (see Chapter11 for entire pedigree), left Chicago on the evening of October 29, 1929 with 75 persons aboard, bound for Milwaukee on a normal cruise run. But the 48 year old dowager would never reach her intended destination. This was in a way prophetic because Thursday, October 29, 1929 was also the day of the stock market crash that ultimately resulted in this Country's Great Depression. The sinking of the *Andaste*, *Milwaukee* and *Wisconsin* would, like the stock market crash, bring an era to an end.

During the night *Wisconsin* encountered a vicious fall storm and began to take on water. Soon the pumps could not keep up with it. By 1:00 AM, October 30 Captain Douglas Morrison ordered the wireless room to send out an S.O.S. and to indentify her position as being 6 1/2 miles off the southern Wisconsin shore. The Kenosha Coast Guard Station responded and came out through heavy seas, along with the tug *Chambers*, to effect the rescue of 59 passengers and crew. The *Wisconsin* went to the bottom in 125 feet of water carrying with her 16 persons, including Captain Morrison.

On that same day—October 30—wreckage from the *Wisconsin* came ashore at Grand Haven—over 80 miles from the site of the disaster—which gives some measure of the force of the storm.

Dense fog settled in over the Lake behind the storm and it was this mariner's nemesis which claimed the fourth and final victim of our story. The 420 foot automobile carrier *Senator* was downbound from Milwaukee to Detroit on a calm sea in that fog the morning of October 31, 1929, with a cargo of 241 new Nash automobiles. Approximately 20 miles east of Port Washington, at 10:30 AM, she collided with the 440 foot ore carrier *Marquette* which was upbound from Escanaba to Indiana Harbor with 7,000 tons of ore. (a point of explanation: mariners consider all Great Lakes waters as flowing to the sea via the St. Lawrence River, so a boat traveling from Chicago to Detroit is moving with the current and is therefore referred to as being "downbound", whereas a vessel going in the opposite direction—Detroit to Chicago—is considered moving against the current and thus is "upbound.") It was a mortal blow for *Senator*. An S.O.S. was sent out immediately and the lifeboats were lowered. She sank in 20 minutes carrying 10 crewmen with her. The first rescue ship on the scene was the fish tug *Deloris H. Smith* which picked up survivors from *Senator*'s starboard lifeboats. The *Marquette* made it to Sheboygan Harbor under her own power and was to continue in service on the Lakes for another 34 years before being scrapped in 1963.

Thus ended one of the most tragic years in the history of Great Lakes shipping. Each of these 4 disasters emphasized all too dramatically how the need for emergency aid to stricken vessels had moved from near shore in the days of the sailing schooners to mid-Lake for the modern day large steel ships. It was not that the shore based Coast Guard surfman was no longer needed, it was simply that his role in maritime safety was changing.

CHAPTER 18

ESCANABA COMES TO
GRAND HAVEN

The disasters of 1929 claimed 103 lives in 7 weeks on Lake Michigan—all of them in the waters within 40 miles either side of a line drawn between Grand Haven and Milwaukee. Loss of the *Andaste* had reverberated in Washington. The subsequent loss of the *Milwaukee, Wisconsin* and Senator was to thunder from those legislative rafters. Senator Arthur VandenBerg introduced a bill in the Senate calling for more protection of sailors and boat owners on the Great Lakes. Michigan Congressmen Carl E. Mapes, of Kent County, and James C. McLaughlin, representing Ottawa County, took up the cause in the House. It did not take long for the bill to become law.

Just as sea disasters of a similar magnitude had provided the impetus for the legislation which led to the organization of the Life Saving Service on the Great Lakes in 1876, these 1929 tragedies spawned a new generation of large, fast Coast Guard Cutters which possessed the ability to make mid-Lake rescues as well as a secondary capability—ice breaking. Appropriations were made for the construction of 6 of these vessels—3 for the Great Lakes and 3 for the Atlantic Coast. The *Escanaba, Tahoma* and *Onandaga* were built in Bay City, Michigan for the Lakes while the *Algonquin, Mohawk* and *Comanche* were built in Wilmington, Delaware for ocean duty. *Escanaba* was first down the ways. Two of the 6 are still afloat today: the *Comanche* is part of the Patriot's Point Naval Maritime Museum at Charleston, South Carolina and the *Mohawk* is privately owned in Wilmington, Delaware.

The contract for construction of the *Escanaba* was let to the DeFoe Shipyard in Bay City on November 10, 1931. Her launching, attended by Chuck Bugielski, took place less than a

"Escanaba"—A proud lady ready to be launched September 17, 1932 - Bay City, Michigan. Courtesy Eda Frickman.

Cutter "Escanaba" launched. Courtesy Eda Frickman.

year later—September 17, 1932. She was commissioned November 23, 1932. Cost of construction was $584,000.

The white Cutter was 165 feet long, had a 36 foot beam, a draft of 13 feet and was powered by a 1,500 horsepower steam turbine—steam for which was supplied by 2 oil fueled boilers—coupled with a reduction gear that reduced the 700 r.p.m. of the engine to 146 propeller revolutions. *Escanaba*'s top speed was 15.5 knots and she had a range of 3,000 miles. She had 3 forward search lights to flood the rescue sight—1 giant and 2 smaller ones. Her armament consisted of two 6 pound guns forward, 2 Lewis machine guns, 12 .35 caliber guns and 30 .30 caliber Springfield rifles—the maximum allowed by international law at that time. She had a complement of 6 officers and 58 enlisted men, who quickly dubbed their ship *'Esky'* "

Escanaba's first officers were Lieutenant Commander Louis W. Perkins in command, Lieutenant P.B. Cronk the Executive Officer, Lieutenant j.g. Edwin J. Roland, Navigator, Lieutenant j.g. M.T. Braswell Engineer Officer, Lieutenant j.g. P.L. Stinson Communications Officer, Ensign J.D. Herrington and Warrant Officer A. Kenny, Assistant Engineer Officer. Grand Haven "adopted" all the crew but 2 of the officers—Perkins and Roland—developed a special relationship with the City which lasted for many years after they left *Escanba*. Roland, who had been captain of the Coast Guard Academy football team, went on to become the first commander of the icebreaker *Mackinaw,* in 1950-54 Superitendent of the Academy and then, as a full Admiral, Commandant of the U.S. Coast Guard from 1962-66 before his retirement. During his years in the Service he returned to Grand Haven several times and enjoyed reminiscing about his earlier days aboard the *Escanaba* in this Port City. Ed Roland was 80 years old when he died March 16, 1985.

Escanaba was due to arrive in Grand Haven on December 8, 1932. In 1930 Captain Preston and surfmen Charles Plowman and Tom Laird had gone to the East Coast and returned, by way of the Hudson River and Erie Canal, with a new motor lifeboat for the Station. It was 36 feet long, powered by a 6 cylinder, 83 horsepower Sterling Petrel engine and the Station crew had it painted, polished and ready to escort *Escanaba* into Port. On the other side of the River Grand Haven High School's 45 member marching band, school children, townspeople and the official welcoming committee, headed by Tenth District

Commander John Kelley, were ready and waiting. But the weather intervened with a northwest gale, so the welcome had to be delayed.

Then on Friday, December 9, 1932 at 10:20 AM the handsome white Cutter made her entery into Grand Haven Harbor escorted by Captain Preston and his crew in the Lifeboat Station's new power boat. Shouts of "Here comes the *Escanaba!*" reverberated along the pier and echoed into every corner of the Community. Bells rang, sirens sounded, flags waved—the whole town was alive with excitement. *Escanaba,* sheathed in ice, which added a silvery sheen to her pristine white hull, saluted back as she made her way down the channel toward her new home. The time worn expression "braving the elements" was not lightly used to describe the welcoming party standing on the pier at Government Basin. The temperature was 10 degrees above zero with a 15-20 mph wind coming down the channel, which in today's windchill vernacular—a phenomena recognized in 1932 but not yet labeled—meant it was the equivalent of 24 degrees below zero. But the occasion warmed everything except the brass musical instruments. Mouth pieces were kept in pockets or gloves in an attempt to keep them warm until that moment when the band would strike up the Coast Guard's new marching song "Semper Paratus", written just 4 years previously—1928—by Coast Guardsman Francis VanBoskerck. It was an entirely new piece of music for the high school band and they had practiced sedulously for this big moment. Band members were Don Badcon, Doug Baker, Louis Osterhous, Jim Lee, Ken Barthel, Stan Baltz, Paul Hosking, Tom Taylor, Leigh Nygren, Phil Rosbach, Ken Arkema, Carl Braun, Bill Fant, Jim VanderZalm, Milton Klow, Paul Holtrop, F. Gallagher, Russ Moss, Lloyd Drause, John VanWoerkom, Alvin Kieft, Bob Warnaar, F. Kendall, Henry Beukema, Neal Addison, Roman Wolnakowski, Arnold VerWoert, Charles Jacobson, Max Peabody, Gerald VanWoerkom, Neal VanZanten, Jim Bitting, Andy VanOordt, Bill VanDongen, B. Klow, Glen Chapman and Al Kieft. Officers were Melvin Waldschmidt, president; Edward Wilds, vice-president; Robert Rosema, secretary; Howard Bowen, treasurer; Louis Showers, librarian; John Long, drum major; Paul Mergener, business manager; Clarence VanAntwerp, assistant manager; and John Holtrop student director.

It was 10:45 AM as *Escanaba* eased up to and docked at the

1928 Grand Haven High School Marching Band - representative of the Bands of that era. Courtesy Grand Haven Area Historical Society.

pier near today's Corps of Engineers facility. Band Director Marshall Richards raised his baton and the musicians raised their instruments; then Richards dropped his baton and the band began to play—but only muffled tones came out of the frozen horns. Neither the valves nor the lips worked. Captain Perkins immediately abandoned the military stiffness and protocol attendant to such Service occasions and by so doing set the tenor for a relationship between the townspeople and "their ship" which would become legendary. He ordered the gang plank lowered and invited everyone to come aboard to the engine room. There the instruments warmed up and the band played with gusto. Perkins, a musician, singer and song writer of sorts himself, loved music. Moreover he was an astute public relations person—a showman that knew his audience and could discern when to grasp the moment. Perkins had, in a sense, reached out to *Escanaba*'s new home and given every citizen a warm, welcoming embrace. For the townspeople, the ship and her crew it was love at first sight.

Captain Perkins divided the crew into 2 shifts and gave shore leave to all those not on duty so they could get to know their new town. For 2 days the "Blue Coats" were welcomed in the downtown stores, a High School basketball game, the Grand Theatre, churches and a dance at the Armory. Of the 58 crewmen, 60% were married and had children, therefore shopping for housing was an important priority. The local real

"Escanaba" crew - 1933, (Circled, left to right, sitting on deck) Joe Bruno, Joe Coon. (Seated) Ed Roland, Eddie Duben. (3rd row) Harvey Miller, Louie Barber, Lester Fortna, Eino Mackie. (Back row) Bob Carter, Bill Combs, "Ding Dong" Bell, Fred Saunders, Bert Ninness, Herm Rogall, Louie Frickman, Mike Alloe, Leo Lake. 1960's photo of Commander Perkins inserted.

estate people had literally done their home work and were very helpful in showing apartments and homes. The officers and their wives alone had 18 children for which housing had to be found. Captain Perkins and his wife had 2 daughters, Patricia Ann, age four, and Sue Denise who was 2 years old.

The only crewman aboard *Escanaba* who was a native of Grand Haven was Evan VanLopik. VanLopik had been yeoman in the Tenth District Headquarters for 6 years and had transferred to the new Cutter in time to be one of its first crew members.

He received an officer's commission in World War II and made the Coast Guard his career.

On the night of December 9 there was a Community Banquet at the Elk's Temple honoring the officers of the *Escanaba*. It was attended by all of Grand Haven's dignitaries, which included Tenth District Commander, John Kelly and his Chief, Abram Wessel, Lifeboat Station Captain, William Preston along with South Haven Station's Captain—and Grand Havenite—William Fisher as well as officers of Rotary and the Chamber of Commerce. The very witty William "Concrete" Connelly, Director of the County Road Commission, served as toast and roastmaster for the occasion. Singing was led by Larry Dornbos. In his remarks to the group, Commander Perkins spoke for *Escanaba*'s crew when he thanked Grand Haven for the welcome, spoke in glowing terms about his men as well as the new ship and explained, "*Escanaba* was built to safeguard life and property on Lake Michigan, to rescue men and boats in case of emergency, and to make such inspections as would keep navigation at a high standard."

Over that December 10-11 weekend hundreds of people made their way to the waterfront to see Grand Haven's new white Cutter. There was no doubt it was a "bond."

Louis W. Perkins was born in Waltham, Massachusetts on March 9, 1894. He entered the Coast Guard August 15, 1916, graduated from the Service's Academy in 1918 as an Ensign and by December 5, 1925 had risen to the rank of Lieutenant Commander. His first command was the Cutter *Unalga* based at Juneau, Alaska patrolling the Berring Sea. At age 38 Perkins was *Escanaba*'s first commander, serving aboard her from 1932 to 1935. With his magnetic personality he immediately became a part of the community and insisted his men do the same. He played guitar and loved to sing, which made him a natural for the Elk's Minstrel Shows. Two parodies by "Perkie" appear inside the back cover—one to his ship, the other to the Coast Guard he served. He was proud of both of them and never lost an opportunity to laud them. What "Perkie" lacked in artistic ability as a lyricist he made up for with enthusiasm. He was the perfect catalyst on the Service side for the evolution of the Coast Guard birthday celebration which was about to take place in Grand Haven in the mid 1930's.

Before retiring Perkins attained the rank of Rear Admiral and it was at that point in his career he was appointed Superintendent of the Coast Guard Academy. He visited Grand Haven frequently and often stayed with his good friend George Pardee, another former Coast Guardsman. Perkins died May 13, 1983 in Kirkwood, Missouri. On August 6, 1983 a section of Grand Haven's Tri-Cities Museum was dedicated to Admiral Perkins at which time his daughter, Sue Perkins Bussen, contributed some of her father's memorabilia including examples of his remarkable macrame—Perkins had no peer in this ancient seaman art of rope knotting and sculpturing.

Just 20 days after arriving in Grand Haven, *Escanaba* was called upon to make a rescue which unquestionably proved her worth to any would-be doubting Thomas. The Wisconsin based Kohler Aviation Corporation provided cross-Lake air service from Milwaukee to Grand Rapids using the 8 passenger, single engine, Loening OL-5 amphibian—identical to the ones used by the Coast Guard. The design of the OL-5 was such that the passengers rode inside the amphibians hull while the pilot and co-pilot were in open cockpits. At 4:15 PM on December 28, 1932 pilot Harry D. Gosset and co-pilot Ben Craycraft took off from Milwaukee for the 50 minute flight to Grand Rapids with a cargo of 4 sacks of mail but no passengers. The temperature was 3 degrees above zero. By 6:00 PM the aircraft was overdue in Grand Rapids so an emergency call went out to the Coast Guard. *Escanaba* called all men back from shore leave and steamed out of Grand Haven Harbor at 7:30 PM cutting its way through the ice field while towing the Lifeboat Station's rescue boat with Captain Preston and his crew. After *Escanaba* had cut through the ice pack Captain Preston released the tow line and headed north of the airplane's course. By then the temperature stood at a very cold even zero. Preston sighted nothing and eventually rough seas and ice coating the boat as well as the men forced them to abandon the search—arriving back at the Grand Haven Station at 2:30 AM. Both Holland and Muskegon Lifeboat Stations had also received the emergency call. The Holland channel was completly closed by ice so they could not join the search. Muskegon was able to get its boat out but they too were unsuccessful and returned to their Station at 1:00 AM.

Commander Perkins headed *Escanaba* on a westerly course playing the Cutter's search lights on the clouds hoping to attract the attention of the airmen somewhere out in that vast darkness if by chance they had been forced down and were still afloat in their amphibian. The two airmen sighted *Escanaba's* lights when it was 12 miles from their downed and sinking aircraft and fired a flare into the air chancing it would be seen at that distance. *Escanaba* saw it. Perkins headed in the direction of the flare and miraculously found the men in their fur lined suits—which saved them from death by exposure—sitting on opposite ends of the Loening's upper wing, balancing the aircraft to keep it afloat. The time was just after mid-night, December 29—Gosset and Craycraft had been sitting in that position for 7 1/2 hours hoping to be rescued.

When the airmen were aboard with the 4 sacks of mail they told their story: about midway across the Lake their engine had failed which forced them down in high winds, a choppy sea and snow flurries. The waves had torn off one of the wing pontoons which made balancing the amphibian very precarious—and that was Gosset and Craycraft's predicament for 7 1/2 hours. Perkins pondered how to tow the $30,000 aircraft to port, but in minutes it sank.

Escanaba searched for Captain Preston's lifeboat for 2 hours—not knowing the surfmen had returned to their Station— but then abandoned the search and returned to Grand Haven at 5:40 AM.

The perfect record of the Kohler Airline during 4 years of continuous service over Lake Michigan without an injury was nearly broken in the narrow escape of pilot Gosset and co-pilot Craycraft. The fact that *Escanaba* was able to find these two men on a vast storm-tossed sea in the dead of night was astonishing and widely heralded. *Escanaba* had arrived on these inland seas none to soon.

One thing not generally known is that when the *Escanaba* arrived at this Port in December 1932 Grand Haven was not necessarily going to be her home port because her permanent duty station had not yet to been determined. She was placed here temporarily because Grand Haven was District Headquarters as well as one of the more active ports on Lake Michigan. The person who had been charged with the responsibility of making a recommendation to the Coast Guard Commandant for the final decision of where *Esky* would be stationed was Lieutenant Commander Louis Perkins. He was given great latitude with no particular time constraints but, since this was an entirely new concept for the Coast Guard on the Great Lakes, Perkins was to wait until the operation sorted itself out so he would then be better able to advise what would be the most effective point of deployment for the Cutter. Perkins liked Grand Haven from the start and he knew the feeling was mutual. Both Holland and Muskegon were larger cities and quite naturally solicited the honor of being home port for the new Cutter. The competition with Muskegon was obvious because the carferry fleet was about to transfer there from Grand Haven. That intercity rivalry was even reflected in Perkie's song lyrics. Perkins knew the longer a decision was delayed the more communities there would be to muddy the water so he decided to try a little lobbying early in the selection process. On January 12, 1933 he wrote the following letter to Coast Guard Commandant, Rear Admiral Harry G. Hamlet:

> Dear Admiral Hamlet:
>   Before writing an official letter covering the location of the Escanaba at Grand Haven, I desire to acquaint you with the situation as it now stands.
>   From such observations as have been made here and at Muskegon, it appears that the choice of this port is most advantageous to the Government. This harbor is much more free from ice than Muskegon, wharfage is available at all times at the Government dock, this space is closer to the City, and it is more convenient in every way.
>   It is hoped that the above may give you an estimate of the situation until additional facts have been produced looking toward a permanent birth for this vessel.

He signed it and sent it off to Washington feeling confident he and his wife could now shop for a home in Grand Haven. He was absolutely right.

Having the *Escanaba* stationed in Grand Haven did, of course, mean quite a boost in the economy at a very critical point during the Depression. Gordon Moore—still living in Grand Haven—was a salesman for Braak's Bakery and was awarded the Cutter's account for all baked goods. It was not only a sizeable account but also afforded him the perquisite of occasionally going out on the white ship.

The USCGC *Escanaba* had many interesting and unusual calls to duty while stationed in Grand Haven but none matched the glamour or international intrigue of her assignment in July 1933, just 6 months after arriving at her new home port. Benito Mussolini had become the Fascist Premier of Italy in 1922 and Adolph Hitler was taking advantage of the 1930's world depression to auger his way to power. Both had grandiose plans for European supremacy. Chicago was celebrating its Centennial with the Century of Progress World's Fair in 1932-33. Italy had a fleet of seaplanes under the command of General Italo Balbo, an aviator and Italian Minister of Air, and it was with this show of air power, in the guise of a goodwill tour, Italy planned a powerful propaganda ploy; Balbo was to command a fleet of 24 seaplanes in a flight from Rome to Chicago to air deliver mail with a commemorative stamp designed specially for the Century of Progress.

Anti-Facist threats from Chicago's Italian community, which vowed to destroy the seaplanes while they were here, posed a security problem for both Italian and United States governments. Captain Perkins' orders from Division Headquarters in Chicago were to proceed to that City with *Escanaba* to control the navigable waters as the air fleet arrived and then provide protective surveillance for the seaplanes during their July 15-19 visit. Implicit in the communique was that any slip in *Escanaba*'s assignment had the potential for international repercussions.

Perkins cleared and patrolled a square mile off the Chicago Municipal Pier so the 24 seaplanes would have a cordoned zone for safe landing and mooring. At night *Escanaba*'s powerful search lights were to illuminate the area for security. Perkins had two interpreters aboard as well as command of a fleet of small boats which were to serve as shuttles for the Chicago Postmaster, pilots and crew. No other craft was to enter that zone without first presenting its credentials to the officers aboard the *Escanaba*.

The 24 seaplanes gracefully landed three at a time and then taxied to their mooring buoys without mishap. Henry White—who lives today in Southgate, Michigan—served aboard *Esky* from the first week of January, 1933 until October, 1935 and vividly recalls the excitement along the Chicago Lake shore when the seaplanes landed between 1:00 and 2:00 PM. *Escanaba* took her station eastward and close by the aircraft. There were hundreds of boaters in the harbor watching the spectacle, one of whom was Colonel Carlo Tempesti of the Italian Air Force and at that time serving as the Italian Consul General in Chicago. There was to be an orderly marine parade of gayly decorated official boats, yachts, launches and barges complete with bands. But at this moment Colonel Tempesti broke ranks and like lemmings every power boat in the harbor followed in a mad dash to be first to the seaplanes. Bedlam prevailed. It was just that sort of confusion which could shield a potential saboteur. Tempesti had the fastest speed boat so he got there first, but in his over-enthusiasm he rammed a hole in the wing of General Balbo's aircraft. Balbo was furious. Captain Perkins—who was a strong, authoritative figure when the need arose—quickly untangled the swirl of well wishers and restored order. The rest of the visit of the Italian Air Squadron passed without incident; the air fleet departed from Chicago for their return transAtlantic flight to Rome on July 19.

Commander Perkins, his crew and *Escanaba* were cited by Coast Guard Commandant Hamlet, Postmaster General James Farley and Chicago's Italian Consul General Tempesti for the exceptional manner in which order was maintained and duty performed during the potentially volatile visit. Perkins was decorated by the King of Italy with Cavliere of the order of the Cross of Italy.

The crew of the *Escanaba* and the surfmen of the Lifeboat Station played major rolls in the Memorial Day celebrations in Grand Haven. The Lake disasters of 1929 still haunted the residents of Grand Haven and each Memorial Day for some years the widows dressed in black would gather on the beach as Captain Preston laid a wreath on the waters of Lake Michigan in remembrance of the men lost in those tragedies. The *Escanaba* crew would parade to the beach for the waterfront ceremony during which they fired a volley in salute. Then they would shoulder their rifles and march up to Lake Forest Cemetery to honor those dead with another fusillade of musketry.

Prior to the 1932 arrival of the *Escanaba* the water that made up Government Pond extended from the Corps of Engineers' buildings down well past today's Escanaba Park seen in the Naomi photo on page 166. Those waters downstream from the main basin were shallow and unusable so they were a convenient dumping ground for channel dredging and were slowly filled in.

Tenth District Commander John Kelley envisioned this spoil area as an ideal landing for Coast Guard vessels if it were properly filled and landscaped. When he received word that Grand Haven was one of the locations being considered for a new Cutter being built in Bay City, he made work of his dream project. Working with the Corps of Engineers and the City, Kelly was able to see his plan take shape, but he would never see it through because he died of a heart attack while attending a community dinner at the Elk's Lodge commemorating Armistice Day on November 11, 1933—just one month before the landing was completed. Kelly was buried in Lake Forest Cemetery.

When finished in December of 1933 the embarkment was a fine addition to the waterfront and an ideal dock for the *Escanaba*. It was appropriately dedicated Kelly Memorial Park, the name it retained for 16 years.

On November 30, 1934 at 10:00 PM a monstrous storm drove the whaleback tanker *Henry W. Cort* onto the Muskegon breakwater. The Lifeboat Station and *Esky* were called to help the crew of the stricken vessel. Henry White had shore leave that night and remembers hearing the recall whistle which called the crew back to the ship. When the Cutter and Captain Preston's surfmen arrived at the scene in Muskegon it was too dark to effect a rescue so it was decided to wait until morning.

Through the murky night the Grand Haven and Muskegon surfmen set up the breeches buoy gear on shore while *Escanaba* stood by the *Cort*. The same mountainous waves which pounded *Cort* made it nearly impossible for *Escanaba*'s wheelman, Jim Binns who was aboard *Esky* 1933-36— married Joyce VanDyke and now lives in Addison, Michigan—to hold a position. When morning light broke, a line was fired to the *Cort* by the surfmen and all 25 crewmen were shuttled ashore by breeches buoy. The only casualty was John Dipert, a surfman from the Muskegon Station, who was lost when Muskegon's lifeboat was swamped and driven ashore. Binns gained great respect for the "bungalow sailors" who were exposed to the harsh elements for more than 12 hours on that rescue mission. Although the event took place 56 years ago, Binns still remembers Captain "Stormy" Preston's swollen, weather beaten face when the surfmen returned from the ordeal.

Escanaba was a popular boat at all the ports on Lake Michigan and served a variety of functional, humanitarian and ceremonial duties. In 1936 she was on constant call for icebreaking at 12 separate harbors during the winter months. In the summer she attended a meeting in Milwaukee of the Mid-West Controllers of Customs, a VFW gathering in Holland, assisted the steamer *Pathfinder* ashore near Mackinac City, had a 2 day stay in Menominee for a 4th of July celebration, a 3 day visit at the Traverse City Cherry Festival and patrolled a Starboat regatta at Benton Harbor as well as the Chicago to Mackinac Yacht Race. Meanwhile *Esky* was in constant radio contact ready to serve any and all marine emergencies. She answered 40 calls for aid—12 from large Lake steamers, 10 from fishing vessels and the rest of a general nature—thus many citizens learned to appreciate this affable, rugged workhorse.

The patrol duty during yacht races was not always just ceremonial. In July 1937 a 60 mph gale hit the Chicago-Mackinac fleet the first night out completely disabling the *Dorello*, a yawl owned by J.M. Corday of Chicago. The crew of the *Dorello* sent up flares which were seen by *Esky*. Before the storm subsided it drove the yawl all the way from Ludington to South Haven and it was there Commander R.J. Mauerman was able to put a boat over the side to rescue the 7 beleaguered crewmen. *Dorello* had no sails left and her cabin was awash but the hull held and was towed into port by *Escanaba*.

Escanaba was a very effective icebreaking machine and proved that it was possible to extend the shipping season nearly year round. Because of her ability to plow through the toughest ice packs she was in almost constant demand. Her first winter in Grand Haven—1932-33—she freed the *Missouri* on January 3, the *Missouri* and *Grand Rapids* were cut loose on February 13 and then later in February it took 3 days to free the *City of Milwaukee*, *Missouri* and *Grand Rapids*. Every winter tested her tenacity and in many cases her rescues were a matter of life and death for those trapped in the deep freeze because the smaller boats, such as the fish tugs, did not have the fuel supply to sustain themselves for days on end so the possibility of death by exposure was a real fact of life for the fishermen. Such was the case in 1935-36, a winter when more than 110 inches of snow fell.

William VerDuin and Anthony Verhoeks were aboard the *C.J. Bos* which was stuck in the ice 12 miles from shore and the temperature had dropped to -24 degrees. Although it may be

"Escanaba" freeing icebound "Missouri" left, and twin stacked "Grand Haven". Courtesy Grand Haven Area Historical Society.

overly dramatic to say they might have perished, it is certainly not an overstatement to say that the arrival of *Escanaba* to free them was timely and much appreciated.

It was this icebreaking capability that allowed *Escanaba* to earn the title of "ship of mercy" when, on January 22, 1934 she broke through the ice pack to carry food and supplies from Charlevoix to the residents and livestock stranded on Beaver Island, located 32 miles offshore.

From 1936 to 1942 the *Escanaba* rescued 27 persons, gave major assistance to 63 vessels while rendering miscellaneous assistance to 17 others with a total of 900 passengers or crew aboard vessels valued at $7.5 million and cargoes at $1.5 million. *Escanaba* was widely acclaimed and with each newspaper story or official communique Grand Haven would be mentioned as her home port. The civic pride Grand Havenites gained from the relationship was immeasurable and the return of gratitude from the City to the Coast Guard was to be everlasting.

Commanders of *Escanaba* were the following:

1932-35   Lieutenant Commander Louis W. Perkins—from the Cutter *Unalga* in Juneau; transferred to Fort Lauderdale.

1935-36   Lieutenant Commander Louis B. Olson—from the Cutter *Senaca* in Mobile: transferred to the

Academy November 5, 1936.

1936-37 Lieutenant Commander R.J. Mauerman—from the Cutter *Icarus* on Staten Island.

1938-41 Lieutenant Commander J.P. Murray

1941-43 Lieutenant Commander Carl U. Peterson—from Newtonville, Massachusetts; went down with his ship June 13, 1943.

Loading relief supplies aboard "Escanaba" for ice bound Beaver Island 1934. Courtesy Eda Frickman.

In the Coast Guard vernacular men who are members of a ship's crew when the ship is commissioned are given the privileged title of "Plank Owner", which literally means they own a piece of the ship. Of the 58 men in *Escanaba*'s original 1932 crew—the "Plank Owners"—the following made Grand Haven their home after leaving the Service; Joe Coon, Louie Frickman, Orville Collins, W.S. "Pop" Rogers, Leo Lake, Louie Barber, Eino Mackie and Joe Bruno. None of these men are living today but their widows—Emilia "Mickey" Coon, Eda "Lindy" Frickman, Catherine Lake and Helen Bruno—were very helpful in piecing this information together. Ethel Conant Pankowski, wife of the late Bernie Pankowski who served aboard *Escanaba* 1933-34, also lent support to this research. Ethel's parents operated Conant's Restaurant, across from the Grand Theatre, in the 1920's and 30's.

Men who are not *Escanaba* "Plank Owners" but served aboard

her between 1933 and 1942 and still live in Grand Haven are Bill Herbst—aboard *Esky* 1936-38, Steve Vozar—1938-43, Ed Lautenschlaeger-1938-40, and Bob Burgess—1938-40. Two Michigan men who served aboard *Escanaba* in those early days are Henry White, now living in Southgate—aboard *Esky* from January, 1933 to October, 1935 and Jim Binns who lives in Addison—from fall 1933 to 1936. According to Henry White, each time he passes the mast in Escanaba Park he recalls a rainy night on a storm tossed Lake when he and shipmate Bill Werner (married Libby Burns, sister of Bobbi Stobbelaar) climbed *Esky*'s rigging to secure the yardarm which had broken loose. *Escanaba* lives on through all of these former Coast Guardsmen.

CHAPTER 19

DEPRESSION DAYS

Grand Haven entered the Depression of the 1930's as one of the busiest ports on the Great Lakes. When the Depression ended so had the Port's glory years. The Crosby Line, which had served Grand Haven for over 30 years, ceased operation in 1925. The Goodrich Line, whose ships had called on this Port for nearly 75 years went bankrupt, the last ship out of Grand Haven leaving December 22, 1932. The carferries, whose black smoke and throaty calls gave a special taste and tempo to this Port City for 30 years, transferred their operation to Muskegon in 1933.

Grand Haven did what it could to forestall the loss of the carferries. Back in the 1890's a swing bridge had been placed across the South Channel, its southern terminus being where First and Madison Streets meet (today's Farmers Market). We will refer to it, therefore, as the First Street bridge. The 1923 City map not only shows the location of that bridge but it also reveals an elaborate street layout on the island which, when developed, would have been accessed by the First Street bridge. Clarence Clover—who still lives in the Grand Haven area—can remember as a young man in the 1920's helping the bridge tender crank open the swing bridge to allow boats to enter or leave the South Channel.

The First Street bridge was so close to the carferry terminus that it presented a river traffic problem besides blocking off valuable boat storage. Therefore in 1930 the Third Street bridge—today's South Channel bridge—was built and then in 1932 the State granted Grand Haven $404—obviously a low Depression bid—to remove the First Street bridge. It was hoped this good faith effort on the part of the City would not go unnoticed by the Grand Trunk Railroad, operators of the carferries.

The Grand Rapids Herald ran a story on June 4, 1933, datelined

233

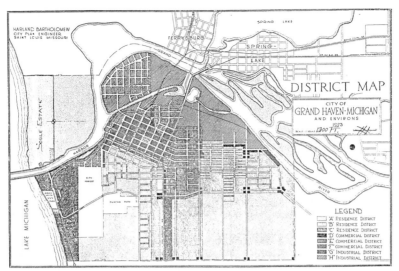

1923 Grand Haven area map showing First Street Bridge at South Channel and 3 bridges over the Grand River— railroad, U.S. 31 and old "Interurban" to Mill Pt. There is no Grand Ave. and there would be no N. Shore Rd. until 1928. Courtesy City of Grand Haven.

Grand Haven, which extolled the virtues of the Harbor stating that ". . .Grand Haven is the port of Grand Rapids just as San Pedro is of Los Angeles. With 2,316,00 tons of freight and 75,000 passengers passing through annually it makes the port the 4th largest on the Great Lakes. . .". It continued on to explain that the Port's tremendous growth was due to the fact it was at the confluence of 2 great State highways, US-31 and US-16, and that on the average 51 freight trucks a day moved between Grand Rapids and Grand Haven which in just the past 2 months had carried 3,000 automobiles to Robbins dock for westward shipment. The article credited Major George L. Olsen, chairman of the Harbor Commission and even had a statement from William Connelly, Director of the County Road Commission,". . .who admits his line is highways but recognizes the value of water highways to connect the concrete ones." It did not miss the opportunity to point out that Grand Haven was the home port for the *Escanaba*, ". . .the newest, largest and most modern of the Coast Guard Cutters" and concluded with the fact that the future of the Port of Grand Haven could not be brighter and to insure its success the City had retained Walter S. Syrett as a port engineer. Well, the Herald story was so slick that one could even suspect it had been written by the Grand Haven Chamber of Commerce and submitted to the paper for publication—which may have been close to the truth.

But removal of the bridge and the June 4th Herald article were too little and too late. The last carferry to leave Grand Haven was the *Madison*, which sounded her farewell—"3 long and 3 short"—at 4:30 AM July 17, 1933.

Besides the fish tugs, the only remaining fleet in Grand Haven Harbor was that of Construction Materials, which still had 4 tugs pushing 13 gravel scows on the River and 4 freighters hauling the aggregate from the Ferrysburg depot to Chicago and other ports. Construction Aggregates' boats make regular visits to Grand Haven today—1990—but instead of gravel, they leave Port with sand dunes in their holds. Recent State legislation will soon put a stop to such operations.

The Goodrich Line assets were sold at auction May 10-15, 1933. The *Alabama*, *Carolina*, *Illinois*, *Christopher Columbus*, *City of Grand Rapids*, *City of Benton Harbor*, *City of Saugatuck*, *City of Holland* and *City of St. Joseph* brought a total of $7,500 with an additional $810,000 in bonds.

Nat Robbins and E.E. Taylor—former Goodrich Line president—formed their own steamship line with the *City of Grand Rapids* and *City of Holland* and began a summer service for Grand Haven from June 30 to Labor Day, 1933. The *Missouri* was added to the fleet on July 10, 1935. Upon *Missouri's* first arrival here, Grand Haven declared a "Nat Robbins Day" in appreciation for Robbins' efforts to revive that nostalgic passenger run to Chicago.

If nothing else the Depression years bred resourcefulness. Unemployment was high and for those so displaced keeping bread on the table presented a daily challenge. William VerDuin was City mayor in 1931-32 and was followed by Lionel Heap, who held the office in 1933-34. One way to supply cheap food was to grow it yourself. Heap reasoned that if given the land the unemployed could help support themselves. Mayor Heap found the land in the Grand River islands between Grand Haven and Spring Lake and started the community gardens. Although it smacked of socialism people accepted the idea because it worked.

Another readily available source of food was fish, consequently the Grand Haven fishermen were active. During 1934-35 the fishing fleet was composed of the following boats; *Arline* operated by Ray and Lawrence VanHall, *H.J. Dornbos II*—the Fase brothers, *Mary G*—Caleb VerDuin, *Harry H.* and the *Reindeer* Wally and Eugene Hill—C.J. Bos- William VerDuin, *Fisherman,*—Claude VerDuin, *Johanna*—Martin O'Beck and *Neptune*Abel Abbinga. This was a very close knit group of men and even though the waters belonged to everyone they honored one anothers "turf" in spite of the competition. Fishermen are the same the world over, of course. Since in most cases the quarry can not be seen, fishermen are attracted to the locations which are producing the best results—the "hot spots." For that reason fishermen are wary and try to keep a low profile when they are having good luck. But the word leaks out so from time to time a region that is producing good catches will attract "visitors." If the visitors play by the rules, generally there are no problems but if they try to get the edge they could be courting trouble. Such was the case for one "visitor" to Grand Haven during those Depression years.

In the summer of 1934 the fish tug *Rogarie Claire*, owned and operated by Clarence Metz from Rogers City, showed up to do some business in the Grand Haven waters. At first the local fishermen treated him very neighborly but then it was discovered the *Rogarie Claire* was equipped with trap-nets. Trap-netters were not popular because their nets afforded them an advantage over those who used conventional nets and besides, the legality of trap-nets was questionable. Metz used the Barn dock to tie-up and it was there on August 10, 1934 that the *Rogarie Claire* exploded and sank. It was never ascertained if the explosion was an accident triggered by lightning or "other causes." Regardless, Mr. Metz went back to Rogers City with no boat and an empty stringer.

The Tenth District took on some added responsibilities in 1933. Redistricting transferred Louisville from the Tenth to the Ninth District but at the same time extended the Tenth's jurisdiction from the tip of Michigan's Lower Peninsula to the tip of the thumb of the Peninsula's mitten which took in the following Lifeboat stations; Sturgeon Bay, Middle Island, Hammond Bay, Thunder Bay Island, East Tawas and Point Aux Barques.

Before we return to the picnics, fetes and festivals let us conclude this chapter with an account of a rescue by Lifeboat Station No. 270—Grand Haven. On September 26, 1930 the stone barge *Salvor* went aground in heavy seas. Captain Preston and his surfmen went 15 miles over storm-tossed Lake Michigan to the scene but it was too dark for a rescue so they were forced to wait until morning. The waves poured over the *Salvor* in the black of the night. To avoid being swept overboard one of the crewmen lashed himself to *Salvor*'s "A" frame while the rest held on as best they could. When morning came Preston went back out to the wreck and convinced 2 of the men to jump. When they did they were fished from the roiling water and taken safely into the lifeboat. The man who had tied himself to the rigging died during the night. Four others were drowned in the *Salvor* disaster which brought the total fatalities to 5.

On Thursday, October 9, 1930 the citizens of Grand Haven, under the auspices of the Chamber of Commerce, had a Testimonial Banquet at the William Ferry Hotel to show their appreciation to Captain Preston and his surfmen. Chamber President was Al Jacobson, Sr., the Toastmaster Kinsbury Scott and the testimonial was given by Major George L. Olsen. Bill Preston was held in esteem and the testimonial dinner was just another way Grand Haven demonstrated gratitude to the Coast Guardsmen. It was a love affair that just kept growing.

On October 24, 1935 Preston was elevated to the rank of Chief Boatswains Mate. He retired February 1, 1939 after 34 years of service. William Preston had joined the Life Saving Service at Chicago in 1904, served at the Beaver Island Station in 1916, Louisville and New York during the World War and had commanded the Michigan City Station since 1919 before moving to Grand Haven in 1922. Captain Adrian O'Beck, who had been a member of the Life Saving crew which participated in the *Ironsides* rescues, died at age 86 on March 20, 1932. Captain John Cavanaugh, who came to Grand Haven in 1888, died April 23, 1936. Captain Billy Walker, who had commanded the Grand Haven Life Saving Station before 1915 and then the Lifeboat Station after 1915, died March 17, 1939. Bill Preston was rapidly becoming the last of a breed from the old life saving days.

CHAPTER 20

FROM FETE TO FESTIVAL

We now return to the history of the Tenth District picnics. To recap, the picnics had begun in 1924 when District Headquarters were located on the second floor of the Masonic building over the Beaudry Dry Goods store. In 1929 Tenth District Headquarters moved across the street to the second floor of the Post Office and by that time the picnics were an established part of District Life.

Beaudry Dry Goods went out of business in 1930 and the space occupied for a short time by the Green 5 & 10 cent Store. The Green Store soon left and by 1933 McLellan's 5 cent to $1 store had moved in. Charles "Chuck" Bugielski, a native of Grand Haven, was working for McLellan's in Benton Harbor in 1933 making $37.50 a week as an assistant manager. That year—1933—the opportunity was presented to Bugielski to transfer to Grand Haven as assistant manager of the company's new store and Chuck accepted the offer.

McLellan's lunch counter was a very popular place for coffee or lunch and was frequented by those who worked in the downtown area, including Elizabeth Fisher and Irene Boomgaard. They recognized the 22 year old Bugielski for what he truly was—a fireball that could get a job done. One day Elizabeth and Irene approached Bugielski with a letter the Tenth District Office had received from Coast Guard Headquarters in Washington. The letter spoke highly of the Tenth District picnics which were focused upon the August 4th Coast Guard birthday and asked for advice from the Tenth District—where it all begun—on how this whole idea could be expanded to gain some positive publicity for the Coast Guard. The Service had just come through prohibition with its share of scars and perhaps was looking for a way to polish its image

The *Escanaba* had been in Grand Haven less than a year and

the euphoria of the townspeople was still fresh. But Bugielski's familiarity with the Coast Guard ran deeper than that. As a young man he had been allowed to accompany the surfmen from the Grand Haven Station on their nightly beach patrols and therefore had seen firsthand their dedication to duty. His interest was keen enough that he attended the christening of the *Escanaba* in Bay City on September 17, 1932. Charlie saw Elizabeth and Irene's behest as a great opportunity for Grand Haven to show, during its own Centennial year—1934, its appreciation to the Coast Guardsmen throughout the District. He took the ball and ran with it. He had no grand plan beyond just a simple community gesture which would say "Thank you and Happy 144th Birthday" to a group of people who had meant so much to this Port City. Elizabeth and Irene had picked the right person to receive their message!

Bugielski wasted no time. He knew the best way for a plan to succeed was to have the right people on the team so he contacted Mel Wright, manager of the Kroger store next to McLellan's, Eldon Nixon, who owned a meat market in the next block and Mrs. Pellegrom and Mrs. Pete VanZylen who were the cooks when community banquets were held at Grand Haven's National Guard Armory. At their first meeting Charlie explained to these 4 people his plan for a potluck picnic at the Grand Haven Lifeboat Station with the main meat course, watermelon and ice cream furnished by the townspeople. In the 1930's surfmen were given a food allowance of 50 cents a day. By pooling their allowance the crew could buy food for the station and have enough left over to hire cooks to prepare it for them. At that time Mr. and Mrs. Witherell, grandparents of Jerry Witherell, were the cooks at Grand Haven's Coast Guard Station and, of course, solicitation of their help and use of the Station facilities would be part of the arrangements. This was to be a one shot deal. There was nothing in the original planning concerning it being an annual event. The committee bought Chuck's idea and came up with a budget of $150. Bugielski headed to City Hall for the answer to that part of the puzzle.

1934 saw this Country in the depths of the Great Depression so $150 was a daring request. But Charlie believed in his mission and was gritty enough to think he could sell the Council on it. Early in 1934 plans were being finalized for the celebration of Grand Haven's Centennial. Mayor Lionel Heap and the City

Council were caught up with Bugielski's enthusiasm and saw his idea as a splendid addition to the Centennial festivities. Charlie came away with the $150. It was to be just the first of a long string of successes for this tireless community volunteer.

In the spring of 1934 Bugielski and his committee sent invitations to every Coast Guard Station in the Tenth District, as well as the *Escanaba*; 77 attended. Ostensibly the 1934 picnic carried on the same theme that had been set in 1924; i.e., it was a Coast Guard "family" affair. However, there was a subtle but significant difference in that it marked the first time a community had sponsored the annual picnic or that there was any sort of concerted community involvement. The townspeople were not there in great numbers, but Charlie Bugielski and his committee were there working, helping, talking and generally letting the Coast Guard people know that Grand Haven cared. It was a success and the Guardsmen accepted the invitation to hold their picnic in Grand Haven again in 1935. Although he did not know it at the time, Bugielski had just worked himself into a permanent volunteer job, one which was to last until Charlie retired from the position in 1981—47 years later. The annual Coast Guard birthday celebration has been held in Grand Haven every year since 1934—56 years.

One week after the Coast Guard birthday celebration Grand Haven staged its own Centennial—August 9-12, 1934. One of the highlights of the week long event was a monstrous 2 mile long parade with 1500 persons taking part and viewed by an estimated 75-100,000 spectators. Director of the parade was Major Olsen, who had staged the City's Memorial Day parades for years, and Olsen had put Bugielski in charge of the Labor section of the Centennial parade. At the conclusion of the procession Olsen was so impressed with the job the young man had done, he slapped Chuck on the back and proclaimed that he—Charlie—was good enough to manage his own parade. Charlie Bugielski directed every Coast Guard procession from 1935 until he retired in 1981—43 highly successful parades. (There was a 3 year hiatus during WW II.)

Following the successful 1934 picnic a committee was established—headed by Major George Olsen—to plan Grand Haven's part in the next year's outing. The 1935 picnic was still basically a Coast Guard family affair but City dignitaries had been invited as well as the committee members and before the day was done Grand Haven had offered to host the 1936 picnic. The Guardsmen and their families heartily accepted.

Lifeboat drills, breeches buoy exercises and rowing practice were still part of station life in 1935. Beach patrol, part of a station's daily routine until 1938, was another duty that harked back to the old Life Saving Service days. At these picnics it was quite natural for men from the various stations to boast of the prowess of their respective crews. But talk was cheap, and as one outrageous claim led to another a challenge to one-on-one competition seemed the only logical way to settle the matter. Thus in 1936 teams of oarsmen, swimmers and Lyle gun squads, all surfmen from the several Tenth District stations, attended the annual affair in Grand Haven looking for some friendly competition. The races and demonstrations were a big hit with the picnickers. News of the impending contests had "leaked" out to the press and, as it turned out, there were as many civilian spectators lined up along the piers on the south side of the River viewing the entertainment as there were Coast Guardsmen and their families at the station on the north side. Nothing can be found concerning the results of that competition but according to Steve Vozar when the *Escanaba* put in at any port around the Lakes a challenge went out to the local Lifeboat station for a rowing race and in 1936 the *Esky* pulling crew were champions of the entire Great Lakes. For lack of better documentation we will assume *Escanaba*'s rowing team took the lifeboat races at the 1936 picnic.

The planners of that 1936 event—Coast Guard and townspeople alike—sensed they had hit upon a whole new theme for the annual birthday celebration.

News of the competition at Grand Haven's 1936 picnic spread to the other stations around the Great Lakes and it was not long before the gauntlet was thrown down by those in the Ninth District in Buffalo and the Eleventh in Green Bay. As was mentioned previously, Chief "Sig"" Johnson had introduced the picnics in those other two districts and, having progressed through a similar evolution, their crews were itching for some outside competition. When the members of Grand Haven's Citizens Committee began planning for the 1937 picnic they struck upon the idea of making the event a full blown celebration with water and land parades, dances, ball games and, of course, surfmen races and demonstrations. And, to be completely

1936 Coast Guard Parade. Courtesy Eda Frickman.

ecumenical—as well as hyping the interest—an invitation was extended to the Ninth and Eleventh District Lifeboat Stations to send their very best.

The 1937 Fete was to be held August 3, 4 and 5, which was a Tuesday, Wednesday and Thursday. The events were held in the afternoon and evening so that as many spectators as possible could enjoy them. With our mind-set today, having a celebration in the middle of the week would not seem to allow for people to come from any great distance to take in the events on a day to day basis, unless, of course, they took three days vacation. Still, a Tribune article proclaimed that "Grand Haven was prepared to entertain 100,000 visitors", so apparently week days presented no major barrier for time or travel. What had started out as a home town affair had very rapidly escalated into a celebration with a passel of popular appeal.

The Grand Haven Tribune published a special edition which included a program for the first "U.S. Coast Guard Water Fete", the Coast Guard's 147th birth anniversary celebration. Grand Haven's 2 year old Waldron triplets Jerry, Joel and Julian—sons of Mr. and Mrs. Adrian Waldron—were pictured with District Commander Ward Bennett as feature attractions in the Fete's big land parade. Tribune headlines announced "Coast Guardsmen Take Over Grand Haven Port." The following is taken from an August 3, 1937 Tribune article by reporter Karl Detzer:

They came by land in gray government trucks on which white life cars, brass rescue guns and gaudy signal flags gave touches of color. They came also in trim white surfboats with yellow oars. A hundred brawny seamen and boatmen picked from the ranks of storm fighters, they brought romance and the tang of adventure to the gaily decorated streets of this harbor town.

For three days they will perform the strenuous and exciting tasks that are their daily life—boat drills and rowing races, lifesaving demonstrations—all the hundred colorful maneuvers that make up the routine of their stations, cutter and picket boats. The program fills every minute of all three days from early morning Tuesday, when the official opening of the celebration was announced by the firing of a salute, till Thursday evening, when a brilliant lighted parade of boats will pass down Grand River. There will be dances, band concerts, dinners for officers of the fleet and even a yachtsmen's regatta.

Lyrical!

Kingsbury Scott, another colorful Tribune writer at that time—brother-in-law of Major George Olsen, one of the organizers of the Fete—added his picturesque style to the building enthusiasm with an article he headlined "Drills And Exercises are Basis for Thrilling Rescue Work in Storms":

Under August skies with the blue-green water of Lake Michigan flashing under the whip of a summer breeze, the United States Coast Guard mobilized here for its 147th birthday, is doing the things its men are trained to do when fall and winter gales scream along the coasts...

Poetic stuff!

Secretary of the Treasury, Henry Morgenthau, Jr., sent all hands a birthday greeting praising the Coast Guard's "splendid record," which, he went on, had always been "marked by honor."

Each afternoon of the Fete large crowds cheered on their favorite teams as the surfmen raced the clock in breeches buoy rigging from the Lyle gun firing until a man came sliding down the hawser. On the first day of the celebration a crew from Lake Michigan stations led with a time of 4 minutes 28 seconds, but before the breeches buoy competition was over on the third day a hand picked crew from Wisconsin stations had won it in the remarkable record of 3 minutes 19 seconds.

Capsize Drill. Courtesy Grand Haven Area Historical Society.

The pulling boat competition was head-to-head from the end of the pier to the South Channel with Holland, Muskegon and Grand Haven crews placing first, second and third in the first day of competition. Surfmen from Holland and Lake Superior's Duluth station took the swimming honors.

The spectacular capsize race over a 1 mile course, during which the lifeboat was capsized and righted three times, was punctuated with roars of excitement from the crowds which lined the piers from Kelly Park to the lighthouse. Columbia Broadcasting was there to beam live coast-to-coast the capsize competition in which the Lake Michigan boats edged out those from Lake Huron. All races were started by Bill Stribley and Captain Preston with Kingsbury Scott, Harold Smith and Claude VanderVeen as judges. Surfboard riding, speedboat racing and music, furnished by the Spring Lake Concert Band, were the civilian contributions to the show.

The gleaming white Cutter *Escanaba* was open for public inspection daily. Honored guests viewed the water activities from her quarterdeck. The Guardsmen were given ample leave time. Officers and men attended dances that continued most of the night.

Every vessel in the Harbor—fish tugs and yachts, as well as the Coast Guard—flew their best parade colors, while downtown store windows displayed an exceptional array of Port and marine memorabilia. One of the unusual pieces on display at the Fete was the original beach cart used by Grand Haven's Life Saving

Beach cart used by Grand Haven surfman as early as 1876. Courtesy Grand Haven Area Historical Society.

Station in such rescues as the *Clara Parker* on November 15, 1883. A one-of-a-kind relic, the cart was sent to a marine historical museum in Baltimore, Maryland for permanent display following the Fete. Reunions of old shipmates and bunkmates— some retired, some still in active service—from stations ranging from Duluth to Buffalo were, for some, the most enjoyable part of the Fete. Reminiscing about the old days in the Service was commonplace.

A memorial ceremony, presided by Mayors Richard L. Cook of Grand Haven and Tunis Johnson of Grand Rapids, was held at Kelly Memorial Park—today Escanaba Park—at which time Mayor Cook presented the Coast Guard a commemorative flag pole erected by the City as a memorial to the Service dead. Captain James Ahern, Commander of the Chicago division, accepted the pole for the Coast Guard in an impressive and colorful ceremony. A kaleidoscopic Venetian boat parade concluded the 3 day Water Fete.

A resolution adopted by Coast Guard officers and men thanked Grand Haven for its hospitality and pledged support to make the next year's event bigger and better. Lieutenant Commander G.E. McCabe of Washington, the official representative of Rear Admiral

August 5, 1937 dedication of flag pole at Kelly Park during Coast Guard Festival Memorial Service. Courtesy Grand Haven Area Historical Society.

Russell R. Waesche, Coast Guard Commander, paid tribute to Grand Haven as the first city on the Great Lakes to stage a celebration in honor of the Service. In response Mayor Cook proclaimed that the City would sponsor the event as an annual Coast Guard birthday celebration. Although reports indicated the crowds were somewhat less than the anticipated 100,000, the Water Fete was, by all measures, a grand success. The Citizens' Committee started planning for the 1938 Fete immediately, which included plans for more events involving the general public so the visiting Guardsmen, who provided most of the entertainment at the first Water Fete, could themselves be entertained.

Viewed from a distance of more than 50 years the 1937 Water Fete—the forerunner of today's Coast Guard Festival—was quite a remarkable event. What made it extraordinary was that nothing about it was contrived; no carnival, no fireworks, no outside name performer, no queen, no fly-over—in short it had absolutely no commercial objective, but in its naivety still garnered national coverage. It was quite simply a public review of the troops—one in which the participants and the spectators both found gratification. The Guardsmen practiced their rescue skills routinely and the Fete gave them the opportunity to show them off. It was an athletic event on nature's own playing field. All Grand Haven needed to do was supply the hospitality, which apparently it did in hometown style. The simple sincerity was magic. It would be difficult to formulate a better foundation for an event which has sustained momentum for more than half a century.

News of the success of the 1937 Coast Guard birthday celebration in Grand Haven spread rapidly through the Service and finally found its way to the desk of the Commandant, Admiral Russell R. Waesche, the first full Admiral in the U.S. Coast Guard. Although he had not attended the first Water Fete in 1937, when invitations went out for the 1938 event Waesche accepted and in so doing set a precedent that has been followed by every Commandant for 52 years, with the exception of Admiral Alfred Richmond who served as Commandant 1954-62.

Rear Admiral Waesche was appointed Coast Guard Commandant by President Roosevelt on June 14, 1936 to replace Rear Admiral Hamlet. His was to have been a 4 year term but WW II extended it until he retired January 1, 1946, which made his tenure as Commandant 9 years and 6 months, just 6 months short of that of Captain Charles F. Shoemaker who served as Commandant of the Revenue Cutter Service for 10 years—March 19, 1895 to March 27, 1905. Russell Waesche was the first Coast Guardsman to achieve the rank of full Admiral.

The first day of the second annual Coast Guard Water Fete—Wednesday, August 3, 1938—opened with a lunch at the William Ferry Hotel for Governor Frank Kelly and members of the State Conservation Commission, the Commission chaired by William H. Loutit. At 3:00 PM there was a dedication of the extension of the Grand Haven State Park. The U.S. Government had owned the original 1.08 acres known as "Lighthouse Acre" since 1838, but an additional 4.24 acres had been secured from private owners and the WPA had done the work of leveling the area. Mayor Richard Cook welcomed the gathering, and although nothing has been found regarding his remarks on that occasion the following appeared in the Tribune prior to the 1938 Water Fete and expresses the feelings of Mayor Cook and the Community at that time:

> For the second consecutive year, Grand Haven will sponsor a U.S. Coast Guard Water Fete in honor of the

birthday anniversary of the United States Coast Guard.

Our entire community is Coast Guard conscious as we realize the splendid service that has been given by this great organization not only to shipping and interlake travel but to the thousands of pleasure seekers who come to our shores in the summer vacation period.

A spirit of fine friendly relationship has existed between the citizens of Grand Haven and the Coast Guard since the time 10th district headquarters was established here over 70 years ago, and it has been constantly maintained down through the years.

May I at this time extend greetings to Admiral Waesche, his aides, and all other Coast Guard officers and enlisted men accompanied by a sincere and hearty welcome from Grand Haven citizens.

Carl Bowen, Director of the County Road Commission, introduced Governor Kelly and William Loutit as the speakers at the Park dedication.

At 4:00 o'clock the competition began which included 100 yard freestyle and relay swimming for men, 50 yard freestyle for women, pulling race between Charlevoix and East Tawas, beach apparatus, canoe races, surf exhibition, picketboat and speedboat races, capsize races between the crews from Grand Haven, Ludington and Holland as well as baseball games. Although nothing was mentioned in the 1938 newspapers, according to Jack VanHoef and Don Constant, birling—log rolling—contests in Government Pond were a big attraction. There was a basket picnic for Coast Guard families and local residents. The day was capped off with a balloon ascension. And that was just the first day.

Thursday, August 4 the ladies toured the beautiful Hopkins Gardens on Spring Lake followed by lunch at the Spring Lake Country Club. The men had lunch at the Armory following which the assemblage visited the *Escanaba*, Admiral Waesche being honored with a 13 gun salute as he went board. The Cutter *Ossippee* from the Soo was in attendance and on public display along with *Escanaba*.

F.C. "Ted" Bolt acted as master of ceremonies for the 2:30 dedication of 2 bronze plaques on Kelly Memorial Park's brick wall, the plaques honoring Captain William R. Loutit and Captain

Nathaniel Robbins IV, the first and second Superintendents of the U.S. Life Saving Service 11th District—Loutit 1877-81, Robbins 1882-98. The castings, donated by the American Legion, were unveiled by William H. Loutit and Nathaniel Robbins V, sons of the Superintendents.

Admiral Waesche spoke to the Guardsmen on the occasion of the Service's 148th anniversary. His address was followed by the memorial service—an integral part of the birthday celebration from the start. And then at 4:00 PM the second day of competition began. In 1937 the pulling boats had raced from the pier head to the South Channel. To provide better spectator viewing the 1938 races started at Kelly Park, rounded a buoy out in the Lake and then came back down the channel to finish at Kelly Park. According to Bill Herbst, the South Haven Station "bungalow sailors" won the 1938 rowing competition against all comers from the Ninth, Tenth and Eleventh Districts.

A sham battle was included as part of the 1938 festivities. *Escanaba* was positioned off shore in a mock attempt to land some men on the State Park beach. On shore to repel the bogus invasion was Company F of the National Guard. Volley after volley was fired from the field pieces on shore and *Esky*'s 6 inchers from the sea, but not a single shell found its mark— because they were all blanks. It was an electrifying "battle" and drew a large crowd.

Attention turned from the beach to the streets and spectators were treated to a colorful, musical land parade. The downtown window displays had an historic theme which lent depth and added meaning to the gala. All of the events were filmed by the West Michigan Tourist and Resort Association.

There was a 6:30 dinner at the Armory for the Servicemen and their families followed by a spectacular Venetian Night parade at the River front. Dancing for the officers and guests at the Spring Lake Country Club and for the enlisted men at the Hyland Gardens—located on the shores of Lake Michigan—lasted well into the early morning hours.

One other feature was added to the 1938 Fete that has become a tradition for every celebration thereafter—fireworks. The City had put a flag pole high atop Dewey Hill—Grand Haven's focal landmark—in preparation for the 1938 Fete's Friday night grand finale. The *Escanaba* had just installed a new 200,00 million candlepower search light and Engineer Steve Vozar was itching

1939 Water Fete Jessie Olsen (middle, back row) was the first Coast Guard Queen. Margaret Johnson Baribeau (front row right) was a member of the court. Courtesy Grand Haven Area Historical Society.

for an opportunity to try it. Vozar fired up the generator which powered the light and at the appropriate moment swept the powerful beam up Dewey Hill to the flag. The gathered masses "ooooh'd" their approval and the fireworks began.

This somewhat detailed description of the 1938 Coast Guard Water Fete has been given here because the pace, pomp and pageantry during the three days of that year's event set the tempo for every Coast Guard celebration which would be held in Grand Haven for the next half century. Each of the next 46 birthday commemorations would have its own uniqueness but the 1938 celebration was the prototype for all the others. The 1937 Water Fete had shown the way but 1938 put some flesh on the bones.

An innovation was added to the 1939 Fete which eventually became a traditional part of the celebration—selection of a queen. The first U.S. Coast Guard Queen was Miss Jessie Olsen— daughter of Major and Mrs. George L. Olsen. (In 1934 Esther DeWitt was crowned Grand Haven's Centennial Queen and even though some of the City's Centennial events took place at Kelly Park and involved the Coast Guard, Esther's reign did not extend beyond the Centennial events) Members of Jessie's court were Mary Ellen Lillie, Phyllis Rescorla, Margaret Johnson and Betty Conant. At that time Jessie's brother, George, was a surfman at the Grand Haven Station. He made a career of the Coast Guard,

"Escanaba" Rowing Crew—1939 Great Lakes Champions. Ed Lautenschlaeger (front row middle). Courtesy Ed Lautenschlaeger.

retiring after commanding the Holland and Charlevoix stations. Jessie joined the SPARS in 1944 and remained in the Service until the conclusion of the war. Jessie Olsen Cole lives today at Houghton Lake, Michigan. Betty Olsen Hickey—Jessie's sister— who had been a member of the Queen's Court during the city's Centennial, still lives in Grand Haven.

It would be 26 years before another Coast Guard queen was crowned. The next Miss U.S. Coast Guard was Miss Nancy Nagtzaam, chosen in 1965, who lives today in Ludington, Michigan.

Admiral Waesche attended the 1939 Coast Guard Water Fete which was replete with picnics, water competition, baseball games, dances, parades and fireworks. Two more bronze plaques—that year contributed by the Grand Haven Rotary Club—were dedicated at Kelly Park to honor Superintendent of the 11th District, Captain Charles Morton—1898-1913 and Commander of the 10th District, Lieutenant Commander G.B.Lofberg—1913-23. But the feature attraction of the 1939 Water Fete was the 3 masted sailor *Oliver H. Perry*, the last of the schooners on the Lakes at that time. The *Perry* had been built in Nova Scotia and was used in African trade prior to the First World War. In the days of prohibition she had been used as a rumrunner from the Azores to the United States' East Coast and it was during one of those forays that she was seized by the Coast Guard. The Government sold her and she was used in the lumber trade on Georgia Bay for a number of years sailing under the name *J.T. Wing*. She was later refitted, took her new name *Oliver H. Perry* and in 1939 was being used as Sea Scout training vessel on the Great Lakes.

Up until 1939 the breeches buoy demonstrations and competition during the Fetes was done on shore. In 1939 the crowds were witness to the real thing. The *Perry* anchored off the State Park and put some men up in the rigging. From shore a Lyle gun fired a line to the schooner and the hawser was secured to the masts so that men in the breeches buoy could slide down the suspension bridge to dry land. It was one of the few times the public could observe an actual demonstration of this rescue technique. It was a sensation and stole the show.

A young man by the name of Glenn Eaton was an enthusiastic spectator in 1939. Glenn had just arrived in Grand Haven as the Forester and Assistant Superintendant of the Civilian Conservation Corps (CCC) Camp in Mulligan's Hollow. This was his first opportunity to observe the Coast Guard birthday celebration but it would not be his last. Eaton later teamed up with Charlie Bugielski and Claude VerDuin and this triumvirate became the managing nucleus of the Coast Guard Festival from 1946 to 1981—35 years of productive teamwork.

One other name which should be included as being one of the stalwart contributors of time and talent in those early days of the Coast Guard celebration is that of Jim VanZylen. Jim, a lieutenant in the Coast Guard Reserves, and wife Beryl served as social host and hostess in the 1940's and 50's.

Military readiness has always been a part of the Coast Guard and the phase of competition not seen by the public during the 1937-40 Water Fetes was the rifle and small arms match firing which took place at the Great Lakes Coast Guard rifle range in Ferrysburg. The dunes were an ideal area for firing small arms in that sand made a perfect buffer for projectiles. This area had been a National Guard firing range as far back as the 1920's and then was converted for Coast Guard use in the 1930's.

Bill Herbst joined Company F of the National Guard on May 4, 1931. Bill was on hand when *Escanaba* arrived in Grand Haven in 1932 and as he saw the white Cutter coming up the Harbor he said to himself, "That's for me." Four openings for surfmen were available in West Michigan in 1934. Gerald "Puffy" Witherell went to St. Joseph. Herbst reported to South Haven for

"Green Ticket" duty on September 19, 1934. Bill Fisher of Grand Haven was captain of the South Haven Lifeboat Station at that time. Bill Herbst was transferred to the *Escanaba* in 1937 and during that summer Herbst, Oscar Smith and Tim "Punchy" McCullough were assigned to the task of converting the old National Guard rifle range—which fired from south to north—to an updated 15 target range which fired from east to west. (Herbst later became skipper of the *Ojibwa*—stationed in Buffalo—and then Ludington Group Commander in 1961-65, before retiring.)

During WW II Coast Guard recruits were being trained in Grand Haven. The Government purchased 80 acres along the North Shore Road from Ralph VanderKolk in 1943, for $1.00 an acre, so that the firing range could be enlarged to accommodate the war- time demand.

Following the war the range continued to be used for training and qualifying—extra pay being awarded for expert proficiency. Each summer as many as 60-70 crewmen of Lifeboat stations and Cutters from Duluth to Buffalo would spend a week at the range firing rifles, pistols, Browning automatic rifles and Thompson sub-machine guns. But residential development put the squeeze on the safety margin needed to operate the range and on March 13, 1970 Ferrysburg was notified by Lieutenant Commander Richard Ahrens of the Ninth District Office in Cleveland that the range was to be closed and the operation transferred to the Great Lakes Naval Training Center near Chicago. Under President Nixon's Legacy of Parks Program for unused Federal land, Ferrysburg made application for the land on December 27, 1972 and received confirmation February 26, 1973. Dedication ceremonies were held during the 1973 Coast Guard Festival at which time John Cherry, Regional Director of the Lake Central Regional Bureau of Outdoor Recreation delivered the deed for the land to Representative Guy VanderJagt who in turn presented the deed to Ferrysburg Mayor, Dave Walborn. Walborn accepted the old range property on behalf of all the people of North Ottawa County and stated that off-road vehicles would be banned so that the land could be used ". . . for recreational purposes in perpetuity." The area was dedicated as Coast Guard Park, complete with the old North Pier light tower as welcoming beacon, on August 4, 1989. Mayor Leon Stille introduced the speaker for the occasion—none other than Bill Herbst, the person who had been a first hand witness to the old rifle range land going full circle.

War clouds were gathering over Europe in 1939. Then, just 1 month after Grand Haven's third Coast Guard Water Fete, Germany invaded Poland—September 1, 1939—and World War II began. From 1939 until the United States was plunged headlong into the conflict on December 7, 1941, this country began to prepare itself for war. North America was insulated from the war by an ocean but as the U.S. began to produce and ship more and more tools of war to its allies, that same ocean became cover for German U-boats which viewed the neutral vessels loaded with war goods as fair game and so month by month U.S. citizens began to "feel" the war in Europe.

Congress brought the Lighthouse Service into the Coast Guard on July 1, 1939. By so doing the Coast Guard assumed the maintainence of some 41,000 aids to navigation—2,000 of those being on the Great Lakes, nearly half of which were lighted. This was done to provide a greater consistancy of port security—a resposibility that shifts to the Coast Guard in time of war.

The Coast Guard Auxillary was organized in 1939. Controlled by the Coast Guard, the Auxillary—which still exists today—was formed as a non-military organization of boat owners to promote safety on the water and assist the Coast Guard in emergencies. The uniforms are similar to the Coast Guard except that the buttons and braid are silver instead of gold. These volunteers took up the slack admirably as the Coast Guard left these waters for war duty.

The Tenth District Headquarters—and Elizabeth Fisher—were transferred to Chicago in 1939. (Headquarters were moved to Cleveland in 1942. Elizabeth Fisher made that move too but after only a few months in Cleveland left the Service and returned to Grand Haven) The Headquarters had been in Grand Haven since 1877—62 years—so the move came as a wrench, but it also put everyone on notice that even these inland seas were part of the grand scheme for war preparation. At that time there were 58 Lifeboat stations—15 of which had radio-telephone capabilities—and 3 Cutters—*Escanaba*, *Tahoma* and *Seminole*—on the Great Lakes. According to Bob Burgess—who served on *Escanaba* 1938-40—an apprentice seaman in 1939 made $21 a month, a Seaman 2nd Class $36, Seamen 1st Class—which required a year to attain—$54 and a Chief—which required 15 years—$125. Half of the pay was received on the 5th of each month, the second half on the 20th. It was the Service's husbandry way of making certain the men always had some cash in their bell-bottoms.

War mobilization put greater demands on iron ore from the Lake Superior region. In 1939 there were 518 commercial Lake freighters and 30 ports—as compared to the Atlantic Coast's 23—which handled 30% of the tonnage moved by the U.S. merchant marine. The character and similarity of the ships and coordination of dock facilities provided rapid turn around time. However, the distances the ore vessels traveled on the Lakes were immense. For example, the distance from Duluth to Montreal is 1334 miles while the distance from Philadelphia to Cuba is just 1300 miles. But the ore boats ran night and day all year so the frequency and consistency of delivery of such a large number of Lake carriers made up for the great distances.

The slow but sure switch to a war footing had an increasing effect on all aspects of civilian life. There was a Coast Guard celebration in Grand Haven in 1940 but it was a stripped down version of the preceding years. During the Memorial Service that year a large stone marker on the lawn in Kelly Park was dedicated. Affixed to the marker was a plaque which read:

To the Enlisted Men of the United States Coast Guard. This memorial is respectfully dedicated by the City of Grand Haven, Michigan, August 4, 1940—Semper Paratus.

Another plaque was added to the brick wall. This 5th plaque honored Tenth District Commander, Lietenant Commander John Kelly—1930-1934. (a slight inaccuracy in that John Kelly died November 11, 1933)

In 1941 the main feature was the Memorial Service. In its 70 years of existance—1871 to 1941, 203,609 sea rescues had been made by the Life Saving Service and Coast Guard—a figure given previously. But these rescues did not come without a price and the annual Memorial Service paid tribute to those Service men who lost their lives in the line of duty that year. The Memorial Service was always an integral part of the annual birthday celebration but, as we shall see, it was to take on even greater significance in the post war years.

All of this war preparation was foreboding but what was more portentous for Grand Havenites was that they could feel that they were about to lose "their ship."

CHAPTER 21

ESCANABA GOES TO WAR

In the fall of 1940 Admiral Waesche began building up the strength of the Coast Guard from the regular complement of 17,000 men. A year later there would be 30,000 who wore the Treasury shield on their sleeves. Every facet of the Service was to feel the urgency of the impending National mobilization for war. On October 6, 1940 *Escanaba* steamed out of Grand Haven headed for dry dock at Manitowoc. She left as a vessel of peace. When she returned 3 months later she was combat ready.

In Manitowoc *Escanaba*'s bottom was removed and re-riveted. In the process the keel was outfitted with the best submarine detection devise available at that time, which was a very crude predecessor of sonar. Her electric generators were wired so as to "degauze" the hull thus foiling the magnetic field that normally surrounded the ship, thereby thwarting torpedoes which used the field as a target. Both wooden masts were removed and replaced by a single metal one. Still, *Escanaba* had not been built as a heavy plated, compartmentalized war wagon and thus remained very vunerable to German torpedoes and floating mines. The wooden decks were replaced with steel. Even the wooden mess table was replaced. Most of the port holes were welded shut. Anti-aircraft guns replaced the 6 pounders on *Esky*'s bow and "Y"-guns for firing depth charges were mounted on her stern. Machine gun and range finder platforms were added as well as ammunition magazines. When the *Escanaba* returned to Grand Haven in January 1941 she was still a white Cutter but with a decidedly different personality. Her crew was mum.

So that *Esky* could carry on her normal duties much of the war gear was removed and stored. But things were not the same. It was like a fighter marking time in his corner waiting for the bell. On August 16, 1941 the Honolulu Coast Guard District was turned over to the Navy and then November 1, 1941

1941 War-ready "Escanaba"—port holes sealed, 2 wooden masts replaced by a single steel one. Courtesy Grand Haven Area Historical Society.

President Roosevelt ordered the entire Coast Guard into the Navy. The Japanese attacked Pearl Harbor on December 7, 1941 plunging this country into the world conflict. The United States declared war against all Axis powers the next day.

Our Nation was in dudgeon. Incidents occur in a person's lifetime which are momentous enough that their indelibility allows them to be vividly recalled years later—incidents which touched the person who lived them so dramatically they can recite exactly where they were standing when they received the news. Three such events which have occurred in the past 50 years are Neil Armstrong walking on the moon, the assassination of President John Kennedy and the bombing of Pearl Harbor.

As with the rest of the Nation, the people of Grand Haven began to prepare themselves mentally and industrially for war. Down at Kelly Park the armament which had been put away just months before was taken out of storage and reaffixed to *Escanaba*. And then one day in March, 1942—with none of the fanfare that welcomed her to Grand Haven 10 years earlier—*Esky* sailed quietly away.

Commander Carl Peterson had received orders to report to the Fisher Boat Yard in Canada near Montreal for *Escanaba*'s final war preparation. There she received additional armament, a protective coat of camouflage and had the rest of her port holes sealed shut. Steve Vozar was aboard *Escanaba* at that time and remembers helping paint the camouflage on the hull. Steve also remembers their first war time rescue. As the Cutter was heading out of Newfoundland on routine patrol she recieved a request to assist in picking up survivors of a ferryboat which had been torpedoed. The *Escanaba* crew rescued 132 civilians. But what stunned Vozar most was the brazenness of the German U-boats— the sunken vessel had been an inter-island ferry which was attacked when only a stone's-throw from the mainland.

Germany had not delayed bringing the action to the American shores once war had been declared. In January, 1942 U-boats sunk 13 tankers off Cape Hatteras. In those early days of the war our total sea coast defense was made up of twenty-three 90 foot and larger Coast Guard Cutters, 42 smaller Cutters and 14 armed tankers loaned to us by the British. Newspapers screamed about the sinkings but cities along the coast kept their lights on— particularly tourist minded Miami—which made target silhouetting an easy proposition for the U-boats. A dim-out was tried first but that was not enough, so by May, 1942 a complete black-out went into effect. Even then, the month of May saw the loss of 41 more ships.

The Coast Guard Cutter *Acacia*—which was *Acacia I*—had been built in 1919 as a mine layer and sailed under the name *General John P. Story*. Her name was changed to *Acacia* and since 1927 had served as a buoy and lighthouse tender in Puerto Rican waters. On March 15, 1942 Kapitanleutnant Albrecht "Ajax" Achilles brought U-161 to the surface along side the defenseless *Acacia* and at 5:35 AM opened fire with his deck guns. Captain Ora C. Doyle, commander of *Acacia*, ordered the ship abandoned and by 5:40 the *Acacia* crew was in lifeboats. *Acacia* sank at 6:25 AM. A PBY spotted the lifeboats and *Acacia*'s crew was picked up by the Navy destroyer *Overton*.

Navy planes sank 2 U-boats in March, 1942. The first surface kill was by the Navy destroyer *Roper*, which knocked out the U-85 in April, 1942. Next, on May 9 the Coast Guard Cutter *Icarus*, under the command of Lieutenant Maurice Jester, rammed and sank the U-352—which was on her maiden voyage—for the fourth kill. On June 13 the Navy's *Thetis* depth charged and sank U-157. And then on August 1, 1942 Coast Guard pilot Chief Henry White (not the same Henry White who served on the *Escanaba*) flying an armed J4F amphibian scored one of the most unique U-boat kills of the war. White and his radioman Boggs spotted U-166 off the coast of Louisiana but the submarine immediately dove for cover. The J4F was not a fast airplane so by the time it reached the sight the U-166 had submerged. Using "Kentucky windage" White estimated the submarine's whereabouts and dropped a bomb—which scored an unbelievable underwater direct hit for kill number six.

In 6 months the U.S. had sunk only 6 submarines—2 by the Coast Guard. But the Germans were building U-boats at the rate of nearly 1 each day, so in the same 6 month period they had launched 123 more. The situation was desperate.

Escanaba entered an arena of the war in which the enemy was seldom seen but the devastation wrought daily was a constant reminder of the enemy's presence. The plan was as old as war itself; the supply lines for the Allied cause were the sea lanes of the North Atlantic where convoys carried food and the implements of war from North America to Europe. Germany's goal was simple—cut the supply line. And there was not a better device to accomplish that end than the instrument of stealth the Germans had perfected, the submarine, or as they called it, "unterseeboot"—the U-boat.

November of 1942 was the worst month of the war for convoy duty. In that month alone the U-boats sank 100 Allied ships in the North Atlantic—more than 3 a day. The Allies were being beaten and were scrambling to develop more sophisticated techniques for undersea detection. The Navy had in its command 6 Coast Guard Cutters of the 327 foot class named for Secretaries of the Treasury which were so able the Navy made them convoy flagships, or command posts. In October, 1942 two of these Cutters—the *Campbell* and *Spencer*—were equipped with the newest submarine espy device referred to as the "high frequency detection finder"—nicknamed "huff-duff."'' Huff-duff was capable of taking bearings on radio transmissions from submarines even at great distances. Huff-duff stations in England, Africa, Bermuda, the West Indies, Canada and the United States recorded all U-boat transmissions and these deverse bearings allowed for triangulation to pinpoint the lurking submarines. All of this was made possible by the fact that the German sealord, Admiral Karl Doenitz, insisted that every U-boat make daily radio contact with his command post in Germany so that he could deploy them according to his most current intelligence on the movement of Allied convoys. In addition the wolf-packs made frequent contact with one another or with Doenitz even while stalking their prey.

The precepts of huff-duff were excellent but putting them to work was to take time and practice. In February of 1943 Ocean Escort Unit A-3, composed of Cutters *Spencer* and *Campbell*, an English Corvette *Dianthus*, 4 Canadian war ships and the Polish destroyer *Burza*—all under the command of U-boat hunter Navy Captain P.R. Heineman on his flagship *Spencer* was covering west bound convoy ON-66 which was made up of 63 merchant ships. On February 18 *Spencer* and *Campbell* picked up submarine chatter on their huff-duffs and by February 21 they knew a wolf pack was prowling on the fringes of their convoy. Observation planes spotted and attacked 3 submarines on the surface so *Dianthus* and *Spencer* peeled away to strike but the U-boats submerged and escaped. Then *Spencer* sighted still another and charged with guns blazing as the submarine slipped beneath the surface. *Spencer* dropped depth charges and returned to the convoy; U-225 never again reported to Doenitz.

The loss of U-225 still left 4 U-boats in the pack and they systematically picked off their prey. U-606 sank 3 ships in a single night. *Burza* sped to the scene and depth charged. In an evasive maneuver U-606 dove to a depth of 780 feet which ruptured her hull and she was forced to come up. The wounded fish popped to the surface near *Campbell* which made a heeling turn and, with guns cracking, rammed the submarine at 18 knots. The U-606 sank with only 12 of her 48 man crew being rescued. Coast Guardsman Captain James Hirshfield, commander of *Campbell*, was awarded the Navy Cross.

By spring of 1943 there were 116 U-boats in the Atlantic. In the first 21 days of March 1943 the Allies lost 85 ships and Hitler was never closer to winning the war. But the skills of the Allies in "spotting" the invisible quarry were rapibly improving. In April of that year *Spencer* was on routine convoy duty and dropped some charges in the calculated location of a lurking U-boat. The computations and deductions were perfect and U-175 was soon on the surface—wounded but still fighting. *Spencer* fired back and then rammed the submarine sending her to the bottom. It was *Spencer*'s second tally but the U-175 guns had killed one Spencer crewman before the submarine went down.

In the aftermath 41 U-175 survivors were picked up.

As it was to be recorded, the dark hours of March and April, 1943 were to give way to a fast brightening dawn. In May 41 U-boats were sunk and then in July another 45 were sent to the bottom. The tide had turned.

The foregoing accounts are cited here to set the scene for the theatre of war in which *Escanaba* was involved. It was hide-and-seek warfare and *Esky* did not have the advanced huff-duff or radar to play the game. At that stage of the submarine blitz the Cutters were kept so busy the only chance they had of being equipped with electronic eye-sight was to be forced into the shipyards for damage repair.

Denmark had fallen to the Germans early in WW II. Greenland—a possession of Denmark and necessary to the security of the Western Hemisphere—was strategic not only as a link in the North Atlantic shipping lanes but also for its production of cryolite which was essential in the aluminum needed for airplane construction. On April 9, 1941 a Denmark in exile-United States agreement to defend Greenland against a German takeover was announced which paved the way for U.S. "civilians"—actually Servicemen who were temporarily "discharged"—to go to Greenland to build meteorlogic stations, reconnaissance posts and airfields. By the time the United States entered the war Greenland was a sizeable Allied base. Provisioning Greenland to maintain it on a war footing required open sea lanes between North America and the frigid outpost and after the U.S. entered the war that job in part was assigned to the Coast Guard Cutters *Escanaba*, *Tampa*, *Comanche*, *Storis*, *Algonquin* and *Raritan*.

While on this convoy duty between Greenland and Newfoundland *Escanaba* had her second call to action on June 15, 1942. She had spent the night on a futile search-and-destroy mission against an elusive U-boat and was returning to the convoy when her crew saw some distress rockets coming from the vicinity of the freighter *Cherokee* which—as it would be discovered—had been torpedoed and sunk. Commander Peterson closed on the scene, put over lifeboats and saved 21 men who were fast becoming numbed in their lifejackets. Although *Escanaba* did not settle the score with that particular submarine she had been successful on 2 other previous occasions. On the first her crew dropped 8 depth charges on a suspected target. The

U-boat broke surface astern the *Escanaba*, rolled over and disappeared. Later that same day a submarine was sunk in just two passes with depth charges. For *Escanaba* the war was only 3 months old and she was already a veteran.

Because of war censorship the people of Grand Haven lost all contact with *Escanaba*. But they had not lost touch with the war. Men left weekly for armed service and plants, which converted to war production, introduced the home front to the three shift day and with it two new terms for its lexicon—the swing shift and the graveyard shift. As the pool of men to fill the jobs declined more and more women began carrying lunch buckets to keep the machines and production humming.

That is not to say the military did not accept women. Early in the war the Army Women's Auxilllary Corps—WACS, and the Navy's Women Accepted for Volunteer Emergency Service—the WAVES, began accepting applicants, so it was not long before women as well as men were marching off to don service uniforms. On November 23, 1942 President Roosevelt established the Coast Guard Women's Auxillary Corps and appointed the former Dean of Women at Purdue University, Dorothy C. Stratton—a Captain in the WAVES—to organize it. Captain Stratton came up with the name SPARS—a deft acronym of the Service slogan Semper Paratus—and chose as the uniform the WAVES attire with the Coast Guard shield replacing the Navy insignia. At first the SPARS were trained at Navy facilities but by mid-1943 the officers were attending the Coast Guard Academy at New London and the recruits at the Biltmore Hotel in Palm Beach, Florida. All SPARS, like the men, enlisted for the duration of the war plus 6 months. Their primary purpose was to relieve men from desk duty and their numbers grew to nearly 11,000. As mentioned previously, Jessie Olsen (Cole) joined the SPARS, as did Carol Dusterwinkle—February, 1943 to June, 1946—and Mildred Dye, both of whom still live in Grand Haven. Barbara Rowe's sister, Eleanor Fabian, also was a SPAR and although she is not a permanent resident, the Fabian's have a summer beach home south of Grand Haven so she can be said to be a Grand Havenite in spirit.

During the Depression years there was a huge number of unemployed young men. Jobs were scarce and when available were doled out to family breadwinners which left precious little to keep the younger work force off the streets. The Hoover administration saw this pool of available manpower as a National asset and in 1933 established the Civilian Conservation Corps— the CCC. Soon CCC Camps were sprouting up all over the country. The purpose of the CCC was to provide work and job training in conserving and developing natural resouces—the land, forests, lakes and rivers. The Camp was staffed by Army personal with technical assistance from civilian employees who were under the War Department—today more diplomatically entitled the Department of Defense. Unmarried young men between the age of 17 and 23, who enlisted for 6 months, were housed in barracks, fed in mess halls and worked 8 hour days conserving and beautifying this Country's land.

Camp Grand Haven—CCC Camp No. 4612 and an Army designation of Company 1320—was the first soil conservation camp to be established in Michigan. Built in 1939 at a cost of $50,000, the camp consisted of 20 some buildings situated at the base of Five Mile Hill—since 1950 referred to as Mulligan's Hollow, named for John Mulligan who settled on this land in the late 1880's. Viewed from the air Camp Grand Haven had the shape of Michigan's mitten.

Blowing, drifting sands and swamp land dominated sections of Robinson, Grand Haven, Olive, Park and Port Sheldon Townships at that time. The West Michigan Soil Conservation District—established under the U.S. Department of Agriculture in 1938, entirely seperate from the CCC—focused its attention on making this land productive. Pete Tullis helped direct this soil conservation project—the CCC lent the manpower. As mentioned earlier, Glenn Eaton came to Camp Grand Haven in 1939 as forester and assistant to Superintendent Gordon Walker and therefore worked side by side with Tullis as trees and beach grass were planted to stabilize the land.

As Army and Navy recruiting stepped up in 1941 the CCC Camps were closed, which included Camp Grand Haven. And then in July, 1942 the Five Mile Hill buildings were reactivated as an advanced boot camp to train Coast Guard recruits. Glenn Eaton stayed on to acquaint the new occupants with facilities of the camp and it was at that time Eaton met Bill Herbst, who had been assigned to the boot camp to get it ready for the recruits as well as be the Gunnery Range Director when training began. The camp accomodated 500 recruits during an 8 week training session which included service protocol and discipline, the

Grand Haven Coast Guard Boot Camp in Mulligan's Hollow, 1942-45. Courtesy Grand Haven Area Historical Society.

manual of arms and military drills, small arms and ordnance proficiency at the Ferrysburg rifle range, communications, marching with full field gear up and down the dune trails known as Little Donkey and Big Donkey or miles on the beach, assault maneuvers, self defense, seamanship, pulling boats, scaling the boarding nets which were over the side of the Navy training ship *Hollyhock* and overnight bivouacs at Camp Kirk complete with war games in full camouflage. The Boot Camp had its own hospital as well as its own brig—the latter located where the ball diamond home plate is today. Over 5,000 men trained at the facility from 1942 to 1945.

Aubrie Goldman and Jack Billups—both former Grand Haven law officers—took their advanced boot training in Grand Haven. Aubrie Joined the Service August 4, 1942 in Chicago and took his first training at Clear Lake near Battle Creek before being transferred to Grand Haven. Both men married local girls.

It did not take long for Grand Haven to make the boot camp recruits feel welcome. On August 4, 1942 a Service Men's Center was dedicated at 105 Washington Street. Commander Lyndon Spencer from the Chicago Division was there as a representative of Admiral Waesche, Coast Guard Commandant, as was Lieutenant R.M. Wadewitz, the officer in charge of the training camp.

In his remarks at the dedication of the Service Men's Center Mayor James VanWessen said, "It is not a happenstance that the training base is located here—we wanted it and we went after it." Mrs. Willette Gale—or "Ma" to the Coasties—was the volunteer hostess assisted by Dorothy Metzler, who was chairperson of the Center committee. Other officers were Reverend R.A. Lewis-secretary and Paul Johnson, Sr.-treasurer. The Art Giesekings, Max Metzlers, Jack Thomas, Jim VanZylens, Carl Linds, Frank Fishers and Dr. and Mrs. E.J. Hoek all played active roles in staging monthly dances, providing reading material, lining up homes for Sunday and special holiday meals and generally taking care of the needs of the trainees. There was a cookie jar at the center that Arnold Braak, owner of Braak's Bakery, and the local women never allowed to go empty. The Service Men's Center stayed open until the end of World War II and in its time was truly a home away from home for Coast Guardsmen who were in Grand Haven.

The camp was closed at the conclusion of the war but the Government moved in again in 1956 when a radar station to detect enemy aircraft was built on Water Tank Hill. Over the years several of the old buildings found public use—one as a Jaycee Club House another as a City police pistol range. Through the efforts of Al Jacobson, Jack Jordan and Bob Yelton the Ski Bowl was started in 1962 and the old laundry house—the only building that had a concrete floor—was used, and is still being used today, as the warming hut. The old barracks slowly fell into disrepair and were finally demolished in 1971 to make way for a park. The 80.5 acre Mulligan's Hollow Park was dedicated by Mayor John Walhout on Saturday, August 25, 1973.

Let us now return to the sea and continue the saga of the *Escanaba*.

CHAPTER 22

ESCANABA IS LOST

I

In the summer and fall of 1942 the bigger and better equipped Cutters were slugging it out with Doenitz's wily U-boats along the main thoroughfares of the North Atlantic sea lanes. The Greenland Patrol was relegated to the older, slower and smaller vessels, which included the *Escanaba*. In that harsh, bleak setting crews had to endure the dangers of storms, fog, and ice as well as the German enemy but, although their beat lacked glory, their lesser role was vital to winning the Battle of the Atlantic.

One of *Escanaba*'s early assignments, according to Steve Vozar, was to help shield a convoy of 16 merchant ships making its way from Greenland to Boston. There were also 4 Canadian Corvettes protecting the convoy but since neither the Corvettes or *Escanaba* was equipped with adequate submarine detection devices such as Huff-duff, the protection they afforded the merchants was deaf and blindfolded. The U-boats had a field day. Only 1 of the 16 cargo ships made it to Boston.

After a merchant was torpedoed the escort vessels would converge on the scene to pick up survivors. Time was of the essence because once a seaman was thrown into that freezing brine his life was measured in minutes. Lights could not be used because that was an invitation to the prowling U-boats to launch another "fish", so the escorts would ease into the zone, often in complete darkness, with nets thrown over their sides which enabled those that were capable to climb aboard. Many would be in a state of shock or unconsciousness from exposure and thus unable to help themselves aboard as their lives slipped away. Vozar's job was in *Esky*'s engine room and he can recall hearing those would-be survivors pounding desperately on the side of the ship.

Crewmen from the rescue vessels would swing themselves

over the side to help men aboard or even tie a line under the arms of those incapable of helping themselves so they could be hoisted aboard. After one pass the rescue vessels doubled back and kept sweeping the zone, often bringing aboard victims that were already lifeless. Anything in an attempt to save one more life. Vozar credits the Canadians with having done a yeoman's job.

All of this was done with knowledge that the same U-boat which sank the first vessel was undoubtedly in the vacinity waiting for a chance at another kill. The survivors were billeted in the warmest part of the ship which was usually down in the engine room. Steve Vozar can remember having as many as 100 wet but thankful men huddled in his work area.

These early rescue attempts made it clear to those aboard *Escanaba* that if more survivors were to be picked out of those icy waters new techniques would have to be devised. This led to *Esky*'s Executive Officer, Robert H. Prause, experimenting with rubber suits in the near freezing water off the dock at Bluie West One, Greenland. What he developed was the prototype of today's wet suit and would prove to be invaluable in the dark days which were yet to come.

Steve Vozar was hospitalized with a back injury which required corrective surgery and so he left *Escanaba* on November 11, 1942—however, he remained assigned to his ship during his extended recovery. He was ashore recuperating when *Escanaba* went down.

On February 3, 1943 the Cutters *Escanaba*, *Tampa* and *Comanche*, *Escanaba*'s sistership, were escorting the troop ship *Dorchester*, with 904 men aboard, and 2 merchant vessels. A gale which had swept down from Greenland sent waves spraying over the Cutters encrusting the guns and depth charge Y-guns with ice rendering them useless. The sea was so rough the convoy had slowed to 11.5 knots and at times live steam was needed to remove the ice to allow for visibility. *Escanaba* was 6,000 yards off *Dorchester* guarding her starboard flank. The violent seas made submarine detection nearly impossible for the meager equipment aboard *Escanaba* and U-456 was able to sneak between the two ships. At 1:02 AM *Dorchester* was hit by a torpedoe which struck such a deadly blow that in 18 minutes she was settling by her bow. The Cutters were unaware that Dorchester had been struck until she began to sink. *Escanaba* and *Comanche* converged on the area in a futile attempt to locate any of the wolf-pack while *Tampa* continued on toward Greenland, 150 miles away, with the 2 merchant ships.

On the *Dorchester* there occurred an act of heroism which will live in the annals of marine history. Four Army chaplains— Reverend George L. Fox, Rabbi Alexander D. Goode, Reverend Clark V. Poling and Father John P. Washington—handed their lifejackets to soldiers and this ecumenical cadre of God's men went down together with the *Dorchester*.

Escanaba and *Comanche* began picking up survivors who were in life boats, clinging to rubber rafts or floating helplessly in the 34 degree salt water. Men from both Cutters donned rubber suits and went into the frigid water to perform the first ever rescues while wearing the new protective apparel. From *Escanaba* Lieutenant Robert Prause, Ensign Richard Arrighi, Seaman 2nd Class Forrest Rednour and Officers Steward 3rd Class Warren Deyampert spent up to 4 hours in the water in their rubber suits assisting the victims in a rescue technique they referred to as under the "counter", or beneath the overhang of the ships stern. This put them dangerously close to *Escanaba*'s propellers but it provided an unobstructed pull straight up from the water and was perhaps the only means of retrieving an unconscious person in high seas without running the further risk of banging his body against the side of the ship with every rolling lurch.

Comanche rescued 93, *Escanaba* 133. For this heroic exploit 6 officers and men were given posthumous awards in August, 1943. Although these men may or may not have been with the *Escanaba* when she sailed from Grand Haven in 1942, they were all remembered as the resourceful, brave and devoted Coast Guardsmen they were. The following is an excerpt from *Escanaba*'s official record which pertains to the *Dorchester* rescues:

> Lieutenant Commander Carl U. Peterson, USCG, commanding officer of the Escanaba, was awarded The Legion of Merit posthumously. He and Executive Officer, Lt. Robert H. Prause, to whom a letter of commendation was awarded, did outstanding jobs of organizing and supervising on the scene all the rescue operations. The handling by Lt. Prause of the survivors and crew members in the water while the ship was maneuvering, plus the prompt recovery of two crew members who were pulled

overboard as they tried to keep the survivors alongside, displayed sound judgment and excellent seamanship. Despite the lack of illumination there was no confusion. Everyone worked with grim determination to cheat the enemy out of as many victims as possible, despite the constant threat of submarine action. Lt. Prause had previously planned the retriever method of rescue and had gone into the icy water off the dock at Bluie West One, Greenland, in a rubber suit with a line attached. The experiment paid great dividends. The total number rescued by the Escanaba was 133 alive, of which one died on board. Twelve bodies were also recovered.

Even when a victim looked dead, he was brought on board and only 12 out of 50 apparently dead thus rescued were actually found to be dead by the ship's doctor, Asst. Surgeon Ralph R. Nix of the U.S. Public Health Service. He worked valiantly, with the assistance of members of the crew and of those survivors who had recovered, on those who showed signs of life and was posthumously awarded a letter of commendation.

Ens. Richard A. Arrighi, USCGR, posthumously awarded the Navy and Marine Corps medal, Aug. 18, 1943, was the first to go over the side as a retriever. This act boosted the morale of the entire crew and gave confidence to the other retrievers. During the early hours of the rescue one lifeboat was contacted which was in fair condition. This boat had picked up the other survivors and was fairly crowded. As the lifeboat was made fast to the Escanaba's side, one of its helpless occupants fell in between the cutter and the lifeboat. This man was covered with oil and the men in the lifeboat simply could not extricate him from his perilous position. Ens. Arrighi, working in the water at the time, swam in between the boat and the ship, pulled the man out so that he would not be crushed, held him up so that a line could be put around him and helped the men in the boat get him aboard. Arrighi was in grave danger of being crushed between the boat and the ship's side, but luckily was spared, only to lose his life in June when the Escanaba blew up. He was in and out of the water rescuing survivors, working in the dark with a rough sea running and quitting only when his rubber suit became worn and filled with water. After that he had to be hauled out of the water and treated for exposure.

The Navy and Marine Corps Medal also went posthumously to Forrest O. Rednour, seaman second class and Warren T. Deyampert, officers steward third class, who worked between three and four hours in the water during darkness pulling rafts in close to the ship, securing boelines about the survivors so that they could be hauled aboard the Escanaba and at times keeping helpless survivors afloat until they could put lines about them. They too were often in danger of being crushed between rafts and the ship's side. Rednour stuck with a raft loaded with survivors as it drifted under the ship counter and the propeller had to be backed to get the raft to a position where the survivors could be unloaded. Deyampert stuck with a single floating survivor as he drifted astern under the counter, in order to keep him clear of the propeller. He disregarded this danger to himself, in order that the survivor might be kept clear of it. Rednour worked the longest of all the retrievers and accounted for the greatest number of survivors, but finally had to quit when his rubber suit became torn.

The rescues by the crews of *Escanaba* and *Comanche* in those icy, choppy seas was remarkable and demonstrated a selfless dedication which harked back to like deeds performed by their predecessor Life Saving Service surfmen nearly three quarters of a century before them. And although 225 men were cheated from death's grip the dawning light revealed the gruesome aftermath—hundreds of bodies of the 678 men who were lost bobbing on the waves in their lifejackets.

Then it was *Escanaba*'s turn.

Escort Task Unit 24.8.2 and convoy G.S. 24 left Narsarssuak, Greenland at 10:00 PM, June 10, 1943 bound for St. Johns Newfoundland. In the Escort Task Unit providing protection for the convoy were the Coast Guard Cutters *Tampa*-the flagship, *Raritan*, *Storis*, *Mojave*, *Algoquin* and *Escanaba*. Among the ships in the convoy was the *U.S.A.T. Fairfax*, a ship the Germans had predicted they would sink. On June 12 the convoy passed through fields of icebergs and "growlers." These together with the dense fog made navigation a dangerous and slow process.

The dense fog had turned to a cold, gray mist by June 13. The water was smooth which indicated the convoy was still in the vacinity of the ice field although the ice itself lay somewhere beyond the mist. The ships closest to *Escanaba* were the *Raritan* and *Storis*.

At 5:10 AM on June 13 the gunners mate aboard the *Raritan* was keeping watch through the starboard porthole in the wheelhouse when he suddenly saw a red smudge reflected in the glass. He turned and saw smoke rising where the *Escanaba* had been. After a moment of shock the general quarters signal key was wrenched over and the terrifying cry of the hooter swept the ship springing all hands to *Raritan*'s battle stations. *Raritan* headed straight for the scene.

Storis, closest to *Escanaba*, reported seeing ". . .a cloud of dense black and yellow smoke and flame billowing upward into the air. . .". None of the vessels had heard the explosion. *Storis* bore down on the site where *Esky* was last seen, while the rest of the convoy continued on, zigzagging to evade further submarine attacks.

Escanaba sank in 3 minutes—too quickly for any sort of a distress signal to be sent. *Raritan* and *Storis* were at the scene in 10 minutes and could find nothing but floatable odds and ends in water thick with black fuel oil. An empty life raft was taken aboard. Then *Raritan* sighted a strongback—a 38 foot log used as a slide to launch lifeboats, one of which *Escanaba* left behind in Grand Haven and is in Ray Mieras' extensive collection of Coast Guard memorabilia—which had 2 men clinging to it who were muttering in a semiconscious, incoherent manner. *Raritan* pulled up to the survivors and crewmen went over the side on the nets to pull the helpless, oil blackened men aboard. The men's clothing was frozen to the wood so the strong-back had to be slid out of their bent grasp. A third person was taken aboard in an unconscious state.

The first two taken aboard the *Raritan* were Seaman 1st Class Raymond O'Malley, from Chicago, Illinois and Boatswains Mate Melvin Baldwin from Staples, Minnesota. When brought aboard they were half dead but first aid, 2 hours of massaging and warm blankets brought them back among the living.

The third person, Lieutenant Robert Prause, was declared dead from exposure. It is ironic that the man who devised the rubber suit "retriever" method of saving those near death from exposure in the icy North Atlantic waters could not himself have been saved by his own innovation. As the *Raritan*'s official log discloses, Prause was buried at sea the next day, Monday, June 14, 1943.

After O'Malley had recovered he said he had passed out just as he saw the *Raritan* and did not remember a thing until he woke up 2 hours later with people rubbing his arms and legs. He then gave *Raritan*'s officers this account of *Escanaba*'s last moments:

> Well, I relieved the wheel about 0445. I made a turn to port about 0500—that is swung from 190 to 140. I heard a burst of machine gun fire. The officer of the deck looked to the starboard wing at the machine gun there, which I noticed was silenced. He then went behind me on the port side of the wheelhouse. There had been about 3 or 4 short bursts of gunfire in this interval. As he walked behind me, the commanding officer and the exec came into the wheelhouse from the emergency cabin. Just then there was a terrific explosion. I was forced upward, but stayed on my feet because I had hold of the wheel.
>
> I hit my head on the overhead. I turned toward the port side and saw the junior O.D. was bleeding from the hair down. We tried to open the starboard door but the knob was gone. We pushed it anyhow and the door opened. When I got out I noticed the deck was blown up in one spot. The starboard wing had blood on his face. I could see fire amidships. The stern was settling. I began to tie on my life jacket. I got two strings tied when I was suddenly washed overboard.

Those who had been fortunate enough to be above deck when the explosion occurred now found themselves in the ice water and faced the brutal reality of death by exposure. O'Malley and Baldwin reached the strongback and were later joined by Commander Peterson and 2 other crewmen. Both O'Malley and Baldwin lost consciousness and when they awoke found themselves aboard the *Raritan*.

It was Ray O'Malley's first and last trip on the *Escanaba*. Of the 103 men aboard *Escanaba*, 101 were lost. Melvin Baldwin died in September of 1964 so today Ray O'Malley is the sole survivor. O'Malley had been in the Coast Guard 4 1/2 years and his first duty on the *Escanaba* was at the wheel when he heard the explosion. He spent 8 years in the Coast Guard and then in civilian life became a Chicago policeman like his father, grandfather and many of his relatives. Ray and his wife Dolly never miss a Coast Guard Festival.

No conclusive evidence has ever been found for the cause of the loss of *Escanaba*. O'Malley has stated that the firing he heard prior to the explosion had not come from *Esky* nor was there another ship within earshot. One remote but possible explanation which was given was that it could have been the hydrophone effect of a torpedoe heard through the loud speaker in the wheelhouse. A torpedoe hit seemed logical because no one disputed the fact that the convoy was in U-boat territory. Other possible reasons were a mine or an internal explosion, such as one of the depth charges stored in the ship's magazine. However no official cause has ever been ascribed.

Escanaba's history and record of its sinking is only one of hundreds in the Navy and Coast Guard files which give comparable accounts of quiet deeds of heroism and devotion ending in tragic loss. The Coast Guard lost 16 Cutters in World War II. *Escanaba* ended her days at position 60 degrees 40 minutes North, 52 degrees 10 minutes West in 3,000 feet of water off the southern end tip of Greénland, 2,000 miles from her Grand Haven home.

II

News of the sinking reached Grand Haven by 10:00 AM that same day—June 13, 1943. It was the top radio story. The Muskegon Chronicle ran an Extra which turned loose the newsboys to chant their sing-song gibberish through the streets bringing war weary people to their windows and doors. Five cents would get you the fine print below the glaring, come-on headlines—ESCANABA SUNK.

Grand Haven received the news with stunned disbelief. It was a deep, personal loss—the kind that makes one want to be alone for awhile before discussing it with anyone. Those men lost had been part of the spirit of the City—good friends. News of the *Escanaba* bored into the soul of the City more than anyone had imagined it might.

Very little was known about *Escanaba*'s whereabouts or war time activities since she left Grand Haven in March, 1942. All anyone knew was the official announcement and the brief information given in the telegrams from the War Department with the too-familiar words, "The War Department regrets to inform you . . ." Three of the crew—Machinist 1st Class Max Bonham, Chief Machinist's Mate Layton Counselor and Chief Machinist's Mate Charles Mickle—were West Michigan men. Their wives, children and other relatives still live in the West Michigan area. For these families—as with all the families of those who had been aboard the ill-fated Cutter—the yellow telegrams brought the fullest measure of war grief.

Navy Communique 417 gave the official news release:
The U.S.C.G. Cutter Escanaba assigned to convoy duty in the North Atlantic has been reported lost. All hands except two enlisted men were lost with the ship. Next of kin have been notified.

The loss of *Escanaba* brought to 99 the number of ships lost by the United States up to that time.

But Grand Haven, like the rest of the Nation, had become toughened to war and after the initial shock was shaken off the townspeople's decision was swift and resolute—there would be another *Escanaba*. Plans were hastily drawn up for an "old fashioned" Coast Guard birthday celebration—something that had been displaced by the war. It would be the kick-off for a War Bond drive to raise the money to build a Cutter to replace *Escanaba*. A goal of $1,000,000 was set, the approximate cost of a replacement vessel at that time. And that was not calculated on the value of the bonds at maturity, that was to be $1,000,000 up front money. Chairman Ted Bolt announced that the bond drive would begin August 4, 1943 and would conclude on or before November 4—just 3 months to raise a million dollars.

It was billed as Coast Guard Day, a one day memorial celebration which was held on Wednesday, August 4, 1943. Although perhaps not intended as such, it had nostalgic overtones that reached back to the roots of the singular relationship between Grand Haven and the Coast Guard.

A parade, which featured the Coast Guard with its own band, marched up Franklin Street to Fifth, over to Washington Street and then down Washington to the reviewing stand in front of the Service Men's Center. Ray O'Malley and Mel Baldwin had been sent here by the Service to be the honored guests—a scenario which would be repeated by O'Malley for the next 47 years.

A lunch was held at the American Legion and then from 1:00-3:00 o'clock the old Water Fete activities—breeches buoy drill, pulling boat races, swimming races, capsize drill—took place at Kelly Park—*Escanaba*'s former home. Between 3:00 and 5:00 PM at the Coast Guard Training Station the public was treated to races on the obstacle course and boxing matches.

At 7:30 PM 20,000 people attended a very solemn Escanaba Memorial Service at Kelly Park. It was at that moment Grand Haven's annual Coast Guard birthday celebration—today's Coast Guard Festival—began to mature in meaning and purpose. After that August 4, 1943 Memorial Service, and events which were to follow in the next 9 months, Grand Haven's celebration had a new direction, a new objective, a new mission—which it has never forgotten. Until then the birthday celebration had been what birthday parties usually are—fun and games—with a nod to those who had been lost in the line of duty. But at that juncture in history we begin to see a change in those roles—a deepening consideration and better understanding of what it meant to wear the Coast Guard shield, to be willing to give the full measure and live up to the old life savers credo, "You've got to go out, but you don't have to come back."

Escanaba was not coming back.

CHAPTER 23

THE AFTERMATH

During the Escanaba Memorial Service August 4, 1943, Chairman Ted Bolt announced the start of the bond drive to build a replacement vessel for *Escanaba*. And as he did he also began what Mayor Marge Boon, 44 years later, would refer to as "One of the most extraordinary civic achievements of World War II."

Within the first hour $15,000 worth of bonds were sold—by the end of the day $40,000 worth. Grand Haven sublimated its grief by becoming totally committed to the cause—every man, woman and child. O'Malley and Baldwin conducted a 2 week campaign as they toured throughout Michigan. Out of State relatives of those lost on *Escanaba* pitched in. Grand Haven was divided into 5 districts and 100 women sought War Bond pledges door-to-door. Every Bond was affixed with a sticker which read "I Remember the Escanaba." The Tribune kept a daily "thermometer" of the progress and by September 22—the half-way date—$563,142 had been subscribed. At that point the City bought $60,000 worth of bonds and by the end of September the $1,000,000 goal had been reached. The drive received extensive publicity and had captured the imagination of people state wide, so even though the goal had been reached the sales kept coming. The final tally was $1,218,301.

At that time the 255 foot Cutter *Otsego* was being built at San Pedro, California. It was the general policy of the Government that war bond dollars could not be earmarked for a particular cause—and with good reason. However, the Coast Guard was so impressed by Grand Haven's bond drive effort the decision was made that the *Otsego* would be renamed *Escanaba*, WPG-64, in honor of her namesake, the former *Escanaba*, WPG-77. *Escanaba II* was launched on March 25, 1946. The ceremony in California was attended by a large delegation from Grand Haven which included Mayor Edmond Wilds, Chamber of

Commerce President Mart Erickson, Matron of Honor Mrs. Blanch H. Turner, Mrs. Patience E. Teschendorf—widow of *Escanaba* crewman , Mr. and Mrs. Edward Soule with their son Thomas and daughter Ruth, Mr. and Mrs. Walter Nilsson, Mrs. Axel Colson, Mr. and Mrs. Angus Little, Mr. and Mrs. Bernard Muller, Mr. and Mrs. Henry McKay, Marian and Myrtle Bavery, Lieutenant Cornelius VerDuin, Mrs. Everett Swemer and Margaret Addison.

The ship was christened by Patience Teschendorf. Mayor Wilds presented a plaque that remained on the ship until it was scrapped, at which time it was removed and returned to the City. It now hangs in Grand Haven's Tri-Cities Museum and reads:

The citizens of Grand Haven, Michigan in a special patriotic drive, purchased U.S. War Bonds totaling $1,218,000 toward the cost of this ship. This vessel replaces the original Coast Guard Cutter Escanaba lost in 1943.

Escanaba II never visited Grand Haven. Her first assignment was Alemeda, California. She later served on the East Coast for awhile and then was decommissioned at Curtis Bay, Maryland in October, 1954. Reactivated August 16, 1966 she was assigned to New Bedford, Massachusetts as one of 21 ships which manned the Atlantic weather station "Delta", located 650 miles southeast of Newfoundland, east of Nova Scotia. Patrols lasted 3 weeks and they could not leave the station until relieved. While headed to the station on December 27, 1970 *Escanaba II* rescued 31 crewmen from the wrecked Finnish tanker *Ragny* in what Commander Lawson Brigham—captain of *Escanaba III* in 1987—described as, "One of the most dangerous and successful rescues at sea in modern times."

Escanaba II was scrapped in 1973.

For weeks after news of the loss of *Escanaba* people strolled aimlessly past Kelly Park—just remembering. Any memento left behind from the Cutter suddenly became a treasure. Kids scoured the hallowed grounds and docks hoping to find any kind of a souvenir. Then someone thought of the wooden masts that had been removed from *Escanaba* when she had gone to Manitowac in October, 1940 to be outfitted for war. Had they been saved? If so, where were they? Mayor Wilds inquired and found that one of the masts had been taken to Battle Creek, Michigan where plans were being made to erect it as a memorial to past servicemen. He also learned of the life raft which had been recovered from the wreckage. Following a good deal of persuasion and politicking—with much cooperation from District Commander Captain E.T. Shanley and his officers in Chicago—the Navy deeded the mast and life raft over to Grand Haven in early 1944. Plans were made to place *Esky's* mast at Kelly Park with the dedication set for Memorial Day. At that time Glenn Eaton was president of the Junior Chamber of Commerce—today's Jaycees—and had been a helpful, enthusiastic supporter in acquiring the trophies. Mayor Wilds solicited the help of the American Legion and Veterans of Foreign War but turned the details of the dedication over to Eaton.

Escanaba's 60 foot mast was set in Kelly Park and dedicated on Memorial Day, May 30, 1944 in a solemn ceremony attended by hundreds. Sally Green, a Chamber of Commerce employee, was flower girl. Captain Ralph W. Dempwolf, Ninth District Commander, addressed the assembly:

> The men of the *Escanaba* had faith. They fought for principles which, even though they were often obscured in the confusion of war, are dear to all of us. Those principles guided their efforts for victory and peace. Let all of us who survive not forget them. Let us never lose the faith that the crew of the Escanaba had in the Service and in their community and in us. Let us go on with the job.

Mayor Wilds dedicated the mast with this pronouncement:

> The full rigged mast, life boat and other rigging of the U.S. Coast Guard Cutter Escanaba are preserved here and will remain through the years as a fitting tribute to a proud ship and her gallant crew.
>
> We dedicate this memorial to those brave men who died while defending the ideals and liberties of the great Nation they served. May it ever remind us of those who so valiantly gave their lives that we might live and enjoy the blessings of freedom and democracy.

The plaque at the base of the mast read simply:

> In memory of the U.S. Coast Guard Cutter Escanaba, lost in action on convoy duty in the North Atlantic,

June 13, 1943.

It had been less than a year since the people of Grand Haven had received the news that *Escanaba*—'Their ship'—had been lost. For them the dedication of the mast was a sanctifying, sobering experience. As mentioned previously, there have been 3 National events in the past 50 years which were momentous enough to be remembered vividly by those who lived though them. For those who lived in Grand Haven through the war years we can add a 4th—the bulletin of June 13, 1943.

A program for the *Escanaba* mast dedication was printed through the efforts of the Junior Chamber of Commerce, under the guidance of its president Glenn Eaton.

Maintenance of the wooden mast is ongoing. Grand Haven's Board Walk along the River was complete in 1984—the City's Sesquicentennial year. As a Sesquicentennial gift to the City, the officers and crew of the Cutter *Acacia*, in cooperation with the City crews, erected an interpretive exhibit at Escanaba Park which describes *Acacia*, her duties and capabilities and provides an ideal waystop today for people strolling the Board Walk.

With Escanaba Park all spruced up, the state of disrepair of the *Escanaba* mast became quite obvious. In 1984 the mast was taken down and completely refinished by Lieutenant Commander Wayne Verry's crew from the *Acacia* on the recommendation of Coast Guard Commandant Admiral James Gracey. When it was replaced, an elaborate rededication ceremony was held on Memorial Day, Monday, May 27, 1985—the 40th anniversary of the original dedication. The 1985 Memorial Day Parade went down Washington Street as usual but then continued on down Harbor Avenue to Escanaba Park. The Parade Marshal was Colonel Nelson Voshel, with Honorary Marshals Alie Tysman, Gerritt Swiftney, Al VanOordt, Major Fred Mastenbrook, Glen Hinkle and Steve Biros. Mayor Marge Boon presided as Ray O'Malley raised *Escanaba*'s call letters up the mast. From a Coast Guard boat flowers were scattered on the river by Rebecca Augustyn, Amanda and Jennifer Bottje, Roberta Easterly, Tiffany Henshaw and Melissa Stille as Jack Melcher sounded Taps. The Grand Haven High School Band, under the direction of Craig Flahive and Mike Reid, played the National Anthem and the High School choir, directed by Shirley Lemon, sang the Battle Hymn of the Republic. Fittingly, a special guest was William Wilds, son of Edmond Wilds who had been Mayor when the *Escanaba* mast was dedicated 40 years ago. The newly painted mast glittered in the sunlight as if in appreciation. Also, at that time the plaque which had been on the large stone in the middle of Escanaba Park and the plaque that had been at the base of the mast were both placed on a single stone which stands today in front of the mast. Grand Haven had not forgotten.

Escanaba's life raft was refurbished in 1987 by Boy Scout David Hoffer, the same year the City planted the shrubs and erected the post and rope balustrade—all of this in preparation for the commissioning of *Escanaba III*. A brass ship's bell was added to the mast which adds a nautical touch—but it is not from *Escanaba*.

Under the direction of Scoutmaster Dan Putman, in 1989 Boy Scout Troop #246 refinished the mast's spar as well as the 40 posts of the balustrade around the mast.

Many people see the mast today but few are aware of the full meaning behind it. It is, in the strictest sense of the term, a shrine. It has been said that minuscule amounts of cremation ashes of former Coast Guardsmen have found their way to the base of the mast as a final pilgrimage. *Escanaba*'s old mast has been the focal point for every annual Coast Guard Memorial Service since it was consecrated 46 years ago. It nobly symbolizes not only the devotion of all Coast Guardsmen who have given the full measure but also the spirit and dedication which created Coast Guard City, U.S.A.

CHAPTER 24

THE POSTWAR YEARS

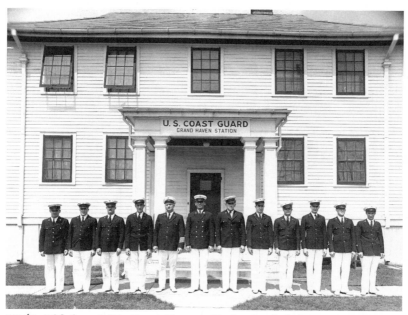

1941 Lifeboat Station Crew. (Left to right) Lou Stormer, Charles Plowman, Henry Marsh, C.F. VanDoorne, Tom Laird, Office in Charge Fred Wendel, George Olsen, Myers, C.W. Fisher, George Edwards, Stanley Loyer and Howard Smith. Courtesy Grand Haven Area Historical Society.

When the productive might of the United States hit full stride it was just a matter of time before World War II would end. Allied victories over German submarines in the North Atlantic, elimination of Nazi airplanes over England, routing of Axis tanks in North Africa and demolition of Italian artillary in Italy ultimately led to D-Day—the Allied invasion of Europe. VE—

Cutter "Tahoma" stationed in Grand Haven December 13, 1945—November 1947.

Victory in Europe—Day came May 7, 1945. Victories in the Coral Seas and Midway, Coast Guard assisted landings on Guadalcanal, Iwo Jima, the Philippines and Okinawa and finally the Atomic Bomb resulted in VJ—Victory over Japan—Day on August 14, 1945. World War II came to an end as World War I had just 26 years earlier—with the victorious Allies achieving unconditional surrender over the enemy.

Everyone scrambled to get back to a peace time footing. Europe, England, Russia and Japan had to dig out. For America the transition was easier—it was a matter of reassigning the postwar resources. On December 13, 1945 the Coast Guard Cutter *Tahoma*—one of *Escanaba*'s 5 sisterships—arrived in Grand Haven. *Tahoma* had been at the Soo and Cleveland prior to World War II. She came to Grand Haven as a seasoned veteran of rugged North Atlantic convoy duty, but had shed her camouflage coat for a glistening white hull and was ready for Lake duty again.

Through the duration Grand Haven had never lost touch with its Coast Guard ties and now it was anxious to resume the unique prewar relationship it had initiated—the annual celebration of the Coast Guard birthday anniversary. But "Water Fete" was dated because many of the old Life Saving Service skills which were still part of the surfman's daily routine in the 1930's were not practiced after the war—"Fete" having gone the way of Lucky Strike green. "Festival" seemed to be term most conventional and fashionable in West Michigan; Benton Harbor-St. Joseph had its Blossom Time Festival, Bangor had its Apple Festival, Traverse City its Cherry Festival and Holland its Tulip Festival. "Festival" better described what the "Fete" had involved into so it was decided the City would rename its annual birthday celebration the "Grand Haven Coast Guard Festival." "

1946 was the transition year and would be the only Festival held while *Tahoma* was stationed here. She left in 1947 and was replaced by the black hulled Cutter *Woodbine*, a buoy tender which made Grand Haven her home for the next 25 years.

By 1948 the Festival began to take on the profile which indentifies it today as one of the premier summer attractions in the Nation. Adhering to August 4 as the focal date, the 1948 celebration took place from Monday, August 2 to Wednesday, August 4. Monday evening there was a reception at the American Legion followed by a buffet dinner.

The 290 foot, 74 foot beam icebreaker *Mackinaw* paid a visit from its home base in Cheboygan, Michigan in 1948, as it would at Coast Guard Festivals for many years to come. Built during the war to assure clear year-round shipping lanes for the iron ore from the upper Great Lakes, when launched at Toledo in 1944 she was the world's most powerful icebreaker. On Tuesday both the *Woodbine* and *Mackinaw* were open for public inspection.

The official party had a luncheon at Schuler's on Tuesday noon and dinner at the Spring Lake Country Club that evening. That same night there was a Window Tour of the downtown stores followed by a Street Dance.

Admiral Joseph F. Farley, Commandant of the U.S. Coast Guard, attended the Admiral's Luncheon on Wednesday aboard the *Mackinaw*. Early that afternoon competition in swimming, diving, water skiing, canoe tilting and fly casting was featured with an added attraction of a water rescue by the Coast Guard. The land parade was followed by the National Memorial Service during which Admiral Farley presented medals and awards to Coast Guardsmen and 2 more bronze plaques were dedicated on the brick wall at Kelly Park. These plaques honored Commanders of the Tenth District, Lieutenant Commander Chester Lippincott—1923-27 and Lieutenant Commander William Wolff—1927-30.

The brick wall which displays these 7 plaques was renovated in 1981 but the plaques remain there today as they were dedicated a half century ago. However there is one plaque missing—an 8th bronze commemorative for the last man to serve as Tenth District Commander before the headquarters were moved from Grand Haven: Lieutenant Ward W. Bennett—1934-1939. It is an oversight which can and should be corrected.

The 1948 Festival was capped off with a Venetian Night Boat Parade and a spectacular fireworks display.

In 1949, as a result of actions taken by Mayor Martin Boon and the Grand Haven City Council, Kelly Park was renamed Escanaba Memorial Park to commemorate the World War II loss of the Cutter and her 101 crewmen. The ceremony to reconsecrate Escanaba's old home took place, appropriately, during the 1949 Coast Guard Festival with Mayor Boon presiding. Commander Kelly himself would have approved of that action.

It is not the purpose of this mongraph to innumerate each of the postwar Coast Guard Festivals or even attempt to credit the hundreds of volunteers who have made them possible. That will be left for another publication by persons who were more intimately involved with the annual celebration. Rather we will conclude this work with an overview of the 40 years from 1950 to 1990—the relative modern history of Coast Guard City, U.S.A.

Charlie Bugielski left McLellan's in 1938 and opened the M and M Variety Store at 711 Washington Street. The Coast Guard Festival has never had an official headquarters of its own, but from 1938 to 1981—43 years—the back room of the M and M Store was the unofficial headquarters. An invitation to Charlie's "office" was a visit to grass roots America volunteerism. Nothing pretentious—just a bare-bones work station that reached out to every corner of the country from one Festival to the next as Bugielski contacted Heads of State, Service brass at all levels, put together parades, airshows, carnivals, drum and bugle shows and—ah yes—those amazing firework finales. When a person visits historic Williamsburg, Virginia and sees the room in which Patrick Henry, et al, plotted the overthrow of English domination one is struck by the modestness of the setting. The reason for the phenomenon is that things which leave such a mark on history are embellished in our minds. The same analogy can be drawn for 711 Washington Street. The Coast Guard Festival announces to the Nation annually that Grand Haven is Coast Guard City, U.S.A. Admirals, generals and world leaders have come to Grand Haven for the event, much of which can be attributed to Charlie "Hustle's" charisma. If ever we were to ascribe a founding home to the Festival it would have to be the back room of Charlie Bugielski's M and M Store. It was no bigger than a mini-van, but out of that humble back room flowed the stuff of which legends are made.

Aside from the Coast Guard and military brass, airshows, big name attractions, drum and bugle corps, carnivals, queens and the fabulous fireworks, the Coast Guard Festival—and Chuck Bugielski—are best remembered for the chimerical parades. They were Charlie's trademark. And if you were to poll the spectators who have viewed these extravaganzas over the years as to their choice for the number one attraction year after year the nod would go to the Scottville Clown Band. This zany group was organized in Scottville, Michigan—8 miles east of Ludington—in 1903 as the Scottville Merchant's "Fun Band", later called the "Ladies Band" and then in 1920 officially took the name "Scottville Clown Band." In the early years the Band appeared at functions in nearby townships and counties. Reorganized after WW II the Band, led by "Drum Major" George Wilson—who still leads the group today—was literally "discovered" by Bugielski and the Clown Band made its first "big" appearance in Grand Haven's Labor Day parade in 1948. Today the 110 members have a demanding summer schedule of 35-40 performances which takes them State wide, but they have never missed a Coast Guard Festival since 1951.

The Scottville Clown Band is such a popular part of the Coast Guard Festival that today it appears twice in the parade; first on a flatbed truck as the first band and then it is driven back so the Band can stroll—to use the term "march" would be an affront— through the parade route as the last musical group. What one tends to lose sight of is that through all of their antics these "clowns" play excellent music. They are, in the vernacular of show business, the "hook" or "top bill.'" No one who is familiar with Coast Guard Festival parades would ever think of leaving without hearing the strains of "When the Saints Go Marching In" or "Basin Street Blues"—2 of the Band's trademark tunes—

The Scottville Clown Band has performed at every Coast Festival since 1951. Courtesy Grand Haven Area Historical Society.

bringing up the rear with "Drum Major" George Wilson "strutting" his stuff with his toilet plunger baton. And there is an interesting analogy for what occurs next. The New Orleans funeral bands play dirges going to the cemetery with the casket and the mourners but when they return the band plays Dixieland, such as "When the Saints Go Marching In." The swaying, dancing, strutting rejuvenated mourners following the band are called the "first line." Invariably there are bystanders and spectators who get caught up in the occasion and take to the street to swing along with the parade. This group is referred to as the "second line." As the Scottville Clown Band passes they pick up their own "second liners" who follow the Band to the official reviewing stand where the Festival parade has its finale.

There the Band serenades the Coast Guard brass and dignitaries with another of their signature tunes—"The Stripper"—during which one of the Band members in female drag does a spoof burlesque tease to the delight, laughter and standing applause of the Coast Guard officers and other dignitaries. It makes a joyous curtain for another successful Charlie Bugielski parade.

In the 1940's Grand Haven City officials and Festival committeepersons began making annual visits to Washington, D.C. to coordinate the August 4th birthday celebration with Coast Guard personnel. One may choose to call it lobbying or politicking but the effort was sincere and at least demonstrated to Coast Guard officials that the road to Coast Guard City was a two way street.

Claude VerDuin went on the Grand Haven City Council in 1948. Claude was no stranger to Washington or to politics. During WW II Secretary of the Interior, Harold Ickes, had appointed VerDuin Deputy Coordinator of Fisheries in the Great Lakes Region. After the war Claude was a lobbyist for the St. Lawrence Seaway for 7 years, Secretary of the Great Lakes Harbor Association and also, for a time, had a position with the Michigan Municipal Utilities. VerDuin was elected Mayor in 1952, serving until 1957. During this time he became Director of the Tri-Cities (Grand Haven, Spring Lake and Ferrysburg) Chamber of Commerce, filling that position from 1955-1970. It was during the 1950's and 60's that the annual trip to Washington took on proportions which significantly strengthened the City's ties with the Coast Guard. As many as 60 persons would make the trip to attend the National Chamber of Commerce Meeting and then call on the Coast Guard Headquarters. This tradition is still carried on today and the friendships which have resulted cannot be over-estimated.

The Coast Guard Academy Band was organized in 1925 but for 39 years had no official status, even though it had played for every inaugural ceremony since Herbert Hoover. Grand Haven was instrumental—no pun intended—in having a bill passed by Congress on April 10, 1964 which changed the Academy Band into the official United States Coast Guard Band. Deeds of this sort on a national scale seem a long way from the 1934 Tenth District picnic—but not really. It is just that Grand Haven has never forgotten.

It was during Claude's tenure with the Chamber of Commerce that the Grand Haven Water Thrill Show became a popular event at the Grand Haven Water Front Stadium and a regular attraction of the Coast Guard Festival. The show was put together by water skier Lyle "Whitey" White assisted by boat drivers Bob Payne and Felix Pytlinske. "Whitey" had no peer when it came to inovative stunts on water skis. He was the first to "water ski" atop an 8 foot ladder—but that was not all. He would then put on his water skiis, jump from the ladder and finish the performance in conventional style. He was also the first person to take off from the water suspended from a lighted kite and soar 30 feet above the craning crowd. He was one of the first to try skiing barefooted, standing on his head or with no hands. "Whitey" was a true showman. Boat jumping by Payne and Pytlinske was also a crowd

(Left to right) Charlie Bugielski, Gerald Ford and Claude VerDuin-1984. Courtesy Claude VerDuin.

pleaser.

Glenn Eaton II was born in Pennsylvania and came to Grand Haven in 1939. After the war Glenn Eaton stayed in the area and went to work for the Anderson-Bolling Company in Spring Lake. But his home was in Grand Haven and so that is where he became politicly involved in public service. After serving 2 terms on the City Council—1956-60—Glenn was elected Mayor for one term—1961-62. He has been a member of the Board of Light and Power for 23 years and even served as Plant Manager—without pay—from time to time.

During Glenn's term as Mayor another tradition was established between Grand Haven and the Coast Guardsmen who serve here—honorary citizenship. The *Woodbine*'s 5 officers and 50 crewmen, as well as the crew of the Lifeboat Station, were made honorary citizens of Grand Haven in a dignified ceremony at City Hall. Eaton kept abreast of what Servicemen were being transferred here and would send them a welcome from the City. Upon their arrival in Grand Haven the Guardsmen were honored in the Council Chambers in the formal presentation of a certificate which bestowed upon them honorary Grand Haven Citizenship. This tradition is carried on today.

The feature which has given depth, meaning and National

(Left to right) Charlie Bugielski, Councilman Virgil Quebeman, and Mayor Glenn Eaton present a banner to Sarnia, Canada, 1961. Courtesy Coast Guard Festival Committee.

purpose to the Coast Guard Festival is the National Memorial Service at Escanaba Park. Glenn Eaton was instrumental in developing this annual commemoration from the dedication of *Escanaba*'s mast in 1944 to the ceremony's present day profundity.

These short biographical sketches give some feeling for the respective roles this triumverate played in the 35 years they worked together to elevate the Coast Guard Festival to a position of National prominence. However it should be understood that their parts overlapped so the total effect was a team effort. It should be further understood that they did not do it all on their own. There were many, many volunteers and committeepersons who assisted along the way, but these three—Charlie Bugielski, Claude VerDuin and Glenn Eaton—were the catalysts behind this remarkable success story. Grand Haven was indeed fortunate to have these 3 dedicated workers at such a critical phase of the evolution of the Coast Guard Festival. Each was honored by being designated the Parade Marshall: Bugielski in 1981, VerDuin in 1985 and Eaton in 1986. Bugielski retired from the Festival Committee in 1981 and was followed by VerDuin in 1983.

Dr. William Creason came to Grand Haven in 1946 after graduating from dental school. During the Korean Conflict—1950-53—Bill was called into the Navy and served as a dentist in Germany. While in a Berlin night club Bill had the opportunity to see a demonstration of a small—approximately 12 feet long—water fountain which had accompanying background music and a backdrop of multicolored lights that played on the screen of water. The height of the water was adjusted by the operator to fit the mood of the music and the hue of the light. The water spigots were in a tank so as the screen of water was shot into the air it fell back into the tank to be recirculated. The effect was very pleasing and after the show Creason was able to inspect the mechanics of the apparatus and talk with the inventor-operator. Bill had no particular use for it at that time, just a fascination. But, unbeknownst to Creason then, the day would come when he would have a very special application for that German minature "musical fountain." Creason left the Navy after the Korean Conflict and returned to his private dental practice in Grand Haven in 1953.

Dr. Bill Creason was elected to the City Council in 1955-56, during the time that Claude VerDuin was Mayor. Claude vacated the office and Bill was elected Mayor in 1957-58 but then left the political arena after serving just one term. When Glenn Eaton was Mayor he called upon Bill to fill the seat of a Councilman who had passed away—Joseph "Sky" Swartz. Creason served out that term—1961-62—and then went on to serve as Mayor for 3 consecutive terms—1963-69.

To anyone visiting or living in Grand Haven in the 1950's and 60's the obvious City blight which needed radical attention was the Riverfront. Up until the 1930's the River area was the hub of Grand Haven's commerce but when the carferries left in 1933—as did the cruise ships when the demand for Lake passenger service disappeared in the 1930's—the entire Riverfront began to fall into a state of disrepair. In the early post-war years the situation was apparent but by the late 1950's it was an embarrassment. Viewing it today it is difficult to remember how decadent it had become. Harbor Industry was the only business on the River that made any attempt at beautification but

1965 Coast Guard Festival lawn party at Creason home. 3rd from left, Nancy Nagtzaam, Miss U.S. Coast Guard. Holding elephant trunk, Gov. George Romney. 2nd from right, Charlie Bugielski. Far right, Mayor Bill Creason. Courtesy Grand Haven Area Historical Society.

Henry Parker's efforts alone were not enough.

Almon and Watson McCall were publishers of the Grand Haven Tribune at that time and were enthusiastic advocates of cleaning up the Riverfront. In a conversation with Mayor Bill Creason in 1958 Almon said, "You know Bill, if you really want to help this town you could put something over on Dewey Hill to draw attention to the Riverfront. Then people would get the idea and before long we'd see some improvements down there." It was not a particularly new idea because it was the focal point of downtown Grand Haven—a landmark that could not be missed. Flag poles had been placed up on the Hill at various times through the years. Ed Kinkema, Sr. had suggested a cross. As mentioned earlier, the whole community turned out on April 16, 1941 to plant pine trees to stabilize the creeping giant. It was not that Dewey Hill had been overlooked, it was just that everyone enjoyed its majesty but had never seriously thought about using

1930's cane pole perch fishing on the South Pier. Courtesy Harold Bretschneider.

in any way other than its natural stateliness to promote the City.

Creason mulled over McCall's comments and thought about the water fountain he had seen in Germany. Claude VerDuin had an active Area Promotion Committee at the Chamber of Commerce and during the period Creason was off the City Council—1959-60—Bill became chairman of that committee. Bill proposed to the committee an idea for a large version—a very large version—of the musical fountain he had seen on stage in Berlin to be placed on Dewey Hill as a means of rallying civic pride to improve the Riverfront. The idea sold but no one was entirely aware of all the details which were ahead.

The first obstacle was that Grand Haven did not own all of Dewey Hill—as had been presumed through the years. Clare Jarecki owned part of it, which was subsequently purchased by Ted Bolt, acting for the Hofma Trust, and then given to the City. The first hurdle had been cleared.

It was initially thought that $17,000 and donated labor would be adequate to prepare the land and build the lighted water display. Creason formed a Fountain Committee of himself, Bill Booth, Clarence Smith, Marshall White, Foster Poe, Glenn DePagter, J.B. Sims, Preston Bilz, Dick Hammer, Bernie Boyink, R.V. Terril, George Purcell, George VerDuin, Walter Bruin, Bob Warnaar, Tom Fullerton and Ron Hartsema. The Gardner-Denver Company—Brice Maddox CEO—contributed substantially to the total effort. After 2 years of meeting, planning, experimenting, hoping and $150,000 later the Grand Haven Musical Fountain had its inaugural showing at 9:30 PM, Memorial Day, Thursday, May 30, 1963. It was resoundingly received.

The viewing was—and is today—free and people had just never seen anything quite like it. And it was not merely a very large version of the musical fountain Creason had seen in Germany but rather a prodigiously large edition of it. The statistics are mind boggling. Water is pumped from the River up to a blacktopped holding basin the size of a football field. Electric pumps in the control room are capable of delivering 300 horsepower and can recirculate the water in the basin at the rate of 4,000 gallons a minute through a maze of pipes 1 1/2 miles long. Water patterns are made by 1,300 nozzles of various sizes which can shoot the water a few feet or 100 feet into the air, make the water look like a peacock tail, or make the spray swing, sway—and even hula. The kaleidoscopic lighting adds a surreal veil to the dancing mist. Possible combinations of color, water height and patterns number into the multi-trillions. An average 20 minute show today takes more than 100 hours to prepare and will have 2,500 to 2,800 Fountain changes. It is all computer regulated but even then the control panel in the submerged pump room resembles something out of the NASA Command Center.

During the Holiday Season no water sprays from the Fountain but the Christmas story is broadcast across the frozen River each night as lights illuminate the Wise Men astride 32 foot camels walking up Dewey Hill, 16 foot shepards watching over 6 foot sheep down near the River, 22 foot angels high up on the Hill overlooking a 28 foot creche on the brow of Dewey Hill. Betty Ellis designed the scene and painted all the figures. The Grand Haven Rotary Club assumes the responsibility of erecting and disassembling the Nativity Scene each Holiday Season— regardless of the weather conditions.

Donated time, talent, equipment as well as dollars made the Musical Fountain possible. A marvel of modern engineering, the Fountain is equally impressive as a monument to civic endeavor and cooperation. The free showings are presented nightly during the summer months and at Christmas time.

Environmental concerns were an upmost consideration in the design and placement of the Musical Fountain. Except for the buildings down at River level which house the banks of speakers little else can be seen. Even the 54 foot "feature" pole at the top of Dewey Hill is retractable and therefore not visible except for special events. The pole can be "dressed" to take on the appearance of a star at Christmas, a cross at Easter or an anchor during the Coast Guard Festival. The mechanism to raise and lower the huge telephone pole—which takes about 5 minutes— was engineered and contributed by the Dake Corporation.

The Musical Fountain accomplished exactly what everyone invovled had hoped it would. It was not only an instant success on its own but things began to happen along the Riverfront.

President Paul Johnson and the other trustees of the Loutit Foundation believed in the Musical Fountain from the start and made signifcant contributions to see it through to its completion. The Foundation then initiated the Riverfront restoration on the east side of the River by purchasing land when it became available and then holding it for future reconstruction and development. The Foundation eventually acquired all of the Riverfront

Paul Johnson hosting officers at the 1964 Coast Guard Festival.

property from Washington to Howard Streets and then improved their holdings by placing over 1,300 feet of sheet piling along the River bank. Today a large portion of that is City owned Bicentennial Park.

In the first years of the "Whitey" White Water Thrill Show and the Musical Fountain the only viewing for these shows was from the banks of the River or from some temporary bleachers which had been set up on the Harbor Industry property. The Grand Trunk Railroad had discontinued passenger service to Grand Haven in 1955 but until 1963 the City's negotiations with Grand Trunk to acquire the Railroad's Riverfront properties had been unsuccessful. During this time The Coast Guard nudged Grand Trunk a little closer toward the "fait accompli" when *Woodbine* Commander, Lieutenant Commander Joe Fox, used his Cutter and crew to remove all of the old, dilapidated Grand Trunk dock piling which was "obstructing" the channel. Completion of the Musical Fountain may or may not have tipped the balance in the thinking of the Grand Trunk officials, but by 1967 the terms of vacating their holdings had been finalized and the Loutit

Foundation procured the Riverfront property. This eventually made possible Grand Haven's Tri-Cities Museum, the Waterfront Stadium, the City Marina and the Sesquicentennial Ferry Landing—the sundial through the efforts of Al Jacobson, the brass Grand River anaglyph through the courtesy of the Grand Haven Brass Foundary, Hung Liang plant metallurgist.

By 1977 the Loutit Foundation had invested $828,100 in the Riverfront, Fountain and Museum. The Foundation's role in the Riverfront beautification can never be overstated.

The Musical Fountain had its shakedown through June and July of 1963 but there had yet to be an official "throwing of the switch." That special occasion was saved for the 1963 Coast Guard Festival—the Fountain's first big time show.

One of the dignitaries who attended the Festival that year was Major General (retired) Benjamin D. Foulois—the Army Air Force's First pilot. In 1910 he had learned to fly by correspondence with the Wright Brothers who also signed his license. As he stated it, "In one day I soloed, made my first landing and my first crack up. Then we threw the text books away—they were all wrong." The 1963 Festival was another great success but everything that year was keyed toward the finale— the official unveiling of the Musical Fountain which was to feature a very special Coast Guard show.

Coast Guard Commandant Admiral Edwin Roland sent as his representative that year Rear Admiral Richard D. Schmidtman. A mock switch had been rigged at the Riverfront reviewing stand for Schmidtman so when the moment arrived the Admiral could throw the arm and "start" the Fountain. There was no wiring that went with the switch so its effectiveness was obviously questionable. Admiral Schmidtman turned to Claude VerDuin and asked, "Is this thing going to work?" VerDuin—who knew the whole procedure was going to be accomplished by a system of prearranged light signals—answered by saying, "Well Admiral, if it doesn't you and I are going to be standing here with a lot of egg on our face." Admiral Schmidtman threw the switch and— there it was. The Grand Haven Musical Fountain sprang to life. And as the strains of Semper Paratus—the finest of all the service marches—came booming across the River in cadence with the colorful dancing water for the first time, Admiral Schmidtman filled with pride turned and said, "Throughout my career I have heard about Grand Haven and the way you folks feel toward the

Coast Guard but I never believed it. Now I believe it. Without a doubt, this has got to be Coast Guard City, U.S.A.!"

Bugielski, VerDuin, Eaton and the press had, for variety sake through the years, used different ways of describing Grand Haven and the Festival—"Coast Guard City, U.S.A." certainly being one of those. So Admiral Schmidtman's artictulation of the term may not have been the first use of the title for Grand Haven but that time it had an official ring. Throughout the Service today Grand Haven, Michigan is known as "Coast Guard City."

Admiral Schmidtman's son, Captain John "Jack" Schmidtman, USCG, was stationed in the Ninth District Office in Cleveland, and came to Grand Haven in 1988 to reenact his fathers "throwing of the switch" on the occasion of the Musical Fountain's 25th anniversary.

The Musical Fountain and Charlie Bugielski's fabulous fireworks have been the finale of the Festival for over a quarter century. The Saturday night crowds viewing the spectacle in the 1960's and 70's were estimated at over 200,000 for any given show. But, as amazing as the crowds of people, were the boats that jammed the Harbor for the closing performance. To say you could have walked across the River by going from boat to boat would not be stretching the truth. The parade of red and green running lights on boats heading for port—Spring Lake, Muskegon, Holland—after the show was a spectacle to behold and went on long after the final crescendo of fireworks had bombarded the night sky. The sensational Saturday night finale— the Waterfront Stadium entertainment, the Fountain Show, the fireworks, the huge crowds, the countless boats—is still the same today, of course, but it was the era of the 60's and 70's which set the pace—the Festival's golden years.

Those were also the years of the great air shows and the astounding Air Force precision flying team—the Thunderbirds. From 1964 to 1970 these red, white and blue star spangled jets flashed over Grand Haven Memorial Airpark in patterns that twisted one's neck to the limit. The Thunderbird F-100 jet which sits on the pylon at the entrance to the airpark was a gift to the City as a gesture of gratitude for the welcome and hospitality the Thunderbird teams received here.

As was inevitable the Jaycees staged a beauty pageant in 1963 to select a Miss North Ottawa County who then was eligible to participate in the Miss Michigan competition. The young lady who was selected added her pulchritude to the Coast Guard Festival and was an honored guest at all the Festival functions. In 1965 the title was changed to Miss Ottawa County and United States Coast Guard. Then in 1970 the queen chosen was Miss United States Coast Guard, a title which harked back to 1939 and is still used today. The following is a chronology of those queens:

YEAR	TITLE	NAME
1939	Miss Coast Guard	Jessie Olsen
1963	Miss N. Ottawa County	Sue Ann Higgins
1964	Miss N. Ottawa County	Lynn Saundes
1965	Miss Ottawa County & USCG	Nancy Lynn Nagtzaam
1966	Miss Ottawa County & USCG	Peggy Ferm
1967	Miss Ottawa County & USCG	Karen Louise Coulson
1968	Miss Ottawa County & USCG	Debby Moore
1969	Miss Ottawa County & USCG	Judy Ann Lockman
1970	Miss U.S. Coast Guard	Jackie Waldo
1971	Miss U.S. Coast Guard	Pam Fisher
1972	Miss U.S. Coast Guard	Cindy Chapman
1973	Miss U.S. Coast Guard	Melanie Johnson
1974	Miss U.S. Coast Guard	Lori Beth Baldus
1975	Miss U.S. Coast Guard	Gabrielle Knue
1976	Miss U.S. Coast Guard	Beverly Simons
1977	Miss U.S. Coast Guard	Dawn Kamp
1978	Miss U.S. Coast Guard	Pamela Jean Angell
1979	Miss U.S. Coast Guard	Rhonda Ann Yedinak
1980	Miss U.S. Coast Guard	Mary Lynn Knoll
1981	Miss U.S. Coast Guard	Jana Lee Mierle
1982	Miss U.S. Coast Guard	Sue Cron
1983	Miss U.S. Coast Guard	Shari Janiszewski
1984	Miss U.S. Coast Guard	Kathlyn Kinzer
1985	Miss U.S. Coast Guard	Kristen Sue DeWall
1986	Miss U.S. Coast Guard	Shawn Mulder
1987	Miss U.S. Coast Guard	Laura Christine Lantz
1988	Miss U.S. Coast Guard	Heather Lee Louisell
1989	Miss U.S. Coast Guard	Beth DeMeester

The Coast Guard celebrated its 175th anniversary in 1965. Denver Todd was an historian, a railroad buff, a fine writer as well as an enthusiastic philatelist. To commemorate the anniversary Denver and his Tri-Cities Stamp Club developed the slogan "U.S. Coast Guard, 1790-1965, Always Ready," to be used for postal stamp cancellations that year. Through the efforts of Grand Haven Postmaster Roy Hierholzer the slogan was approved for 29 cities from Washington, D.C. to Honolulu, Hawaii but the coveted first day cover was run through the Grand Haven Post Office on August 4, 1965.

Then after 177 years in the Treasury Department, on April 1, 1967 the Coast Guard became part of the Department of Transportation. Administratively things changed somewhat but operationally it was business as usual.

The Nation celebrated its Bicentennial in 1976. It was also a special year for the Grand Haven Coast Guard in that it was the observance of the 100th anniversary of the founding of the old Life Saving Station on the north side of the River mouth. The occasion was marked here in Grand Haven by a visit on August 5, 1976 from the 238 foot, 3 masted square rigger Norwegian training ship *Christian Radich*—one of the many tall ships which were in this country to celebrate our Nation's Bicentennial. As she came in from the north through the summer haze she was a striking anachronism with all of her sails set in full glory. What also struck one was the fact that the wind was out of the southwest and the *Christian Radich* was heading straight into it—a very difficult assignment for a square rigger. Upon docking at Escanaba Park, Mastercaptain Kjell Thorsen revealed his secret—diesel power. The sails were just for show—and what a show it was. It was quite a contrast with the *Mackinaw* and the

Cutter "Mackinaw"

Christian Radich docked near one another—a capsulization of a century of sea technology and history and a very fitting way to commemorate the 100th anniversary of the founding of the Life Saving Service in Grand Haven. The following are the men who served as Keeper or Officer in Charge from the days of volunteers to the present:

YEAR	TITLE	NAME
1871-76	Volunteer	Captain Richard Connell
1876-81	Keeper	Captain Richard Connell
1881-85	Keeper	Captain John DeYoung
1885-89	Keeper	Captain Thomas Beavais
1889-1908	Keeper	Captain John Lysaght
1908-14	Keeper	Captain William Walker
1915-22	Officer in Charge	Captain William Walker
1922-39	Officer in Charge	Captain William Preston
1940-45	Officer in Charge	Chief Fred Wendel
1946-56	Officer in Charge	Chief Bill Woods
1956-60	Officer in Charge	Chief Keller Harmon
1960-62	Officer in Charge	Chief Rex Caulson
1962-64	Officer in Charge	Chief Guy Lozo
1964-68	Officer in Charge	Chief Anthony Fargnoli
1968-70	Officer in Charge	Chief George Baum
1970-73	Officer in Charge	Chief Dennis Bauchan
1973-76	Officer in Charge	Chief Ed Salyi
1976-80	Officer in Charge	Chief T.J. Thompson
1980-82	Officer in Charge	Chief Frank Tupa
1982-85	Officer in Charge	Chief Blaine Mack
1985-88	Officer in Charge	Chief Jim Green
1988-	Officer in Charge	Chief Robert Harko

Harko is the present Officer in Charge. Bauchan, Thompson and Green made Grand Haven their home after retirement—as have 50 some other ex-Coast Guardsmen over the years.

It was learned in 1971 that the *Woodbine*—WLB-289—would be leaving Grand Haven—her home port for nearly 25 years—to be decommissioned. The 180 foot Cutter had been built in Duluth in 1942 and served in the Pacific in World War II during which time she had received 2 battle stars. The *Woodbine* had replaced *Tahoma* when she arrived here in November of 1947. On January 25, 1972 Bernie Boyink, Director of the Community Center, held a public farewell party at the Center during which

Coast Guard Festival Retiree's Party at the Herbst home. Some of these men were Surfmen in the 1930's. (Left to right front row) Clarence VanDoorne, Rudy Styphanie, Vic Radulski, Charlie Plowman, Jim Gilligan, George Baum and John Van Ingham. (Back row) Harold Rohr, Matt Kaluske, Guy Lozo, Glenn McGeorge, Pop Rogers, Orville Collins, Lou Frickman, Joe Bruno, Bert Wicks, Cash Slaghuis and Bill Herbst.

Mayor John Walhout presented certificates of honorary citizenship to *Woodbine*'s 4 officers, 2 warrant officers and 44 enlisted men. This was the same civic minded crew which had helped with the Nativity Scene and assisted in preparing the North Ottawa Community Hospital for an open house.

Woodbine sailed out of Grand Haven Harbor for the final time on January 26, 1972 at 10:00 PM and blinked her lights to the crowd of 50 who were there to see her off. Poignantly, she had to break ice to leave her home for her final voyage as a Coast Guard Cutter. She made a stop at Sturgeon Bay, Wisconsin to transfer some gear to the Cutter *Mesquite*, which was to assume *Woodbine*'s duties of servicing nearly 150 buoys in Lake Michigan waters, and then dropped the ship's mascot—a "Heinz 57 variety" dog called "Angel"—at the Frankfurt Station before heading for her decommissioning in Detroit.

Cutter "Woodbine" stationed in Grand Haven 1947-1972. Decommissioned Feb. 15, 1972. Courtesy Grand Haven Area Historical Society.

Decommissioning ceremonies for the *Woodbine* took place at the Coast Guard station on the Detroit River near Belle Isle on February 15, 1972 and were attended by approximately 100 people. Captain Joe Fox—former commander aboard the *Woodbine*—represented Admiral William Jenkins, Commander of the Ninth District. Attending from Grand Haven were Mayor John and Beverly Walhout, John and Paula Montgomery, Paul and Maxine Rose—both Paula and Maxine served as chaperons for Miss U.S. Coast Guard in past years—Miss U.S. Coast Guard Pam Fisher, her mother Doris and chaperon Edith Pershing, Dave Evans, Welsey Scriptsma and children, Reverend Roy Wagner and George Pardee. The *Woodbine* had these 14 commanding officers while stationed in Grand Haven:

YEAR	COMMANDER
1947-48	Captain W.B. Millington
1948-49	Commander Urial H. Leach, Jr.
1949-51	Commander F.A. Goettel
1951-53	Commander J.J. Thuma
1953-55	Commander Earnst H.Burt
1955-57	Commander F.B. Carter
1957-59	Lieutenant Commander T.C. Peacock
1959-61	Lieutenant Commander J.J. Brunk

1961-63	Lieutenant Commander Joseph C. Fox
1963-65	Lieutenant Commander Anthony F. Fugaro
1965-67	Lieutenant Commander Donald Cunningham
1967-68	Lieutenant Commander J.R. Mitchel
1968-70	Lieutenant Commander D.N. Sessions
1970-72	Lieutenant Commander Stanley Powers

The *Woodbine* was given to the Cleveland Public Schools by the Coast Guard to be used as a training ship. However the operating expenses ate away at the Cleveland Board of Education budget and in 1978 she was sold at auction to B and B Wrecking for the scrap value of $37,500. Two years later the scrap company sold it for $290,000 to Andy Machinery of Brownsville, Texas for use in commercial trade. Today the *Woodbine* is still afloat and being used as a fishing boat in Alaska.

Except for the duration of World War II, Grand Haven had not been without a Coast Guard Cutter for 40 years. Whether or not a Cutter would be assigned to Grand Haven to replace the *Woodbine* was questionable—her departure left an uneasy void. In the spring of 1972 Mayor John Walhout received confirmation from his good friend Congressman Guy VanderJagt that the tug *Raritan*—WYTM 93, stationed in Milwaukee since 1962—would be transferred to Grand Haven.

After leaving Milwaukee *Raritan* put in at Muskegon and then at 6:45 PM on Monday, July 10, 1972 left Muskegon bound for Grand Haven with an entourage of dignitaries from Coast Guard City. The group was composed of Mayor Walhout, City Councilmen Ted Parker, Cliff Pfaff and Bill Boonstra, City Manager Daryl Tammen, Glenn Eaton, Miss U.S. Coast Guard Pam Fisher and her chaperon Edith Pershing and Fred VandenBrand of the Tribune. As *Raritan* came up Grand Haven Harbor she was escorted by 75 boats, welcomed by the horns and flashing lights of the many cars that jammed the parking lots, a water salute from Joe Bruneau, Dick Robinson and the rest of the crew from the City Fire Department, sirens, whistles and a Chuck Bugielski thunderous pyrotechnical greeting from flag bedecked Dewey Hill. *Raritan* acknowledged the reception with 5 blasts of her horn. She pulled up to her new home at Escanaba Park at 8:00 PM where she was welcomed by 2,000 people and an official greeting party composed of Beverly Walhout, Ferrysburg Mayor Dave Walborn and his wife Pat, Spring Lake Village President

Cutter "Raritan" stationed in Grand Haven 1972-79. Courtesy Grand Haven Area Historical Society.

John Mastenbrook and his wife Rose, Claude VerDuin, Reverend Dick Rehm and Lieutenant Commander R.E. Ahrens, Commander of the Muskegon Group Command. It was another typical show of appreciation for what the Coast Guard meant to Grand Haven.

Named for an Indian Nation in New York, the 110 foot Cutter was christened *Raritan* at the Defoe Shipyard in Bay City, Michigan on April 22, 1938. Primarily a search and rescue vessel, the icebreaker was suitable for sailing in any weather. It was appropriate that *Raritan* should come to Grand Haven in that she had been the ship which rescued the 2 survivors when *Escanaba* went down in the North Atlantic on June 13, 1943. Therefore it was somehow historically fitting that she would end her career here.

Raritan remained in Grand Haven until 1979. When she was decommissioned on May 14, 1988 the speaker at the ceremony was Dr. West who had been the Executive Officer aboard *Raritan* when she went to the aid of *Escanaba* on June 13, 1943. *Raritan*'s name boards, battle ribbons and bell were presented by Vice Admiral Clyde Lusk, from Washington, D.C., to Museum

Tour of Governor's Island, New York, c. 1970's. (Clockwise from plaid jacket) Charlie Bugielski, Mayor John and Bev Walhout, John Fortino, Adm. Rae, John MacLean, Fran and Ave Casemier, Frieda and John Miller, Bob Bolt, Roy Hierholzer, Claude and Fern VerDuin, George and Rose Donner, Jean Verseput, Don Hughes, Bud Bleyert, Barb Kameraad, John and Jan Rohr, Jerry and Marsha Witherell, Marge and Jim Oakes, Eunice Behrens, Marge Boon, Minn and Bert Reuderdahl, Sandy and Dave Klaassen, Bob and Jan Hendricks, Les and Jo Enninga, Joan and Capt. Arnold Danielson and Ed Cook.

Director Molly Perry at the Memorial Service during the 1988 Coast Guard Festival. They are now part of Grand Haven's Tri-Cities Museum's Coast Guard display. Commanding Officers of *Raritan* while she was in Grand Haven were:

YEAR	COMMANDING OFFICER
1972-73	Chief Warrant Officer Thomas J. Nalley
1973-76	Chief Warrant Officer Gail Daugherty
1976-79	Chief Warrant Officer Thomas J. Nalley

Grand Haven's fifth Cutter, the *Acacia*, arrived in Port during

Cutter "Acacia" has been based in Grand Haven since 1979. She wears the Coast Guard stripes authorized for all service vessels in 1967.

the spring of 1979. Thus, during John Walhout's tenure as City Mayor, Grand Haven became the duty port for 2 Cutters—*Raritan* and *Acacia*. And that did not come about by accident. Walhout served as Mayor for 9 consecutive years—longer than any person in the history of Grand Haven. (If one counts consecutive years of service on the Council and as Mayor the nod goes to Marge Boon with 16 years—8 years on the Council followed by 8 years as Mayor.) John capped a half century of Mayors and City Councilpersons—dating back to 1930—who had a sense of history regarding the relationship of the Coast Guard and Grand Haven. It was their leadership, their trips to Washington, their hospitality to all Coast Guardsmen, their friendships with people in Washington and the Coast Guard, their dedication and concern that helped make the difference. We have mentioned Mayors but let us not forget the Councilpersons, listed here chronologically from 1930: Bruno Peter, Garret Boiten, Baltus Pellegrom, Peter VanZylen, N.F. Yonkman, John J. McCracken, Henry Ringelberg, Harold Westerhof, Martin Kieft, John Roossien, James VanWessem, J. Walter Boyd, Percy Tatroe, Earle Hill, Henry Casemier, William Swart, Frank Meyer, Harm Roossien, Ben Zenderink, Louis

Breitels, Russell VanderVeen, James Ledinsky, Bert Singerling, Jacob Toxopeus, Howard Zuidema, Joseph Swartz, Harold Fisher, Virgil Quebbeman, Thomas Fullerton, George Purcell, David Pushaw, Paul Luytjes, Norman Engleright, William Boonstra, Robert Dillenback, Cliff Pfaff, Ted Parker, Paul Rose, Jack Smant, Paul Verseput, Peter Manting, Peter Bol, David Klaassen and Don Wessel. For these men "Grand Haven" and "Coast Guard" were the same—inseparable.

Up until 1972 the Coast Guard Festival was a City function. In that year a nonprofit corporation—the Grand Haven Coast Guard Festival, Incorporated—was organized to remove the City from the potential problems of liability. This was at a time when Charlie Bugielski, Claude VerDuin and Glenn Eaton were still the guiding triumvirate behind the Festival so even with the new modus operandi it was, for all intents and purposes, still business as usual. However, in 1981—after 47 years of devoted service to the Coast Guard Festival—Chuck Bugielski retired from his parade duties but still continues to direct the fireworks finale. VerDuin left in 1983 but remains on as a consultant for the Festival Committee. Eaton has yet to retire from the Committee but instead has chosen to limit his role as his time will allow.

As these three stalwarts were stepping down, two people came onto the City scene who tutored under them and took up the reins to fill a number of the vital functions Bugielski, VerDuin and Eaton had performed through the years. Marjorie "Marge" Boon was elected Mayor in 1980—the City's first female Mayor— the same year that Larry Deetjen took the position of City Manager. For the next 9 years they teamed in their respective roles to achieve yet another distinguished chapter in the historic relationship between the Coast Guard and Grand Haven. They entered into Festival business willingly when asked but left the main chores to regular Committee members. They were most effective in affairs of State and in this capacity broadened and resurfaced the roads to Coast Guard Headquarters, the halls of Washington and the chambers in Lansing that had been so capably established by Bugielski and Mayors Cook, Wilds, Martin Boon, VerDuin, Eaton, Creason and Walhout in the years before them. Together Boon and Deetjen established a network of contacts which were very useful in the work of the Festival Committee. In addition they selflessly volunteered in whatever manner they could locally to insure the success of the annual celebration. In the early 1980's there were 4 City Councilmen—Don Wessel, Dave Klaassen, Paul Rose and Paul Verseput—who had Coast Guard enthusiasm coursing through their veins either congenitally or acquired. They sensed the proficiency of the Boon-Deetjen team and assisted wherever they could.

The effectiveness of this Mayor-City Manager team extended well beyond the annual Coast Guard Festival. In the early 1980's the Coast Guard began building 13 new 270 foot, helicopter equipped, state of the art vessels referred to as The Famous Glass Cutters—named for former historic Coast Guard Cutters. Four were to be built in Tacoma, Washington— *Bear*, *Tampa*, *Harriet Lane* and *Northland*—and the remaining 9 were to be built at the Robert Derecktor Shipyard in Middletown, Rhode Island— *Thetis*, *Forward*, *Legre*, *Mohawk*, *Seneca*, *Campbell*, *Spencer*, *Tahoma* and *Escanaba*, the latter to be known in Grand Haven as *Escanaba III*—or, as Clarence "Tad" Poel correctly made the familial link in his Tribune "Focus" column, the new *Escanaba* was *Esky I*'s granddaughter.

The keel was laid for *Escanaba III*—WMEC 907—in 1983 but plans had yet to be made for her christening. Jim Ward of the Coast Guard Public Realtions Office in Washington suggested to Larry Deetjen that since only a woman could christen a Cutter and because of Grand Haven's historic ties with the *Escanaba*'s, he—Deetjen—should begin making suggestions where they would be most effective that Mayor Marge Boon be the person for the honor. Admiral Jim and Randy Gracey had become good friends with Maurie and Marge Boon when Gracey was Commander of the Ninth District in Cleveland in 1981. In 1982 Admiral Gracey was elevated to the position of Commandant of the U.S. Coast Guard. And so it was in 1984 that Admiral Gracey extended an invitation to Mayor Boon to accept the honor of christening the new *Escanaba*. Marge gladly accepted and began making plans for the Saturday, August 24, 1985 ceremony which was to be held at the Derecktor Shipyard in Rhode Island.

The Derecktor Shipbuilding Company sent a selected number of invitations to people in the Grand Haven area. However the Coast Guard and Robert Derecktor were both astonished but pleasantly surprised when 33 arrived from Michigan and 2—Grand Haven's adopted citizens Ray and Dolly O'Malley—from Illinois. They were provided seating on the foredeck of *Escanaba III*—a very honored vantage point. In attendance from the Grand Haven area were Mayor Marge and Maurie Boon, their daughter Christine who was the Maid of Honor for the ceremony, Dennis and Dawn Boon and their son Eric, Don and Dorothy Wessel, Dave and Sandy Klaassen, Larry and Lynn Deetjen, Denver and Ruth Todd, Harold and Marguerite Swartz (Harold being the master model ship builder who's beautiful scale models of the *Escanaba*, *Raritan*, *Acacia* and *Escanaba III* can be seen in Grand Haven's Tri-Cities Museum), Terry Judd, Jim and Lois Christman, Ernie and Doris VanDam, Fred and Pat Borchers, Bill and Carol Bedford, Jim and Edie Swart, Bernie and Ethel Pankowski (Bernie having served on the first *Escanaba* in 1934-35), Ralph and Rose Secory and Martha and Leighanne Boomgard.

The twin christening of *Escanaba III* and *Tahoma II* was attended by about 1,000 people and the address for the occasion was given by Rhode Island Senator Claiborne Pell. Pell was a member of the Coast Guard in World War II and for that special occasion he was wearing the shoes which had been issued to him back in his Service days. He concluded his appropriate remarks by quiping, "I hope today's Cutters hold up as well as these shoes."

But Mayor Boon's comments about the first *Escanaba* and the historic significance of that day's christening ceremony to all of the people of Grand Haven gave real depth and meaning to the ceremony. Looking at the Cutter Marge closed her emotional remarks with a request which was hard to ignore:

> Before you settle down into your new port I would like to challenge you to visit Coast Guard City, U.S.A.—Grand Haven, Michigan—to gain a fuller understanding of the words spoken here today. You have a proud heritage to live up to young lady. . .We know you will develop your own personality and accomplish tasks your predecessors were incapable of, but please never forget your roots. You belong to us. No matter where the winds of time take you, you are ours. We love you now and we will more than love you as you enter our Harbor with your flags flying. Then we can all echo," Welcome home *Escanaba*."

Wearing protective glasses and gloves Mayor Boon said, "I christen thee *Escanaba* in the same name of the United States of

Christening of "Escanaba III", Middletown, Rhode Island, August 24, 1985. Mayor Marge Boon and Maid of Honor Christine Boon.

America," smote *Escanaba III* a crashing blow on the point of her bow with a bottle of champagne—and gave a "thumbs up" to the cheering Grand Haven delegation who were high up on the Cutters deck.

Mrs. Benedict Stabile, wife of the Vice-Commandant of the U.S. Coast Guard, Vice Admiral Stabile, christened the *Tahoma*, the second Cutter in the dual ceremony.

Escanaba III was only 60% complete when christened. Her completed cost would be $54,723,694, as compared to *Esky I* which was built for $584,000 and *Escanaba II* that had a price tag of about $1.5 million. When completed *Escanaba III* was to have all the state of the art navigational devices, armament as well as search and rescue equipment—which included a helicopter with its own shipboard heliport and retractable hanger. She would carry a compliment of 15 officers, 10 petty officers and 84 crewmen.

The plans from the start were to commission *Escanaba III* in the Boston area where she would be stationed. At every opportunity Marge Boon, Larry Deetjen, City Councilmen or Festival Committee members would insist that this new *Escanaba* should come "home" for that very special occasion

"Escanaba III" deck during christening, August 24, 1985. (Left to right) Ray O'Malley, Sandy and Dave Klaassen, Lois and Jim Christman, Bernie Pankowski, Lyn and Larry Deetjen, Ralph and Rose Secory, Edie and Jim Swart, Fred Borchers, Denver and Ruth Todd, Marguerite and Harold Swartz, Doris and Ernie VanDam.

in the Cutter's life—anywhere except Grand Haven would be inappropriate. The message got through. The man to make that decision was Commander of the Atlantic Area Fleet, Vice Admiral D.C. Thompson.

Sixty three persons, Association of Commerce and Industry members, local officials, Festival Committee members and others, attended the April, 1987 Association of Commerce and Industry—a.k.a. Chamber of Commerce—Annual Washington Trip. Special arrangements were made for the group to tour the Coast Guard facilities on Governor's Island, New York. During the tour Admiral Thompson told Mayor Boon of a decision he had made. Marge asked if he minded if the group shared the news. Thompson said, "Not at all." Boon climbed up on a chair, whistled the group's attention and then Admiral Thompson told the assemblage that the *Escanaba III* was to be commissioned in Grand Haven in August of that year—1987. Furthermore, Mayor Boon was asked to be the commissioning sponsor for the Cutter. The groups cheers said it all. Thanks to friendly persuasion for a cause which seemed right—*Escanaba III* was coming home.

At 12:00 noon on Thursday, August 27, 1987 *Escanaba III* sailed into Grand Haven Harbor led by 2 smaller Coast Guard boats spraying a water salute and was followed closely on her stern by the *Mackinaw*. A Grand Haven Lifeboat Station boat had shuttled 50 local dignitaries out to *Escanaba III* so they were aboard to enjoy the full tenor of the historic occasion as she slowly and majestically eased her way into Port. Among these were former *Escanaba I* crewmen Steve and Sadie Vozar, Ed Lautenschlaeger, Bernie and Ethel Pankowski and Bob Burgess. The Musical Fountain played Semper Paratus as an army of local boats swarmed around the mother drone and were swept along as vicarious escorts. Hundreds of waving people lined the piers and Board Walk, many carrying love signs such as "Welcome Home Esky." For some it was a time warp of 45 years which harked back to a time when another *Escanaba* came into the Port of Grand Haven on a cold and icy December day. *Escanaba III*'s Commander, Commander Lawson W. Brigham, and her crew understood that for a twinkling they and their ship were surrogates and in that guise were thoroughly transfixed by Grand Haven's response to " *Escanaba*'s homecoming." Which *Escanaba*, for that moment, was in the mind of the beholder. Each played out their role in total respect for the other.

Upon docking, relatives of the crew of the original *Escanaba* were given a special tour of the new *Escanaba*. Relatives of the original 1932 crew included Ann Donnelly and children—wife of the late Orville Collins, the late Louis Frickman family—wife Eda Frickman and 2 sons, the late Louis Barber family—wife Joyce Barber and children, the late Joe Coon family—wife Emilia Coon and a son. Relatives from later crews were also honored guests and included the late Emmanuel Ninnes family—a son and a daughter, the late Leo Lake family—wife Catherine Lake and children, the late Layton Counselor family—wife Doris Coster, the Bill Herbst family, the Steve Vozar family, Jean Lautenschlaeger and family, and the Robert Burgess family. *Escanaba III* and the *Mackinac* were open to the public all 3 days they were here.

A Memorial Service was held at Escanaba Memorial Park at 4:30 PM on Friday, August 28 during which the names of each of the 101 men lost aboard the first *Escanaba* were read and as they were a crew member from *Escanaba III* placed a red carnation at the base of *Esky*'s mast in cadence with a rifle salute sounded from the deck of the new Cutter. The flag was lowered to half staff where it remained until the commissioning ceremonies the next day.

The Grand Haven Area Historical Society made a special effort to find those in the area who had purchased War Bonds during World War II to help build the *Escanaba II*. Bond drive participants who could be located were Louis VanSchelven, Claude Verduin, Glenn Eaton, Albert and Doris Knuth, Al VanBemmelen, Jeannette Pofahl, Maurice Boon, Al and Helen VanOordt, Ben and Ann MacNeill (Ann remembers as a 13 year old saving money from picking blueberries to buy her $25 Bond), Cornell Beukema, Joe Bruneau, Bud Sherwood, Don Wessel, Lou Wessel, J. Nyhof Poel, Herb Hierholzer, Paula Wuennecke Olthof, Charles and Ruth Nash, Stanley and Gertrude Thoroughman, Kathy Arkema, George Bennett and Gary Byl. The Knuths still had some of the Bonds they purchased, one of which is on display at Grand Haven's Tri-Cities Museum.

Escanaba III's commissioning ceremonies began at 11:00 AM, Saturday, August 29, 1987 with more than 1,000 people in attendance. Mayor Marge Boon, the Cutter's sponsor, opened the ceremony with, "Welcome home you gorgeous creature." She then made all of *Escanaba III*'s Plank Owners—the vessel's first crew—honorary citizens of Grand Haven. Boon next presented Commander Lawson Brigham a world clock for the Cutter and said, ". . . anywhere she goes, the Escanaba will know the time in Grand Haven. And every time she puts to sea the citizens of Grand Haven will be with her." Brigham greatfully accepted the gift on behalf of his crew and then further commented that Grand Haven had staged one of the largest commissionings of the decade. Ray O'Malley spoke of the fate of the original *Escanaba* and concluded,". . . May every ship that leaves port return safely."

Rear Admiral Arnold Danielson, Commander of the Ninth Coast Guard District, addressed the crew, reminded them of their mission to ship and Country and then closed with, ". . . give your very best, just as those on the first Escanaba did." With her crew standing at attention in Escanaba Park, the Union Jack on her bow, the Coast Guard ensign and commissioning penant flowing on the mast, the Grand Haven flag along with the rail bunting and hoisted signal flags in full glory, the national ensign—the

American flag—was ceremoniously hoisted on her stern mast, the first watch posted, the first official entry was made in the ship's log and at that moment—just minutes before noon— *USCGC Escanaba*—WMEC 907 entered the United States Coast Guard Service. Admiral Danielson gave the command, "Crew, man your ship!" Officers and crew—98 Plank Owners—broke ranks and scampered up the bow gang plank to their stations. It was a stirring, once-in-a-lifetime experience for Grand Haven.

The Grand Haven High School Band played. Long lines of people waited for a tour of the white Cutter and before the day was finished *Escanaba III* had hosted 5,234 visitors.

The commissioning and the events surrounding it were inspiring and made one very proud. When it came time for "goodbye" there was an air of finality. As *Escanaba III* sailed out the channel the next day, it was not difficult to turn back the calendar and wonder what was in the minds of those in 1942 who watched another *Escanaba* leave the Port of Grand Haven. For many it was hard to turn away.

Escanaba III visited the City of Escanaba and Toledo before reporting for permanent duty in Boston where she remains today. A teletype message was received at the Muskegon Group Command on Sunday—the day after *Escanaba III* left Grand Haven—and was forwarded to Mayor Boon through the Grand Haven Lifeboat Station. It was from Commander Lawson Brigham and read:

> To say simply "thank you" in response to the overwhelming outpouring of love and hospitality we received while in your fine city seems too little.
>
> Even though we have departed the geographic limits of Grand Haven we know we have not sailed beyond the boundaries of your thoughts and prayers.
>
> The memories of our arrival, welcome, the Memorial Service for the Escanaba, our commissioning ceremony and the tremendous send-off will stay with us for years to come.
>
> Please pass to your citizens our most heartfelt thanks for all they did to make us feel at home. We were honored to include them in a truly historic and memorable occasion for the United States Coast Guard.

Admiral James Gracey was Commandant of the U.S. Coast

Guard from 1982 to 1986. During his command plans were being formulated for the Service's Bicentennial. Marge Boon and Gracey had talked informally about Grand Haven's role in the celebration and Gracey had intimitated that it could be a major one. Mayor Boon discussed the possibilities with the City council, Larry Deetjen and the Fesival Committee. It was decided if Grand Haven was to request the 200th celebration be held here, the City and Festival Committee should be prepared to be totally committed to the challenge; if the request were granted the entire Nation would be focused on Grand Haven come August 4, 1990, and that would be no time to contract a case of stage fright. All parties agreed and Mayor Boon sent the request to Admiral Gracey. Before he stepped down as Commandant, Admiral Gracey announced the Coast Guard's Bicentennial would begin the first week of August, 1989 in Newburyport, Massechusetts—sight of the launching of the Service's first Cutter, *Massachusetts*, in 1790—and would be culminated on August 4, 1990 in Grand Haven, Michigan, Coast Guard City, U.S.A. It was an honor Grand Haven was prepared to meet.

At this same time—1986—big changes were being planned for the Coast Guard facilities in Grand Haven. On the boards was a $2.3 million Multi-Mission Station to be built at Government Pond to replace the 64 year old Lifeboat Station at the North Pier. In addition City Manager Larry Deetjen was negotiating to have the District Group Command relocated here from Muskegon. (Group Command is the facilitating agent for personnel and payroll records, acts as purchasing agent and provides engineering and electronic support for the Coast Guard stations at Frankfort, Manistee, Ludington, Muskegon, Holland, South Haven, St. Joseph, Michigan City, Indiana as well as Grand Haven. Since 1/3 of all pleasure crafts registered in the United States are on the Great Lakes, these lifeboat stations still provide an important water safety function. In 1988 the stations in this Group Command made 1107 calls, saved 52 persons while assisting 2,700 others. Group Command's landlord—the Naval Reserve—in Muskegon was changing its operation therefore the Coast Guard was casting about for a new home for the Command.) Deetjen eventually involved State Representative Alvin Hoekman, Congressman Fred Upton and Guy VanderJadt, Grand Haven's Economic Development Corporation and 3 men who were quite familiar with Coast Guard and Riverfront development projects from years back—Glenn Eaton, President of the Board of Light and Power, Paul Johnson, President of the Loutit Foundation and Bill Creason who at the time was President of the Grand Haven Area Community Foundation. Deetjen juggled several balls in the air at one time, but after long hours of strategizing—and heavy finacial commitments from the Loutit Foundation and the Grand Haven Area Community Foundation— the Board of Light and Power relocated from its administrative offices opposite Escanaba Park to allow Group Command to move in, the Lifeboat Station moved to its new facility at Government Pond and the Loutit Foundation ended up with the old Lifeboat Station at the North Pier as the residue from the arrangement. The Loutit Foundation recouped only a portion of its obligation when it sold the old Lifeboat Station property privately in February, 1990 for a reported $325,000.

The remarkable part of the whole arrangement was that it involved absolutely no Grand Haven tax dollars. What also is interesting is that the City was not used as a "pass-through" agency because, had it been, the whole complicated arrangement would have—since the negotiations involved Riverfront property—required a vote of the people. It was a masterful job on the part of City Manager Larry Deetjen of diplomatically coordinating Community cooperation with politics and the unbelievable maze of bureaucratic red tape. Grand Haven came out the richer in that when completed the complex of buildings and patrol boat docks grouped around Escanaba Park makes a beautiful Coast Guard "campus." Louis Campau and Mr. Wadsworth could look back from 150 years and be quite proud of the development of their Additions.

Lieutenant Commander Larry Mizell, the Group Command's Officer in Charge, moved his operation into the new facilities— now designated as "Group Grand Haven"—on December 21, 1988.

On May 17, 1989 the crew of the old Lifeboat Station began moving to the new Multi-Purpose Station. And they did it in typical Coast Guard style to save Government dollars—using vans instead of hiring a moving company. The colors were first raised at the new Station June 5, 1989.

Formal dedication of the 2 facilities took place, June 28, 1989. It was during those ceremonies that Lieutenant Commander Mizell was presented a new set of shoulder boards by Admiral

Dedication of Grand Haven's Coast Guard Campus, June 28, 1989—Multi-mission station on Gov. Pond to the left, Group Command officers right of the flags off the picture. Courtesy Grand Haven Tribune-photographer Andy Loree.

Richard A. Appelbaum, Commander of the Ninth District, which elevated Mizzel to the rank of Commander. The new shoulder boards were affixed to Mizell's uniform and sealed with a kiss by Mayor Marge Boon. However it would not be until May 26, 1990 that Mizell would have his "Wetting Down" party—the occasion which "officially" consummated his new stripes.

Riverfront beautification had been continuous since 1963. In 1984, the year of Grand Haven's Sesquicentennial, dedication of the Board Walk—or more properly, the Lighthouse Connector Park—on August 18, 1984 provided the finishing touch along the Riverfront. It is a 1.5 mile promenade which extends from Channock Pier on the east to the end of the South Pier and is enjoyed by thousands of vacationers, visitors, strollers and joggers each year. In 1983-84 the Corps of Engineers was working on a $3.5 million pier and River revetment reconstruction project and Larry Deetjen saw this as an ideal time to tie in some Riverfront beautification. The idea for a Board Walk caught on like wildfire. Its timing was absolutely perfect for a couple of reasons; first it was a natural walkway used by many already but just had never been properly defined. Secondly, people were caught up in the enthusiasm of the Sesquicentennial and needed a good excuse to in some way contribute to the celebration. Ken Formsma chaired the committee which staged a whirlwind fund raising campaign punctuated with innovative promotions and an unbelievable amount of public participation resulting in contributions of $200,000. It was a winner from the start and Formsma was the perfect person to spark its success. Today people point to the Board Walk and the wall of names of contributors with great pride. It is another of Deetjen's impossible dreams.

All of these foregoing events which took place in the decade of the 80's paved the way for Grand Haven's part in the Coast Guard's big Bicentennial Celebration August 1-4, 1990. It is ironic that the 2 people who were so instrumental in bringing this honor to Grand Haven would not be able to preside over the Celebration in their official positions. Such is the fate of politics—the results do not always conform to what would seem to be good reason. But then, if everything in life was logical it would be the man who rode sidesaddle.

The Cutter *Acacia* was a 180 foot buoy tender out of the same mold as the *Woodbine*, launched from the same shipyard in Duluth September 1, 1944, just 2 years after *Woodbine*. Her name while under construction was *Thistle*, but in keeping with the Coast Guard tradition of naming its vessels for past famous Cutters, she was christened *Acacia* to honor the first *Acacia* which, as mentioned previously, was sunk in Carribean waters by a German U-boat on March 15, 1942—the first Cutter to be lost in World War II.

In 1986 *Acacia* was one of 5 buoy tenders on the Great Lakes which serviced 2,200 floating buoys and markers. Ship personalities are generally reflected through their commanding officers. *Acacia* has had fine officers and crew and has been an honored member of the Grand Haven family since her arrival 11 years ago. Her commanding officers while stationed in Grand Haven have been:

YEAR	COMMANDING OFFICER
1979	Lieutenant Commander Jerald B. Rainey
1979-81	Lieutenant Commander James J. Shaw, Jr.
1981-84	Lieutenant Commander Paul Barlow
1984-87	Lieutenant Commander Wayne Verry
1987-	Lieutenant Commander James M. Dwyer

In November *Acacia* "dry docks" 200 lighted buoys from Chicago to Escanaba and replaces them with smaller winter markers. Then in March the lighted buoys are reset. In addition to these regular duties, in 1983-84 her crew completely refurbished the lighthouses at Manistee, Frankfort as well as Grand Haven.

Grand Haven celebrated its Sesquicentennial in 1984. As mentioned previously, in September of that year Lieutenant Commander Verry and his crew presented the City the interpretive display of *Acacia* which now stands in Escanaba Park and is appreciated by thousands who stroll the Board Walk.

In 1986 *Acacia* had engine problems which nearly ended her career. She was a 42 year old matron and Commander Verry expressed the concern that unless funds were made available for new engines her days were numbered. The Coast Guard made the decision to stay with *Acacia* and the people of Grand Haven collectively breathed a sigh of relief. When *Acacia* returned from Manitowac with her new engines on March 26, 1987 she was welcomed by a large homecoming crowd, a fire hose salute, music from the Musical Fountain and signs of appreciation that she was back home. Commander Verry commented, "The crew was very impressed. Most of our assignments are in small communities that include us as part of the community, but none of them make us feel as welcome as Grand Haven."

On December 2, 1987 *Acacia* left Grand Haven to go to the Miami area for a 4 month assigment of drug interdiction duty and law enforcement in the Carribean. This anti-smuggling duty harked back to the Coast Guard roots 197 years ago. Chief Warrant Officer Robert Harko, today the Officer in Charge of the new Multi-Mission Station, was the self appointed "morale officer" aboard *Acacia* during the crew's Holiday Season away from home.

Acacia's sister Cutter *Mesquite*, which had been stationed in Charlevoix, ran aground December 5, 1989 off Keweenaw Point while on buoy duty in Lake Superior. She was declared unsalvagable, decommissioned and pulled to deeper water where she will serve as an underwater reef and dive sight. The unfortunate aftermath of *Mesquite*'s misadventure was that because of, as Ninth District Commander Admiral Appelbaum put it, "operational necessity" *Acacia* was reassigned to Charlevoix to take *Mesquite*'s place. *Acacia* left the Port of Grand

Haven for the last time June 14, 1990.

At this time it is questionable whether or not another Cutter will be designated for Grand Haven. If it should pass that none is assigned here, it will be the first time the Port will have been without a Cutter in 58 years. For some this would seem the end of the City's long standing relationship with the Coast Guard, but that is hardly the case. The new Multi-Mission Station and Group Command Headquarters bear witness to the Service's commitment here. The Coast Guard has been and will continue to be an ever evolving Service—only time will tell if the Port of Grand Haven will be home for another Cutter.

CHAPTER 25

COAST GUARD CITY—
FACT OR FICTION?

We conclude this work by settling the issue of the basis for Grand Haven's appellation "Coast Guard City, U.S.A."

There is a popular belief among the citizen's of the Grand Haven area that somewhere in the Congressional record there is a Bill which was passed by Congress in the late 1940's or 1950's that has buried in it some "fine print" which recognizes Grand Haven as the official sight for the annual commemoration of the United States Coast Guard's birthday anniversary. This supposed Bill carries an endorsement by Representative Gerald Ford—then a Representative for the Congressional District that included Grand Haven—and this piece of legislation states that all branches of the armed forces will be honored each year on Armed Forces Day—this to end the confusion and competition of having seperate celebrations for the Army, Navy, Air Force, Marine Corps and Coast Guard. However, since the Coast Guard was under the authority of the Treasury Department and only quasi-military during peace time—being a part of the Navy only in war time— the Coast Guard, this imaginary Bill continues, shall have its own observance separate from Armed Forces Day and this Coast Guard celebration will be held in Grand Haven, Michigan on or near August 4th each year.

The legend gets a bit hazy at this point as to whether the title "Coast Guard City, U.S.A." was bestowed upon the City in this first piece of legislation or if another Bill was passed to so honor Grand Haven. Regardless, somewhere it was voted upon by Congress, so the thinking goes, that Grand Haven was designated as "Coast Guard City."

In an effort to explore this issue letters were written to Congressional Representatives Guy VanderJagt and Fred Upton as well as Senators Carl Levin and Donald Reigle on August 10, 1989 spelling out to them the thinking recited above and asking their assistance in researching the Congressional record in reference to this matter. Representative VanderJagt's office conducted a thorough investigation of the subject and represents the best effort available concerning the matter. What follows is a summation of that work.

Until 1947 there was a Department of War and a Department of the Navy which handled all military affairs. Each branch of the armed forces feted its Service on a seperate day each year; e.g., Army Day was celebrated April 6—the anniversary of the U.S. entry into World War I, Navy Day was October 27—the birth date of Theodore Roosevelt, its champion, and Air Force Day was the 2nd Saturday in September—close to the date when it was established as a seperate service on September 18, 1947. On July 26, 1947 Congress approved the National Security Act which, among other things, coordinated the Army, Navy and Air Force into a single National Military Establishment under the Department of Defense. According to the 1989 edition of Chase's Annual Events, Army Day, which had been authorized in 1936, continued to be recognized through 1949. Armed Forces Day came into existance in 1949 with a proclamation by President Harry Truman. The purpose of the proclamation was to coordinate the observances of all Service branches on a single day.

Gerald Ford had been elected to the House of Representatives in 1949 with an upset victory over incumbant Barnie Jonkman. Ford's campaign had a good deal of support from the Grand Haven area, especially from some men who were fellow University of Michigan alumni—Miller Sherwood, Paul Johnson, Jr. and Chuck Jacobson. Ford was quite familiar with the history of Grand Haven's Coast Guard Festival and saw Truman's proclamation as having the potential of dampening the Coast Guard's enthusiasm for the Grand Haven celebration. He was also very aware that on August 4 of that year—1949—Congress had restated the Service's 150 year policy and in so doing interjected language which made the Coast Guard ". . .a military service and a branch of the armed forces of the United States at all times. . .". So, according to Claude VerDuin, although Gerald Ford was a freshman Congressman, he had the courage to voice his opinion on the matter and suggested that festivals and celebrations for branches of the Service which had an established tradition should be allowed to continue.

It should be pointed out that proclamations are a priviledge of the Executive Branch of the Government and are not acted upon by Congress, therefore they have no legal status—thus Armed Forces Day was not and is not a public holiday. But that is not to imply the President can not be influenced by what Congress has to say on the subject.

Whether or not Truman had included the Coast Guard in his original thinking is not certain, but when he issued Proclamation 2873—which set the date for the observance of the first Armed Forces Day as Saturday, May 20, 1950—a part of the lengthy text read:

> . . . As Commander in Chief of the Armed Forces of the United States, I direct the Secretary of Defense and the Secretaries of the Army, Navy and Air Force to mark the designated day with appropriate ceremonies, and to cooperate with civic authorities and civic bodies in suitable observances. . .

The Coast Guard was not mentioned and perhaps it had never intended to be included in the observance. However, in the book, "All About American Holidays" by Maymie Krythe, in 1962 New York City had an Armed Forces Day celebration which featured a queen for "each of the 5 Armed Forces—Air Force, Navy, Army, Marine Corps and Coast Guard." But Chase's 1989 edition lists the Coast Guard as having its own special day on August 4. It indicates the day is observed to celebrate the anniversary of the founding of the U.S. Coast Guard, August 4, 1790. However there is no mention of where the celebration takes place. Apparently Mr. Chase has not gotten the message.

So at least, according to VerDuin, a portion of the legend is true in that Gerald Ford—the 38th President of the United States in 1974-77—spoke his piece on behalf of the Coast Guard Festival at a time when he thought it was necessary. Although not recorded anywhere, perhaps what he had to say to Congress and President Truman back in 1949 had the desired effect.

Now let us consider the second half of the assignment—the origins of "Coast Guard City." The Congressional Research Service can find nothing in the way of legislation pertaining to "Coast Guard City" so we can dismiss the Halls of Congress as the genesis of the term. However, the Coast Guard Congressional and Governmental Affairs Staff shed a little more light on the subject in the following letter sent to Guy VanderJagt:

Dear Mr. VanderJagt:

This responds to your inquiry concerning a request by your constituent, Dr. David Seibold, for clarification of the origin of Grand Haven, MI, being named "Coast Guard City, USA."

Mr. Claude VerDuin, of Grand Haven, Michigan, who has been involved in the Coast Guard Festival since inception, and our research supports the Congressional Research position on the subject.

We believe it was in the early 60's when a Coast Guard Flag Officer said in remarks that because of all the attention the city paid the Service each year that it truly was, "Coast Guard City, USA."

Subsequently, about ten years ago, our Coast Guard Band Director, Lieutenant Commander Lewis J. Buckley, USCG, wrote a March dedicated to the city entitled, "The Coast Guard City USA, March."

While a formal proclamation may never have been issued, our Service fondly thinks of Grand Haven as Coast Guard City, USA.

We hope this is of some assistance to your constituent.

Sincerely, James Hall for Thomas Schaeffer.

The Flag Officer referred to in this Coast Guard Staff letter is Admiral Richard Schmidtman. The circumstance, as mentioned previously, was when he "threw the switch" to start the Musical Fountain in 1963. That was the milestone occasion for Grand Haven when the label "Coast Guard City" seemed to stick. But when did the City actually earn the title? Grand Haven's natural setting in the dunes with its pristine beaches make it a veritable pearl, but that is not it. And it runs deeper than the parades and fireworks—but they help. Could it have been the dedication of *Escanaba*'s mast in 1944? Or does it go back to the Memorial Service following the loss of *Escanaba* in 1943 which sparked the drive to build *Escanaba II*? Or perhaps it all began in 1934 when Grand Haven organized the first Tenth District-City picnic. Maybe, quite simply, the love affair had its start with the arrival of *Escanaba* in 1932. Then again it could have been in 1924

Coast Guard City, USA. Ray O'Malley paying tribute to lost shipmates at the Annual Coast Guard Festival Memorial Service, as he has since 1943. Courtesy Coast Guard Festival Committee.

when the Tenth District Offices in Grand Haven proposed the idea for the first District picnic. Or could it have had its roots back in 1873 when that volunteer surfman walked out into the crashing waves and extended his hand for the first time to save a victim of a sunken ship? Or was it all of these—and more?

Maybe the "more" is the secret ingredient—especially if "more" can be translated as "spirit." Grand Haven never started out to become Coast Guard City but it did start out with a spirit—and it's the spirit here that counts. Because if spirit is applied to what resources are close at hand, everything is still possible. Grand Haven just never forgot. For that reason there can be no doubt it truly is "Coast Guard City, U.S.A." And what's more, Grand Haven has a song to prove it!

BIBLIOGRAPHY

Altoff, Gerry T. "Oliver Hazard Perry
and the Battle of Lake Erie". *The
Michigan Historical Review* Fall
1988. Historical Society of
Michigan, Ann Arbor, Michigan

*American Heritage Pictorial Atlas of
U.S. History* McGraw-Hill

Bennett, Orlie Lewis. "Shipping In the
Port of Grand Haven 1820 to 1940".
Grand Haven, Michigan

Binns, James. Interview. February 1990,
Addison, Michigan

Bloomfield, Howard U.L. *Compact
History of the U.S. Coast Guard.*
Hawthorne Books, Inc., N.Y., N.Y.

Brown, Melissa. *The Loutit Legacy* The
Loutit Foundation. Grand Haven,
Michigan

Bugielski, Charles. Interview.
September, 1989, Grand Haven,
Michigan

Burgess, Robert. Interview. March 1990.
Grand Haven, Michigan

Chicago Daily Times. June 18, 1943

Chrysler, Don. *The Story of the Grand
River.* Grand Rapids, Michigan,
1976

"Coast Guard History". U.S. Coast
Guard Public Information Division

Coast Guardsman's Manual. 6th Edition. U.S. Naval Institute. Annapolis,
Maryland

Conger, Norman B. "Wreck and Casual-
ty Chart of the Great Lakes, 1874".
The Weather Bureau. Department of
Agriculture. Lake Marine Service.
Available from the Historical Society
of Michigan, 2117 Washtenaw, Ann
Arbor, MI 48104

Creason, Dr. Wm. M. Interview. March
1990, Grand Haven, Michigan

"*Eagle:* The Extraordinary Classroom".

USCG Academy. New London, Connecticut, 1973

Eaton, Glenn. Interview. August 1989,
Grand Haven, Michigan

Elliott, James L. *Red Stacks Over the
Horizon.* The story of the Goodrich
Steamship Line.

Fisher, Elizabeth. Interview. July 1989,
Grand Haven, Michigan

Grand Haven Tribune 1910-1990

Grand Rapids Herald 1933

Grand River Times 1851, 1852

Gurney, Gene. *United State Coast
Guard, A Pictorial History* Crown
Publishers, Inc., N.Y., N.Y.

Halbertstadt, Hans. *USCG.* Presidio
Press, Novato, California

Heckman, Rear Admiral A.A., USCG.
"Remarks Given at Official Transfer
of USCG Rifle Range Property to City of Ferrysburg, Michigan".
Cleveland, Ohio, 1973

Herbst, Wm. Interview. January 1990.
Grand Haven, Michigan

Jacobson, Alvin Jr. Interview. May 1989,
Grand Haven, Michigan

Johnson, Paul. Interview. May 1989,
Grand Haven, Michigan

Kitchel, Dr. Mary S. *Spring Lake Community Centennial 1869-1969*

Kloepfer, Gertrude. *Grand River
Packet* 1982, 1983, 1985, 1986.
Grand Haven Area Historical Society

Latey, H.N. *Robbins Family of Cape
Cod* Library of Cape Cod History
and Genealogy

Lautenschlaeger, Ed. Interview. March
1990, Grand Haven, Michigan

Lillie, Leo C. *Historic Grand Haven
and Ottawa County.* Grand Haven,
Michigan, 1931

McLellan, Captain C.H. USRCS. "The Evolution of the Lifeboat" *Marine Engineering,* January 1906

Mansfield, J.B. *History of the Great Lakes* Chicago: J.H. Beers & Co., 1899

Marquette Michigan Historical Society. "Life Saving Station in Marquette"

Muskegon Chronicle 1914-1990

Noble, Dennis L. "Great Lakes: A Brief History of U.S. Coast Guard Operations" USCG Bulletin, 1989

O'Brien, T. Michael, Photojournalist First Class, USCG. *Guardians of the Eighth Sea, A History of the United States Coast Guard on the Great Lakes*

Preservation News. February 1990. "Great Lakes Salvage Rights"

Raritan. Official Log. Sunday, June 13, 1943 & June 14, 1943

Ratigan, Wm. *Great Lakes Shipwrecks and Survivals.* Grand Rapids, Michigan: Wm. B. Eerdmans Publishing Co., 1969

Time-Life Books *Epic of Flight—The Road to Kitty Hawk* 1979

U.S. Army Corps of Engineers. *Archeologic and Historic Bulletin,* March 1988

Ver Duin, Claude. Interview. August 1989, Grand Haven, Michigan

Ver Duin, Robert. Interview. August 1989, Grand Haven, Michigan

Vozar, Steve. Interview. February 1990, Grand Haven, Michigan

White, Henry. Interview. March 1990, Southgate, Michigan

INDEX